Nature, Landscape and People
Since the Second World War

Nature, Landscape and People Since the Second World War

Edited by T.C. Smout

Tuckwell Press in Association with the Royal Society of Edinburgh
and the Centre for Environmental History and Policy at the
Universities of St Andrews and Stirling

First published in Great Britain in 2001 by
Tuckwell Press
The Mill House
Phantassie
East Linton
East Lothian EH40 3DG
Scotland

ISBN 1 86232 147 7

British Library Cataloguing in Publication Data

A catalogue record for this book is available
on request from the British Library

Typeset by Hewer Text Ltd, Edinburgh
Printed and bound by The Cromwell Press, Trowbridge, Wiltshire

Contents

Contributors   vii
Introduction   ix

1. The National Parks and Access to the Countryside Act
   of 1949 – its Origins and Significance *John Sheail*   1

2. Impressions from an Era *R.E. Boote*   13

3. Toxic Chemicals and Wildlife: Raising Awareness and
   Reducing Damage *Norman W. Moore*   25

4. New Pressures on the Land: Recreation *Michael Dower*   32

5. The Rise of the Environmental Movement,
   1970–1990 *Robin Grove-White*   44

6. Managing the Countryside in a Period of Change –
   1970–1990 *Adrian Phillips*   52

7. Post-War Changes in Forest Practices and
   their Effects *William E.S.Mutch*   70

8. Applying Ecology to Wildlife Conservation: Have Attitudes
   Changed? *Charles H. Gimingham* and *Michael B. Usher*   79

9. Public Perceptions – Have We Helped Them Over 50 Years?
   Ian Mercer   97

10. The Legalities and Perceptions of Marine Conservation
    Lynda M. Warren   106

11. The Challenge of Change: Demands and Expectations
    for Farmed Land *Janet Dwyer* and *Ian Hodge*   117

12. Beyond NIMBYism: The Evolution of Social Attitudes
    to Biotechnology *Joyce Tait*   135

13. Can Ecologists Recreate Habitats and Restore Absent
    Species? *J.A. Thomas*   150

14. Recreation and Conservation in the Countryside:
    Policy Challenges *Nigel Curry*   161

15. Biodiversity into the Twenty-First Century *Derek Langslow*   181

16. Beyond 2000: A New People's Charter *Roger Clarke*   186

17. Delivering Benefits Globally, Nationally and Locally
    Roger Crofts   195

18. Vision and Reality: A Perspective of Conservation Past,
    Present and To Come *Martin Holdgate*   219

    Index   235

Contributors

Bob Boote is former Director General of the Nature Conservancy Council, Chairman of the Council of Europe Committee for the Conservation of Nature and Natural Resources, and Vice-President of the International Union for Conservation of Nature and Natural Resources.

Roger Clarke was a Director of the Countryside Agency from 1984 to 1999. From 2000 he has been Chief Executive of the Youth Hostels Association (England and Wales).

Roger Crofts has been Chief Executive of Scottish Natural Heritage since its establishment. He is Visiting Professor of Environmental Management at Royal Holloway and Bedford College, University of London; Honorary Professor of Geography at the University of Aberdeen; Chair of the IUCN UK Committee and Chair of the World Commission on Protected Areas: Europe.

Nigel Curry is Professor of Countryside Planning and Head of the Countryside and Community Research Unit, Cheltenham and Gloucester College of Higher Education. He has held visiting posts at the Universities of Lincoln, N.Z., Zürich, Switzerland, the Queen's University of Belfast and the Open University. His principal research interests are concerned with access rights to land.

Michael Dower was National Park Officer of the Peak District from 1985–1992, and Director General of the Countryside Commission 1992–1996.

Janet Dwyer is a Senior Fellow at the Institute for European Environmental Policy (IEEP) in London, where she leads research into agriculture, environment and rural development policy. She has qualifacations in biology and agricultural economics and was a Senior Policy Officer at the Countryside Commission from 1991–1998.

Charles Gimingham was Regius Professor of Botany in the University of Aberdeen until his retirement in 1988. He is past President of the British Ecological Society, served on the NE Regional Board and Scientific Advisory Committee of Scottish Natural Heritage, and for 11 years was a member of the Countryside Commission for Scotland.

Robin Grove-White is Professor of Environment and Society at Lancaster University. He was Director of the Council for the Preservation of Rural England (1981–1987) and a Forestry Commissioner (1991–1998).

Ian Hodge is Gilbey Lecturer in the Department of Land Economy, University of Cambridge. He has published on a range of issues in environmental management, property institutions and rural development. He is currently a member of English Nature's Socio-Economic Advisory Group, the Ministry of Agriculture's Economist Panel and the MAFF Task Force for the Hills.

Sir Martin Holdgate has been centrally involved in national and international conservation for over 35 years. He was Deputy Director (Research) in the Nature Conservancy, the first Director of the Government's Central Unit on Environmental Pollution and of the

NERC Institute of Terrestrial Ecology, Chief Scientist in the Department of the Environment and for six years Director General of IUCB – the World Conservation Union.

Derek Langslow was Chief Executive of English Nature, 1990–2000 and is currently a Director of British Waterways and Harwich Haven Authority, and a member of the Agriculture and Biotechnology Commission.

Ian Mercer is Secretary General of the Association of National Park Authorities, formerly Dartmoor National Park Chief Officer and Chief Executive of the Countryside Council for Wales. In his youth he managed nature reserves – Slapton Ley and Malham Tarn.

Norman Moore, former head of the Toxic Chemicals and Wildlife Section of the Nature Conservancy, is a professional conservation biologist who studies the effects of agriculture and other impacts of mankind on wildlife.

William E. S. Mutch is retired, and was formerly Head of the University of Edinburgh's Department of Forestry and Natural Resources. President of the Institute of Chartered Foresters, 1982–1984; member of the Countryside Commission for Scotland, 1988–1991; Board Member, Scottish Natural Heritage, 1992–1994.

Adrian Phillips was employed at the Countryside Commission 1968–1974 and (as Director General) 1981–1992. He is now a part-time Professor of Countryside and Environmental Planning at Cardiff University.

John Sheail is a Senior Principal Scientific Officer in the Centre for Ecology and Hydrology (Natural Environment Research Council), and Deputy Head of the Monks Wood site. An historical geographer, he is External Professor of Geography in the University of Loughborough.

T. C. Smout is Historiographer Royal in Scotland and co-founder of the Centre for Environmental History and Policy at the Universities of St. Andrews and Stirling. From 1992–1997 he was Deputy Chairman of Scottish Natural Heritage. He is the author of *Nature Contested: Environmental History in Scotland and Northern England since 1600* (Edinburgh U.P., 2000).

Joyce Tait is Director of the Scottish Universities Policy Research and Advice Network in the Research Centre for Social Science at the Univeristy of Edinburgh.

Jeremy Thomas is a research scientist specialising in the ecological factors causing change to European wildlife. He is currently Head of NERC's Biodiversity and Conservation Management Section, having studied originally under Professor Norman Moore at the Nature Conservancy's Monks Wood Experimental Station.

Michael B. Usher is currently Chief Scientist of Scottish Natural Heritage, having previously worked on the staff of the University of York for 24 years. He is an ecologist and conservation scientist with a wide interest in environmental issues both in the United Kingdom and abroad.

Lynda Warren is Professor of Environmental Law at the University of Wales Aberystwyth and specialises in marine and nature conservation law and policy. She is a council member of the Countryside Council for Wales.

Introduction

THE ESSAYS IN this book originated in a conference to celebrate the fiftieth anniversary of the National Parks and Access to the Countryside Act of 1949, one of the great statutes of the reforming post-war Labour government, and the legislation that provided the cornerstone both for rural recreational management and for official nature conservation in this island. The meeting was held under the auspices of the Royal Society of Edinburgh, in association with the Institute for Environmental History at the University of St. Andrews, and it was supported by the British Ecological Society and the country agencies. The idea for the meeting came from Professor John Sheail of the Institute for Terrestrial Ecology, who, with Professor Fred Last (as Chairman), Dr. Alison Gimingham, Professor John Beck, and the editor, subsequently formed the Organising Committee. We were three days in our deliberations, the second being occupied by a field excursion to Loch Lomond where we learned much about contemporary problems in an area of great beauty under intense pressure, about to be declared Scotland's first National Park half a century after the enabling legislation for England and Wales.

Our conference – and thus this book – otherwise addressed two broad themes. The first dealt with the past, the fifty years since the 1949 legislation. The second dealt with the future, with prospects for nature conservation and rural recreation in the twenty-first century. 'This meeting could not have come at a more appropriate time', said Sarah Boyack, the Scottish Environment minister, in her opening remarks. What is inevitably missing from the book (apart from any account of our Loch Lomond experiences) was what to all was a highlight – Magnus Magnusson's videoed interviews with Max Nicholson and John Berry about the early days of the Nature Conservancy. As Roger Crofts, the Chief Executive of Scottish Natural Heritage, observed at the meeting, one of its benefits was to bring home the sense of what modern practitioners owe to great figures who took the first steps on the road. Happily both Berry and Nicholson were able to attend.

At the start of the conference, John Sheail (Chapter 1) reminded us how easy it is to simplify history by the comfortable use of hindsight. The making of the 1949 Act was a complex compromise, steered through Parliament in difficult political and economic circumstances. It neither fulfilled nor completely disappointed the ideals of the founding fathers – Dower, Tansley, Huxley and the rest. In the 1950s and 1960s much of the progress in nature conservation was due to the astuteness of Nicholson, who knew, from his own experience as a former senior civil servant, how to cope with his fellows, but much was also achieved by the simple iterative processes of trial and error. On the recreation side, this was especially true in the gradual self-definition of National Parks.

Bob Boote and Norman Moore (Chapters 2 and 3) told their stories from the perspective of long and distinguished careers that began in the newborn Nature Conservancy. Boote, who ultimately became Director General of the Nature Conservancy Council and also played a large role in international conservation, stressed the achievement of others in those early years and the fine line between administration of government policy and campaigning. Campaigning at home and abroad, he emphasised, is intrinsic to nature conservation. It is hard to imagine a conservation agency at the present time being allowed the leeway that the pioneers arrogated to themselves: this was the editor's experience in Scotland, where the Scottish Office's reins held a tight bridle to SNH in the 1990s and the situation in Wales when John Redwood was Secretary of State was even more unhappy. Boote also emphasised the importance of science within NC, and Moore reinforced this. As the scientist perhaps most deeply involved in the affray over pesticides in the 1960s, he spoke with especial authority.

Moore's recollections carried two strong messages: first, on the need for good, independent and objective science, and especially for a new national watchdog to keep an eye open for environmental trouble; second, on the need for English Nature, Scottish Natural Heritage and the Countryside Council for Wales to speak out when unacceptable compromise bad for the environment is proposed. 'It was probably easier for us in the 1960s,' Moore said, 'but I believe that we did get the balance better than we do today.' Murmurs of support for both his points showed he was not alone in either.

Michael Dower's contribution (Chapter 4) switched the focus of the conference to the changing role of National Parks and the altering pattern of recreation in England and Wales. It is given to few (other than monarchs) to attempt to fulfil the vision of their own fathers: he showed how socio-economic change altered the context between John Dower's day and his own period of command in the Countryside Commission. The story of countryside recreation is one of greatly increased leisure bringing greater pressures, yet also of social exclusion, so that much pressure is not yet realised: the previous government showed no interest in bringing the excluded into the country, while the present one is cautiously moving towards greater inclusion, though possibly with more rhetoric than action. What is the appropriate use of the countryside and who is to judge? There are few bigger political conundrums.

The nature of socio-economic change was further explored in a most thought-provoking contribution, from Professor Robin Grove-White of Lancaster University, considering the growth of the environmental movement since the 1970s (Chapter 5). It is hardly enough, he suggested, to trace the rise of conservation concern back to such dramatic external events as the Torrey Canyon oil-spill, the advent of acid rain or the BSE crisis. It also, and more profoundly, involves the broader societal dissatisfactions of citizens about control of their own environments, and therefore of their own lives. Cogently argued science, even if sometimes necessarily based on circumstantial evidence, is often more than adequate to suggest the urgent need for enhanced action or control, but nothing happens because of social, political and institutional vested interests and inertias. Environmental protest and discontent are not necessarily mindless lashing out against 'progress', as opponents perceive it, but rather incorporate a highly motivated, popular quest for a society from which the citizen is not alienated and about which he or she is not cynical. Politicians do not know how to deal with this dilemma, because obsession with growth ('It's the economy, stupid') blinds them to its seriousness. However, unless they become more perceptive, we shall have more eco-warriors and more potentially violent confrontations as at the World Trade Conference in Seattle in 1999, in place of constructive addressing of the dangers that confront us all. Professor Grove-White's paper certainly struck a chord with the editor, who joined the Green Party only because he is tired of single-issue politics.

Professor Adrian Phillips of Cardiff University (Chapter 6) traced the trends in managing the countryside in the two eventful decades beginning in 1970. At the start, it was still assumed in the UK that farming was for food production (virtually at any cost), that experts (officials and scientists) knew best, and that the external world of Europe and beyond was of small and tangential importance. By 1990, huge change and damage had been inflicted on the countryside but conservation had become a great popular cause. The agencies had to devise ways of working with an increasingly diverse range of stakeholders, including powerful voluntary bodies, farmers, landowners and crofters. Simply by virtue of being understaffed and having fewer powers, the Countryside Commission may have been better placed to develop constructive ideas about this than the Nature Conservancy Council – for the former, it was co-operate or wither.

Switching from farming to forestry, Bill Mutch (Chapter 7), offering a lifetime's experience in the industry, traced its history from the start of the century in order to emphasise its dependence on the vagaries of state intervention. The Forestry Commission itself was a state creation: its change of direction in 1957, from planning to provide a strategic resource to attempting to meet almost impossible financial targets, was state-driven. Private forestry largely depended from 1960 on a regime of tax breaks not modified until the budget of 1988. More recently, concern about biodiversity has sent forest policy towards multipurpose objectives, but Dr. Mutch warns from historical experience, that this will not necessarily last.

Two distinguished ecologists working from a Scottish base, Professor Charles Gimingham of the University of Aberdeen and Professor Michael Usher, Chief Scientist of SNH, gave a masterly survey of developments in ecology in relation to wildlife conservation over the past thirty years, too long and closely structured to summarise quickly (Chapter 8). They suggested the 1970s were a *decade of ideas*, incorporating truly global perspectives and the notion of biogeography in the development of ecological theory, introducing the concept of adaptive strategies in plants and animals, and developing multivariate analysis for practical research use. The 1980s were a *decade of questions*, exploring the problems of minimum viable populations (or maximum tolerable ones), the question of non-native species and how they become a threat, and of the effects of pollution carried by air and water on the global ecosystem. The 1990s may be seen as the *decade of biodiversity*, and the one to come, hopefully one of the holistic and systematic application of ecological knowledge to all environmental problems.

At this point in our deliberations the conference adjourned, as explained, to Loch Lomond, to consider what we had learned and to relate it all to the contemporary situation in the field. When we returned, the emphasis was more on the present and the future than on the past, but not immediately or entirely so. Ian Mercer (Chapter 9) shared sometimes bruising lessons from the Countryside Council for Wales and his less controversial experience as Secretary-General of the Association of National Park Authorities. He asked if we had, over the last fifty years, improved public perceptions of the conservation cause. His answer was resoundingly negative. The muddled way in which legislation has developed since 1949 has led to a disorderly and piecemeal legal framework that is bound to confuse the public. He gave a plea for government to construct a logical and ordered system for countryside and biological conservation that will command respect in a modern democracy. Professor Lynda Warren of the University of Wales at Aberystwyth gave an equally critical account (Chapter 10) of the neglect of marine conservation since 1949, at least until very recently. Even now, the lack of a solid science base from which to choose sites and the multiplicity of interests involved in the marine environment make the present site-based approach inappropriate. Again, only fundamental reappraisal will bring progress.

Dr. Janet Dwyer of the Institute for European Environmental Policy, London and Dr. Ian Hodge, of the Department of Land Economy, Cambridge explored the current and future demands and expectations for farmed land (Chapter 11). The 1947 Agriculture Act encouraged rural society to regard the countryside as 'the factory floor', but pressures from all directions, linked to proposals in CAP reform and trends towards globalisation in the food trade, are pushing the agricultural industry towards change. Such pressures are ambiguous in character and uncertain in outcome, but they may well lead to multifunctional goals in land management of which nature conservation and rural recreation will be two. They may even re-open the ancient question about the nature of landed property and the character of popular rights; a trend towards a new 'duty of care' on the part of the farmer and landowner is evident not only in the UK but elsewhere in Europe. The experience of such countries as Switzerland, for instance, may have much to teach us.

Another highly topical issue was discussed by Professor Joyce Tait of Edinburgh University (Chapter 12). She explained how conflicts initially affecting relatively small numbers of people could accelerate into conflicts of a more entrenched and intractable nature affecting national or even international issues, for example over genetically modified crops. The conflict has drifted into areas not crucial to the relatively simple one of the use or otherwise of GMOs. It now involves, for example, a discussion on the future of world farming and who controls it, partly because of the absence of appropriate fora for citizens to discuss the bigger issues. It was exactly the kind of situation envisaged earlier by Professor Grove-White.

No-one doubts that the twenty-first century will see increasing pressure on the natural environment, almost irrespective of the future of farming and genetic modification – for example, from climate change and rural development pressures. What can we do in the positive sense? Dr. Jeremy Thomas of ITE brought his unrivalled experience to bear on the problem of how practical it is to re-introduce vanished species and ecosystems to the British countryside (Chapter 13). He argued, first, that it should be attempted, since human beings have been interfering with ecosystems and other species for so long that arguments about 'naturalness' ring increasingly hollow. Next, he showed that with good science it could indeed be done, using as examples recent successes in the reintroduction of the large blue butterfly and the creation of a rich grassland community on a former arable desert at Twyford Down. But to do this successfully demands an investment in the science and in logistics which will not come cheap. To the editor's mind it is extraordinary how we grumble at paying a few hundred thousand pounds to, say, reintroduce the sea eagle or the beaver, while accepting a MAFF bill of many millions on the ill-considered experiment on the effects of local extermination of badgers on the incidence of bovine tuberculosis.

On a completely different tack, Nigel Curry (Chapter 14) asked about the compatibility of the government's approach to access – top-down compulsion to force universal access to open land by legislation – with 'a longer term shift in governmental style' towards 'participatory action, community involvement, devolved power and local autonomy'. What was really wanted, he argued (for England and Wales, which formed the focus of his paper), was a properly funded rights-of-way network.

Then came the turn of those charged to manage the conservation agencies to present their vision for the future (Chapters 15–17). Derek Langslow for English Nature gave a very upbeat account of what the next fifty years might be like, building on the work of the nature conservation pioneers of 1949: the success of the peregrine rather than the precipitate decline of the corn bunting, points the way to what the future could hold for biodiversity. Roger Clarke for the newly-formed Countryside Agency and heir of the Countryside Commission presented a set of ideas for continuing the aims of the 1949 Act by building on the concepts of 'countryside character' and 'environmental capital'. He recommended that they should be given a form of legal under-pinning that would sharpen the rôle of town-and-country planning in respect of sustainable development, and place a statutory duty of care on farmers to maintain the quality of the countryside. Roger Crofts for SNH in a similar vein argued that successful delivery of environmental benefit lay in integration of environmental concerns with wider social and economic benefit, putting sustainable development and people in the forefront of every environmental concern. For him, partnership was of the essence, and high levels of scientific knowledge had to be joined with high levels of managerial and negotiating skills – not to compromise the natural heritage cause, but to bring it to fruition.

Was there a missing note in the harmony of these vision statements? For some present it was the absence of any reference to what might be called 'nature for nature's sake', the 'reverence for life' of such diverse environmental philosophers as Albert Schweitzer, Aldo Leopold and Arne Næss. Yes, nature is for people, but, as importantly, nature has intrinsic value: nature is for itself. Many will consider that we have a duty towards the other species of the earth precisely because we have developed and enjoyed such a unique capacity to do them harm. Not to recognise these moral and spiritual aspects is to reduce the agencies from guardians of our local biosphere to mere implements of a narrow government concern, firefighters to put out the flames of rural conflict. Increasingly society will notice if the conservation agencies do not live up to something loftier than that. A million people did not join the Royal Society for the Protection of Birds simply because birds are good for tourism.

Sir Martin Holdgate, with his experience of research and policy, was the ideal person to conclude our deliberations, not least from his perspective as former Director General of the International Union for the Conservation of Nature. Notions of nature, he said, have historically tended to be nature-centred or people-centred, yet the vision of the founding fathers of the 1949 Act was for a 'national biological service' which would holistically embrace both nature and people and provide the state with the expert foundations for a unified rural policy encompassing landscape, wildlife and recreation, placing 'sustainable development at the heart of national policy'. For all sorts of political and bureaucratic reasons, reality did not work out so grandly. Something smaller and more fragmented emerged, often doing outstanding work despite its handicap, and increasingly exposed to issues of global pollution and resource depletion. In some ways we have come full circle, returning to the concerns of the founding fathers for ecology used to benefit the whole of society, and back to the imperative need for a strong, genuinely independent science base.

In the various debates that punctuated the conference, many who spoke from the floor shared the anxiety of the final speaker about the future of ecological science as a discipline sufficiently funded, and sufficiently integrated with decision-making, to provide as good a base for conservation action as we had in the past. Another theme that came up more than once, yet did not have a platform speaker to articulate it, was concern over the quality of the modern voluntary body in the environmental field. There was a sense abroad that some of the biggest had become too often insensitively aggressive and unscrupulous with the truth, treating science selectively and preferring propaganda to balance. Also, those bodies that care about pollution are usually remarkably indifferent to the problems of biodiversity, and *vice-versa*. Whether or not these feelings were fully justified, the fact that so many participants articulated them ought to be a sobering matter. Without absolute respect for good science on all sides, environmentalists, sooner rather than later, will completely forfeit the respect and confidence of the public.

A meeting of this sort incurs debts too numerous to mention, but the work of Professor Last as Chairman of the Organising Committee, and of Heather Mantell and Sandra Macdougall of the RSE, cannot go unpraised. Forth Valley Enterprise and Dumbartonshire Enterprise, with SNH, sponsored the field trip to Loch Lomond. SNH, English Nature and the Countryside Agency have generously subsidised this volume. Margaret Richards laboured unstintingly over the text. I thank them all most profoundly.

Chris Smout
Centre for Environmental History and Policy
Universities of St. Andrews and Stirling

1

The National Parks and Access to the Countryside Act of 1949 – its Origins and Significance

John Sheail

THE FIFTIETH ANNIVERSARY of the National Parks and Access to the Countryside Act, and conferment of a Royal Charter on the Nature Conservancy, provide an obvious pretext for probing more deeply the pattern and unity of purpose, and perhaps the confusion and acrimony, that led up to and, more particularly, followed, those events. Rather than being judgmental, the challenge of this paper is to recall what it felt like to be part of that process of evolution and development, which has caused the countryside and coast, and therefore part of ourselves, to be what we are some half century later.

BEFORE 1949

It is deceptively easy to find a compelling logic to the pattern of events that led up to the present-day conservation, or environmental, movement. No published review of that movement seems complete without reference to the founding of the National Trust in 1895, or the conferment of a Royal Charter on the Society of Birds in 1904 (MacNaghten and Urry, 1998). If we probe deeper, we are often impressed by the breadth of interests that informed members of the early natural history, antiquarian and preservationist bodies. The *Annual Report* of the Yorkshire Naturalists' Union for 1906 recorded how 50 members (rising to 150 on Bank Holiday Monday) spent the Whit Weekend exploring the distinctive coastline of Flamborough Head. Besides making their 'scientific finds', members discovered the names of a starch and a lungtonic company laid out in white stones on the turf, large enough for the words to be read from a great distance. A letter written by the Honorary Secretary to local newspapers had the desired effect of provoking such a sense of outrage that the Naturalists' Union was later able to claim that it had prevented the whole headland from being 'spoiled by hideous advertisements'. The two companies vigorously denied any responsibility for placing the advertisements. The boulders were soon taken away (West Yorkshire Record Office, Leeds, Yorkshire Naturalists' Union MSS, 10 and 36–7).

The founding of the Council for the Preservation of Rural England (CPRE), in 1926, is invariably cited as further indication of mounting public-concern. More land changed hands in the years after the catastrophic loss of human life in the First World War, than at any time since the Dissolution of the Monasteries. Some 2 per cent of England was built over between the two world wars. Never before, nor since, has so much land been developed so rapidly (Dewey, 1997). Furthermore, rising affluence, greater leisure time, personal mobility both contributed to, and heightened awareness of, the dramatic changes perceived to be taking place in the countryside and on the coast. It was the age of the charabanc and motor-cycle and side-car. It was not just a question of aesthetic sensibilities being offended by the holiday shacks and shanties that might be erected on the sand-dunes of Lincolnshire, or the plotlands in south Essex, but their impact on the value of other properties.

Not only did such building development cease in the Second World War, but plans for post-war reconstruction offered obvious opportunity for re-appraisal. It was more than just a matter of ensuring that 'never again' was there a resurgence of suburban sprawl (Hennessy, 1992). The skills and expertise gained from the collective process of fighting a successful war might be used to create 'a new (peacetime) Jerusalem'. It found obvious expression in the New Towns Act of 1946, and the Town and Country Planning Acts of 1947. There was also recognition, to use modern parlance, that 'the quality of life' could never be improved without more conscious effort in 'wealth creation'. There were the Agriculture and Forestry Acts. Never before had Government invested so heavily and directly in assisting rural industries to adjust and modernise, and thereby produce the raw materials needed by the nation at large, and the employment opportunities for a prosperous country-side. And finally, the National Parks and Access to the Countryside Act gave both statutory recognition and unprecedented resources to a burgeoning, albeit still minuscule, Third Force in the countryside, alongside farming and forestry, namely that of outdoor recreation and amenity and wildlife protec-tion (Cherry and Rogers, 1996).

The more active members of the inter-war professional and voluntary bodies both encouraged, and were themselves a resource to be exploited by, ministers and their officials, searching for ideas as to post-war reconstruction that would catch the public imagination. Lord Reith had been appointed Minister of Works and Building in October 1940 and, through his own persistence, secured 'personal responsibility' for planning 'the physical re-construction of post-war Britain' (Cullingworth, 1975). His difficulty was to identify issues that did not fall within the purview of other ministers. National parks and nature reserves had obvious appeal. An official in Reith's Ministry,

H.G. Vincent, learnt that John Dower, the Secretary of the CPRE's Standing Committee on National Parks, had been invalided out of the Officer Reserve. As political interest developed, and most obviously with the appointment of W.S. Morrison as Minister of Town and Country Planning in March 1943, Dower was asked to write a comprehensive study of the purpose, management and location of a series of parks, which the Cabinet's Reconstruction Committee approved for publication the day before the War in Europe ended (Minister of Town and Country Planning (MTCP, 1945)).

NATIONAL PARKS AND NATURE RESERVES

Dower and his generation have since been criticised for focusing on national parks, and thereby causing too little attention to be given to the plight of the more typical countryside and coast. But it may be argued that, far from requiring apology, it was an inspired move in the sense of providing an initial goal, that could be so easily visualised and, therefore, comprehended. The suggestion that Dower thought of nothing else but national parks is refuted by his own publications and personal papers, and wartime Ministry files. In a lecture to the Lancashire CPRE, on 'rural planning and preservation', in July 1939, Dower emphasised the importance of dealing not only with the 'extraordinary' country and 'wilder' country, but also with the 'ordinary' countryside that characterised much of Britain. Vincent wrote, in October 1943, of how he relied on Dower for guidance on all aspects of rural and coastal planning (Sheail, 1995a).

The current research of Julian Burcher is also pointing to much else. There was nothing backward-looking, or obsessively rural, about Dower. As a practising architect in the inter-war years, he had pioneered the design of aerodrome buildings, and experimented with the use of steel and other materials that would provide not only considerably-improved living conditions, but the means by which families might live at the highest densities possible within towns and cities. Only in that way could the demand for land and, therefore, the costs of housing be minimised, and the urban infrastructure be made considerably more efficient than one which sprawled through suburbs, or spread as if tentacles along the principal arterial roads. But if over 80% of the population was to live and work in towns and, optimally, in high-rise buildings, there must be even greater opportunity to relax and enjoy the amenities in the countryside. Not only was access to the countryside essential to the spiritual and physical wellbeing of those living in cities and towns, but the revenue derived from daily and longer visits would bring much-needed diversity to the employment otherwise provided by farming, forestry and the extractive industries in the countryside.

But why was there such an apparent obsession for creating national parks in the upland and more remote areas? Dower and those that followed him certainly had a close knowledge and deep-seated love of such countryside, but there was an economic reason too. Where say the Surrey and Sussex County Councils had demonstrated both a willingness and ability to protect and enhance their respective areas of the North and South Downs, Treasury officials acknowledged, in 1938, how such intervention was beyond the means of rural areas where the population was so sparse and, therefore, the rateable income of local authorities so very low. Had it not been for the re-armament programme, and then war, some form of national park might well have emerged in the early 1940s, whereby the Exchequer might complement what had become possible through green belts and other planning devices in the Home Counties (Sheail, 1981).

There has also been criticism of the ecologist's apparent obsession with nature reserves. Certainly, there was a self-serving element, in the sense that such reserves as Wicken Fen, near Cambridgeshire, had demonstrated the value of such properties in providing security of tenure in carrying out long-term ecological survey and experimental work (Sheail, 1987). As they began to help compile lists of national habitat reserves, such leading ecologists as A.G. Tansley, Charles Elton and Cyril Diver realised that, where they had made little headway in competing with agronomists and foresters in acting as 'expert' advisers in farming and forestry, ecologists were pre-eminently well-placed to provide the under-pinning required for the preservation of wildlife on reserves and in the wider countryside and coast. As laboratories and classrooms, such reserves would provide the expertise and experience required for giving general advice as to how the nation's wildlife and physical landforms might be managed (Sheail, 1995b). As the finest examples of Britain's plant and animal life, such areas as Wicken Fen, or the Parallel Roads of Glen Roy, would come to be regarded in the same light as, say, a cathedral or medieval castle, as a national treasure. The ecologist would be their 'expert' custodian (Tansley, 1945).

POSTPONEMENT

But there are dangers in assuming such initiatives evolved inexorably out of the spirit of the times. Close heed has also to be taken of the actual structures of the decision-making process and of the way personalities exploited the opportunities that arose within what political scientists refer to as 'networks'. The larger decision of the Cabinet's Reconstruction Committee, in early May 1945, had far-reaching implications for both recreation and amenity, and for nature conservation.

The main purpose of the Minister's seeking consent for the publication of the Dower report was to provide the rationale for appointing a preparatory National Parks Commission in 1945. The Chancellor of the Exchequer and Minister of Agriculture objected, however, arguing that the kind of executive role intended for the Commission should be exercised by a minister and that, in any case, there were far more pressing priorities for the countryside by way of food production. The Minister of Town and Country Planning was simply invited to appoint a National Parks Committee to explore the practicality of national parks (Cherry, 1975). There was a loss of momentum. By the time the Committee under Sir Arthur Hobhouse, and its Scottish equivalent under Sir J. Douglas Ramsay reported, in 1947 (MTCP, 1947 and Secretary of State for Scotland, 1947), Dower had died and Patrick Abercrombie and other key figures had become even more heavily immersed in urban and other planning issues. Significantly too, the local-authority associations had secured a much larger role under the Town and Country Planning Acts. Although the stridency of the Standing Committee on National Parks ensured there was a Bill, highly effective lobbying by the local government bodies during the parliamentary stages ensured that planning powers remained firmly with the local authorities. The powers of the National Parks Commission were emasculated. Such a humiliating episode for the Minister, Lewis Silkin, was well-noted by the Scottish Office.

The impact of the delay for nature conservation was considerably more positive. A Wild Life Conservation Special Committee had been appointed in 1945, under the Chairmanship of Sir Julian Huxley, to study the practicality of national nature reserves. It included such leading figures as Tansley, Elton and Diver. A comparable committee for Scotland was appointed under the distinguished zoologist, James Ritchie. Where the advocates of national parks and access to the countryside appeared simplistic in believing their goals would be realised, once the necessary statutory powers and Exchequer monies had been obtained, the two wildlife committees saw this as only the beginning of the considerably greater challenge of demonstrating a competence to use such resources. Knowledge, understanding and ability to predict the outcome of conservation management and advice were so rudimentary that research should be the paramount consideration (MTCP, 1947 and Secretary of State for Scotland, 1947).

As first enunciated by a Committee on the Machinery of Government, in 1918, that met under the Chairmanship of Lord Haldane, Government research took two forms, namely operational and more fundamental research (Minister of Reconstruction, 1918). Haldane's Committee had recommended that operational research should remain an integral part of the relevant Government department. By such reasoning, if a National Parks Commission had been constituted in 1945, nature-conservation research would have occupied a position within the Commission and, therefore, the Ministry of Town and Country Planning, analogous to that of pest-infestation research within the Ministry of Agriculture and Fisheries. It was the achievement of first the British Ecological Society, and then the Wild Life Conservation Special Committees under Huxley and Ritchie to persuade Herbert Morrison, the Lord President of the Council and, therefore, the science minister, in the post-war Labour Government, of the need for longer-term, more wide-ranging, research. There was so much synergy between the need for reserves and an advisory service, and for a major and most urgent expansion of field facilities in biological research and teaching, that nothing less than a research council was needed.

Through the considerable skills of two key personalities, nature conservation became therefore a responsibility of the science sector, rather than the planning sector, of Government. Those two principal-figures were Max Nicholson, the ornithologist on Huxley's Committee and, more crucially, the most senior official in Morrison's Office of the Lord President of the Council (Nicholson, 1987), and secondly John C.F. Fryer, the Secretary of the Agricultural Research Council who, through his personal research-interests, had acquired firsthand knowledge of the opportunities and constraints of reserve ownership and management (Sheail, 1993). Appointed by Royal Charter in May 1949, the Nature Conservancy took its place alongside the Medical Research Council and Agricultural Research Council. It was to give advice generally, establish a series of nature reserves, and thirdly undertake the relevant research, over and above what might otherwise be expected of what was, in effect, an ecological research council. Its powers to hold and manage land were conferred by the National Parks and Access to the Countryside Act of 1949. Whereas national parks were confined to England and Wales, nature reserves (being a responsibility of the Lord President of the Council) could be established in Scotland.

THE NATURE CONSERVANCY

Abercrombie (1937) had written earlier of how the greater challenge was not to promote, but to implement what had been sanctioned. For the National Parks Commission and Nature Conservancy, it was not simply the struggle to create a critical mass of expertise and experience, but to assert influence among well-established vested interests. Such tasks were made considerably harder by the straitened economic circumstances of the country and political desire for 'retreat from New Jerusalem' (Jefferys, 1997).

For the Conservancy, there was a pressing need to establish its credentials as a research council. The priority rapidly extended beyond establishing well-founded research stations. As the pace of land-use change increased, so there was urgent need for a series of national nature reserves and for an effective advisory service that took account of not only habitat destruction but also the increasingly ubiquitous incidence of pollution. Everyone was a pioneer – whether serving as a member of the Nature Conservancy or one of its committees, a headquarters' officer, a scientist on a research station, or member of the regional conservation staff. Priorities had to be set, procedures developed, personal contacts established and, above all, the respect of those in the research and land-agency fields won. As Chairman of the Scientific Policy Committee, William H. Pearsall (a Professor of Botany in the University of London) played a considerable role in developing the Conservancy's scientific identity. His memoranda on the aims and practice of reserve management were models of how such a diverse range of interests might be accommodated (Clapham, 1971). It was by no means enough to erect a reserve notice and 'leave it to nature'. Composed of so many species, for which there was only the most rudimentary understanding as to their preferences and needs, a reserve needed perhaps as much skilled observation and management as any farm or timber crop (Sheail, 1998).

A paradox developed. As measured by the criteria of its founding fathers, the wisdom of creating such a hybrid research-council seemed amply borne out. In research, the Conservancy made a significant contribution to the UK's participation in the International Biological Programme (IBP). Besides establishing over a hundred national nature reserves, the Conservancy was a leading participant in such ventures as National Nature Week and 'The Countryside in 1970' conferences, that played so large a part in raising public awareness and understanding of the concept of nature conservation. However, by the conventional measures of the wider fields of science and government, such achievement caused the Conservancy to appear even more anomalous. Its participation in IBP simply illustrated how much more could be attained if Conservancy scientists focused all their energies on what should have been the priority of a research council, namely long-term, fundamental research. Such a deficiency was all the more serious, given the conclusion of the Advisory Council for Scientific Policy that, whilst the balance of effort in civil science was broadly satisfactory, there was increasing anxiety as to 'the promotion of research into natural resources'. By creating a new research council that included the geological and marine sciences, Government would establish a body more comparable in size and standing with the Medical and Agricultural Research Councils. By including the Conservancy as a component body, it would have gone some way to eliminating such an anomaly under 'the Haldane principle'. By such reasoning, the Conservancy became a Charter

Committee of the Natural Environment Research Council (NERC) in June 1965 (Sheail, 1998).

Misgivings as to the Conservancy persisted. In the same way as there was no need for the Medical Research Council to run the hospitals so, it was argued, the Conservancy did not have to own and manage the reserves, in order to use them as laboratories and class-rooms. The closely-applied research arising from the Conservancy's 'catalyst' functions, such as the Broads Study and conferences, showed every sign of increasing as 'The Countryside in 1970' conferences attracted even greater public-interest in the management of the countryside and coast. Where both the Medical and Agricultural Research Councils had an obvious concern for improvement in their respective fields of health and farming, such promotional activities could be left to the relevant Departments, professional bodies and interest groups. The response of the Conservancy was to insist that there was nowhere else in Government where such operational research and management, and the public understanding of its science, might be pursued. That position began to change in the late 1960s, as the essentially urban-focused Ministry of Housing and Local Government, gave way to what ultimately became the Department of the Environment (DOE).

The way was open for NERC to pursue terrestrial ecological research under the Haldane principle, with operational research being pursued within the DOE, most obviously through a grant-aided body with executive responsi-bilities for the reserves and provision of an advisory nature-conservation service. The mounting tensions between the Nature Conservancy and NERC and, more constructively, the introduction of the customer/contractor prin-ciple, following the Rothschild report of 1971 (Lord Privy Seal 1971 and 1972), provided both the pretext and mechanism for abolishing the aberrant Nature Conservancy. A Nature Conservancy Council (NCC) was established, as a grant-aided body of the DOE. The Conservancy's Research Branch remained within NERC, where it became the larger part of a new Institute of Terrestrial Ecology . That Institute would pursue both fundamental studies and the applied research commissioned by the NCC and other 'customer' bodies (Sheail, 1992).

OUTDOOR RECREATION

Scotland generally receives little more than token acknowledgement in accounts of national parks and access to the countryside. Its pioneering role is overlooked. In fact, it is impossible to understand the breadth and significance of the Countryside Act for England and Wales, of 1968, without close reference to the aspirations and circumstances of the Countryside (Scotland) Act, promoted in the previous year.

Where the failure to promote a National Parks Bill for Scotland is commonly attributed to apathy, if not outright hostility, contemporary files of the Scottish Office departments reveal how ministers and their officials concluded that, where regulation and conservation by local government might succeed in England, Scottish parks would require much greater leadership and investment from central government, if they were to have an economic as well as social purpose in meeting both urban and rural needs. In as much as neither the Treasury nor parliament was likely to sanction a more centralised body for Scotland, wholly financed from central funds, little more could be attempted than for the Secretary of State to issue 'national park directions', whereby the relevant county councils were required to give notice of any application for planning consent that might impair amenity and, therefore, the 'ultimate possibility of a national park'. Such areas included Loch Lomond and the Trossachs (Scottish Record Office (SRO), DD 12, 3009–12).

Although a Countryside (Scotland) Bill was drafted as early as July 1960, much more was needed to secure priority in the legislative timetable and Exchequer support. As the Chief Planning Officer of the Department of Health for Scotland, Robert Grieve, remarked, in January 1962, the Highlands and Borders might have a deep place in the heart of the Scots, but there had always been difficulty in finding something on which to hang 'a genuinely inspiring and positive plan'. As Grieve emphasised, that 'new dynamic force' was at last emerging in the form of tourism. Like the motor car, the rapid increase in tourism could no longer be ignored (SRO, DD 12, 2624, 2656–8 and 3011). For Scottish Office officials, there were obvious advantages in expanding their relationship with the amenity and local-government bodies to include tourism, the industry that, above all others, offered a unique opportunity to diversify and, therefore, revive the economy of the remoter areas. No other interest group could speak so authoritatively as to visitor and tourist preferences and, therefore, the balance to be struck between preservation and development (SRO, DD 12, 3009 and T 224, 1055).

Such expert input was especially welcomed by the Scottish Office, whose officials increasingly warned of the embarrassment that would arise if England embarked on further 'countryside legislation'. Although there was 'no great demand for Scottish national parks on the English model', a ministerial brief of March 1964 warned of growing anxiety over what was happening to the countryside. There was increasing concern as to how the countryside might accommodate and benefit from visitors who came increasingly by car. And crucially for the Scottish Office, there was now an academic rigour to what was being proposed. Not only were officials impressed by both the substance and the impact of Michael Dower's description of a 'Fourth wave' of recreation breaking over the countryside and coast (Dower, 1965), but the report of a 'Countryside in 1970' Study Group for Scotland proved of seminal importance. The Chairman of the Group was Robert Grieve, who had taken up the Chair of Urban and Regional Planning at Glasgow University. The report emphasised how Scotland contained by far 'the biggest reserve of open unspoiled hill land and coastal territory in Britain'. Some of the more remote parts fell within the rare category of 'wilderness'. The same physical structure also meant 80% of Scotland's population lived within the Central Belt, parts of which were the most heavily urbanised in Britain. The fact that everywhere was within 30 miles of such upland beauty meant 'a potentially explosive situation existed'. The growth of Britain's motorways was bound to increase tourist pressures on Scotland. The Study Group sought a positive response through 'the integrated multi-purpose development' of farming, forestry and recreation. Its principal recommendation was to establish a countryside commission for Scotland. The publication of the Study Group's findings, and the support obtained from Scottish MPs, marked an important political watershed (SRO, DD 12, 2926 and 2959).

In striking contrast to the 1949 Act, the Scottish Bill passed its parliamentary stages with ease. A member of the largest landowning-family in Scotland, the Earl of Dalkeith, welcomed the measure for the way it anticipated and prepared the countryside for the increasing pressures of an urban population, without frustrating 'the business of the land' (Parliamentary Debates (PD), Commons, 749, 1654–5 and 1663–4). Not only was every interest-group persuaded of the penalties of doing nothing, but the Scottish Bill appeared considerably more pro-active than the 1949 measure in attempting to cope with the side-effects of leisure and recreation, activities that otherwise represented a wholly-welcome advance in economic and social well-being.

THE HISTORICAL CONTEXT

The National Parks and Access to the Countryside Act of 1949 has assumed considerable symbolic-importance as marking the beginnings of a Third Force in the countryside, alongside farming and forestry. With the conscious modernisation of those industries, recreational, amenity and wildlife interests began to establish their presence in the most tangible form possible, through the designation of their respective properties in the form of national parks and nature reserves. As Lewis Silkin asserted, in moving the Second Reading debate, it was not so much a Bill as 'a people'charter' for 'everyone who likes to get out into the open air and enjoy the countryside' (PD, Commons, 464, 1469–70; Blunden and Curry 1990).

If such exaggerated expectations were essential for raising the political consciousness to a point where priority might be given to such legislation, there was inevitably much disillusionment as seemingly common-objectives collapsed before the disparate views of a pluralist society. Policies might become so adaptive and flexible in operation that the question might be asked as to whether the situation would have been significantly different, if there had been no National Park Commission. In posing such a question, Gordon Cherry, in his Cabinet Office 'Peacetime History' of national parks and access to the countryside, doubted whether any other body than a national parks commission could have established the parks with such urgency or motivation. Above all, the parks and the Commission articulated the hopes and aspirations of many years of active and sustained lobbying (Cherry, 1975). It is here perhaps that the Act's real significance may be found. It brought to a conclusion the almost heroic efforts of those comparatively few individuals, whose advocacy was so closely informed by the experiences of the inter-war and wartime periods.

In the event, it was the hard-won expertise and experience gained by the National Parks Commission, Nature Conservancy, and Scottish Office, over some two decades, that brought such a profound change in perception of the twentieth-century countryside and coast. Through such 'learning by practice', the years around 1970 continue to have such a considerable influence. As well as the Countryside Acts, the Nature Conservancy Council Act, and re-organisation of Government research and development, significant advances were made in the 1960s in the concept and practice of conservation management and research. Pollution became recognised as not only an urban, but a rural and indeed ubiquitous, phenomenon. European Conservation Year in 1970 was, perhaps, the most successful year of its kind, in terms of raising public awareness and interest. The voluntary conservation movement considerably expanded, both as existing voluntary bodies were at last reinvigorated and new forms of organisation began to emerge. Some quarter-century later, we continue to draw heavily on the aspirations and assumptions of those pivotal years of change.

REFERENCES

Abercrombie, P. (1937). Administration of schemes prepared by joint committees. *Journal of the Town Planning Institute*, 23, 85–98.

Blunden, J., and Curry, N. (eds) (1990). *A people's charter?* HMSO, London.

Cherry, G.E. (1975). *Environmental planning. Volume II. National parks and recreation in the countryside*. HMSO, London, 157–8.

Cherry, G.E., and Rogers, A. (1996). *Rural change and planning. England and Wales in the twentieth century*. Spon, London.

Clapham, A.R. (1971). William Harold Pearsall, *Biographical Memoirs of Fellows of the Royal Society*, 17, 511–40.

Cullingworth, J.B. (1975). *Environmental planning. Volume 1. Reconstruction and land use planning, 1939–1947.* HMSO, London.

Dewey, P. (1997). *War and progress. Britain 1914–1945.* Longman, London, 156–78.

Dower, M. (1965). *The fourth wave. The challenge of leisure.* Civic Trust, London.

Hennessy, P. (1992). *Never again. Britain 1945–1951.* Jonathan Cape, London.

Jefferys, K. (1997). *Retreat from New Jerusalem. British politics 1951–64.* Macmillan, Basingstoke.

Lord Privy Seal (1971). *A framework for government research and development.* HMSO, London, Cmnd 4814.

Lord Privy Seal (1972). *Framework for government research and development.* HMSO, London, Cmnd 5046.

MacNaghten, P., and Urry, J. (1998). *Contested natures.* Sage, London.

Minister of Reconstruction (1918). *Report of the Machinery of Government Committee.* HMSO, London, Cmd 9230.

Minister of Town and Country Planning (MTCP) (1945). *National parks in England and Wales.* HMSO, London, Cmd 6628.

MTCP (1947a). *Report of the National Parks Committee.* HMSO, London, Cmd 7121.

MTCP (1947b). *Conservation of nature in England and Wales.* HMSO, London, Cmd 7122.

Nicholson, M. (1987) *The new environmental age.* University Press, Cambridge.

Secretary of State for Scotland (1947). *National parks and the conservation of nature in Scotland.* HMSO, Edinburgh, Cmd 7235.

Sheail, J. (1981). *Rural conservation in inter-war Britain.* University Press, Oxford.

Sheail, J. (1987). *Seventy-five years in ecology: the British Ecological Society.* Blackwell Scientific Publications, Oxford.

Sheail, J. (1992). *Natural Environmental Research Council – a history.* NERC, Swindon.

Sheail, J. (1993). The management of wildlife and amenity – a UK post-war perspective, *Contemporary Record. The Journal of Contemporary History,* 7, 44–65.

Sheail, J. (1995a). John Dower, national parks, and town and country planning in Britain, *Planning Perspectives,* 10, 1–16.

Sheail, J. (1995b). War and the development of nature conservation in Britain, *Journal of Environmental Management,* 44, 267–83.

Sheail, J. (1998). *Nature conservation in Britain – the formative years.* Stationery Office, London.

Tansley, A.G. (1945). *Our heritage of wild nature: a plea for nature conservation.* University, Press, Cambridge.

2

Impressions From an Era

R.E. Boote

INTRODUCTION

MY LASTING IMPRESSIONS of the Nature Conservancy and its successors are those of the survival of the organisation, key sites, the wider countryside, research, relationships and campaigning – all of special relevance today.

A major factor for anyone writing about the nature conservation movement is that of achieving a perspective over the tumultuous changes that influenced it after 1945 and of comprehending its vast ramifications. Most of the issues touched on here were often in play concurrently and usually interacting within a flow of events whose priority varied from time to time.

A minor factor, perhaps, is that these impressions are not those of one who was a naturalist or budding scientist from boyhood. I came from a background of economics, local government and planning, with different aims and expectations. Yet I came to value very much the often passionate commitment of my colleagues and consider this to be one of the great and unyielding strengths of the NC and its successors. And I would emphasise that Members of the Conservancy and its committees – eminent scientists, leading land-owners and professional people – shared this commitment. They gave freely of their time, talent and knowledge to staff and, in turn, listened to and learned from them. A great debt is owed to these dedicated, unsung and unpaid, volunteers.

This commitment led to an ethos which I claim to have been a key element in the vast transformation of thought and action to which the survival of a statutory organisation for nature conservation has contributed and in which it now occupies an essential and significant role – one still cherished by many.

SURVIVAL

Survival of the organisation is dominated in the records by the name of Max Nicholson. From the outset, the NC and its aims and policies were opposed or challenged on numerous fronts and Max had few allies, initially, in Whitehall. John Sheail (1998) documents this authoritatively; for example, the views held by some MPs and landed interests and some in Whitehall that conservation was a back-door form of land nationalisation and that the NC – if it were to continue – should only operate under rigorous scrutiny and constraint.

These and other antagonistic views emerged in the numerous reviews of the first thirty years, as identified by Sheail. In particular, some in Whitehall took the lead in ensuring that resources of finance and staff were never adequate to the tasks and that NC policies and activities relating to sites, land management and such issues as pesticides were contested at every level (Sheail, 1985).

Survival also had a personal edge. Following advertised national competition, I had been recruited as a Principal in 1954. Yet it was not long before my colleagues and I at HQ, and in some Regions, were subjected to grading inspections by Treasury officers seeking to downgrade the level of our posts. These candle-end savers seemed, in their work, to be natural descendants from the Spanish Inquisition. The personal aspect was ever present. Some colleagues overheard guests from Whitehall at the NC's Tenth Year Celebration saying that there would not be another ten years – and they were nearly right! Until the advent, in 1963, of the Countryside in 1970 Movement there was little effective strength in professional and public support for conservation, despite the lead of some voluntary bodies, such as the Royal Society for the Protection of Birds. In some areas, the public and local press saw the NC as a cross between naturists and nudists – both of whom were found on a few reserves!

On such major issues as pesticides and pollution, emerging in the late 1950s, initially most concern, and later backing, came from the representative bodies of racing pigeon fanciers, fishermen and some hunting and shooting groups. However, some action over pesticides and pollution and other general environmental issues became increasingly difficult for vested interests to resist after the publication in the UK in 1963 of *Silent Spring* by Rachel Carson. As John Sheail points out in his seminal work on pesticides (1985), this book led to much fury – not unlike that around GM products today. As I had been a member of the Advisory Committee on Poisonous Substances from 1956, I had some authority, as well as much satisfaction, in pointing out to the Chairman in 1963 that some of the Committee's scientists were being much more emotional than they accused Rachel Carson of being (Sheail 1985, p. 90). And another quote from Sheail (p. 232) is relevant to the survival of NC: 'Whilst the shape, size and endeavours of the Nature Conservancy do not constitute the story of the pesticides/wildlife debate, its existence counted for a very great deal'.

The NC was probably the first agency of government to have a formal statement of PR Policy (1958/9). In preparing this, I took advice from the Institute of Public Relations (I was an Associate) and quite naturally purloined phrases from Keynesian economics, such as the 'multiplier effect'. There had also developed direct contact with the media, a tight-rope operation in view of the certainty that some interests would always be offended in the many faceted aspects of conservation. A liaison group was set up with journalists dealing with environmental issues, but this lacked continuity because of constant changes in personnel in the media. Nevertheless, much of special benefit was achieved, especially in the numerous activities for and after The Countryside in 1970 Movement. This involved major conferences in 1963, 1965 (plus the Keele Conference on Education in 1965) and in 1970. It also involved some thirty reports by specialists groups, over 350 organisations and around 1,000 representatives. It was led and serviced throughout by staff from the NC with support from other bodies, notably the Council for Nature and the Royal Society of Arts.

Overall, during the first two decades, despite the batterings on the organisation and the intrigues against it, a vast amount was achieved at home and abroad, as clearly documented by Sheail (1998) and Holdgate (1999). These achievements were critical to wildlife and their habitats, to research into related issues, and, ultimately, to the acceptance today by so many that the enjoyment of nature is more than the province of specialists and activists, but is an integral part of the culture of each and everyone.

KEY SITES

Conservation aims and the selection of key sites to fulfil them (in part) were gifted to the nation in superb prose by the Command Papers 7122 (1947) and 7184 (1949). Implementing these as a programme requiring finance and staff proved difficult, in some cases intractable. At the end of the first decade, the NC was disappointed in progress, with less than half of the Command Papers' sites established as National Nature Reserves. But these sites (all SSSIs) were an impressive selection which would contribute to the safeguarding of many of the major habitats characteristic of the land – the full coverage of which had to await the completion of the Nature Conservation Review in 1977 (which had its genesis in an Acquisition and Management Review initiated in 1965) and the Geological and other major appraisals then in progress.

The safeguard as NNR of the sites listed in the Command Papers had to surmount many hurdles of which attitudes were often the problem. One senior NERC official asked in the late '60s: 'wouldn't 10 to 12 NNR be enough?' Happily, the roll-call of NNR was then, and is now, impressive; superb sites in Scotland (some large, some small); an excellent range in Wales; and many key areas in England. These are clearly documented in the NC Annual Reports to Parliament, which testify to the achievement of a network of NNR – backed by LNR and other SSSIs – still without parallel elsewhere.

Management of NNR, and also that of some special SSSIs, initially was *ad hoc*. It was based largely on the interests of scientists already involved with the sites and on the immediacy of problems on them. However, in the late '50s and early '60s management regimes had been codified with pro formas, prescriptive aims and methods particular to the habitats. In this, research stations and centres often took the lead, but as scientific capacity increased in the Regions it became more of a shared undertaking. And the formation of Habitat Teams for the Nature Conservation Review and various internal forms of organisation (the Acquisition and Management Group, Training Sessions and so on) led to the development in depth of ideas and practices relevant not only to NNR but to the management of habitats in the wider countryside.

WIDER COUNTRYSIDE AND SSSIS

From the outset, those involved in the NC and its partnerships knew that the setting-up of NNR could never, of itself, guarantee the conservation of the nation's heritage of wildlife and their habitats. This needed to embrace habitats in both town and countryside and must include geological and geomorphological features for their fundamental and intrinsic significance.

Some reserves, especially in Scotland, were large enough to resist – at least initially – some of the external factors affecting Britain's land. These included pressure of land development for water, forests, urbanisation, access and tourism, and intensification of agriculture (hastened by the European Common Agricultural Policy). But nature conservation needed to be within a holistic approach of sympathetic land use and management based on reason and persuasion.

These thoughts for the wildlife and habitats of the wider countryside found expression in numerous ways: the Protection of Birds Acts; the official Committees on Agricultural Chemicals; the Red Deer and Red Grouse reports; work with wildfowlers on species and habitats; conservation clauses in development legislation; the NC Report to the Royal Commission on Commons; the Survey of the Inland Waters of the West Midlands; the Report on Broadlands; and the numerous Reports of the specialists groups of the '1970' Movement. Many of these brought into sharp focus for practical application the need to devise ways and means of ensuring multiple use in time and space of natural resources – a task likely to be with us for ever.

A glance at the breadth and depth of these numerous reports shows that the NC's aims and leadership permeated all recognisable aspects of the wider countryside – as well as the coast and some essential qualities of urban areas. Increasingly, as the statutory organisation, the NC advised on, and contributed evidence to, enquiries about a wide range of developments and projects: these included the Dungeness nuclear power station; the Third London Airport; barrages at Morecambe Bay and the Wash; and the future of such national 'jewels' as the New Forest – all of significance to people in town and country. Formal evidence was also given to several Parliamentary Select Committees, including two on Land Use.

With this background, as Chairman of the Council of Europe Committees responsible for European Conservation Year 1970 (ECY) and the European Conservation Conference in February, 1970, I chose with my continental colleagues the four major themes of the impacts on the natural environment of Urban Agglomeration, Industry, Agriculture and Forestry, and Leisure. And ECY 1970 was not, as the 1995 Year, an explicitly nature conservation year, but ranged widely over these major issues which had, by then, given more than adequate warning of the massive influences they would exert on the environment.

The Command Papers and the National Parks and Access to the Countryside Act, 1949, had provided, respectively, the idea and a practical instrument for the health of key sites in the wider countryside, namely the Sites of Special Scientific Interest. Action to safeguard these had started in the '50s, made progress in the '60s and accelerated in the '70s.

SSSIs, from the outset, increasingly assumed value in relation to measures to implement planning legislation, but their importance exploded as land use became more intensive, particularly in agriculture and forestry, leading inexorably – despite much opposition – to the 1981 Wildlife Act. Today, the SSSI is an essential element in the health of the wider countryside with its safeguarding equipped by stronger legislation and more resources, even if still inadequate for the challenges of the twenty-first century. Overall, SSSIs, and various international designations of similar intent, are essential measures towards achieving the major goal of the pioneers – that nature conservation is integral to the economic, environmental and social policies of the nation.

RESEARCH

All the achievements of these fifty years depend, in large part, on research. From the outset the NC was fortunate in that it had the goodwill and co-operation of the wealth of talent in the natural sciences available in the country, Many famous names served on the Council and its Scientific Policy Committee. Tansley, Elton, Pearsall, Fraser Darling, Wynne-Edwards, Ritchie, Ford, Richards, Dudley Stamp and many others contributed directly and through their leadership of specialist centres and University departments to the fund of knowledge for co-operation in nature conservation. This was, even in the early years, more than adequate for advising on specialist issues and for surveying and managing sites of prime importance for conservation – but the resources of finance and staff were cruelly inadequate, other than for the most immediate of tasks.

Inevitably, research at the Conservancy's widely located Merlewood and Furzebrook Research Stations in England, at Bangor in Wales and the two centres in Banchory and Edinburgh in Scotland, was based at first around specialists working in their chosen fields, though all contributed to the science base for effective coverage and management of habitats in the UK.

A wide range of investigation was fostered by the Council's judicious use of studentships, grants and contracts, securing co-operation from University and Field Centres throughout the country and, of special importance, fostering scientifically-qualified personnel equipped to carry forward the remit of the NC. In Scotland, names such as Duncan Poore, Donald McVean, David Jenkins and Adam Watson spring to mind. Research was initiated in zoological issues (especially ornithological), botanical (such as plant distribution) and coastal physiographical work – all of which was to contribute substantially to the Council's legislative and advisory functions.

The teams which were to make Monks Wood Experimental Station internationally renowned were set up in 1960 – moving into new buildings there in 1963. They were charged specifically to apply much of the knowledge available to conservation management and to investigate some of the critical issues of the time – notably pesticides, with work on the vital role of hedgerows in the countryside also being started. Many of the studies, but pre-eminently those on pesticides, took the NC and its successors into the realms of public policy and led to confrontations and campaigning.

In the UK, from 1965, NERC strengthened the Conservancy's research work into nature conservation and from 1973 (after the 'split' – see Sheail 1998) that of its Institute of Terrestrial Ecology. The Institute also received contracts from the new, independent Nature Conservancy Council, between whom personal contacts of scientists remained strong.

All through these early decades the corpus of rigorously-researched scientific knowledge and the experience of specialist management of scientific sites was increasing. This combination in one organisation was then unique worldwide. For example, in Scotland, John Berry was blessed to have students on specialist problems and an operational staff, though small in number, of diverse and wide-ranging talents and capacity – such as Thomas Huxley, John Arbuthnott, Joe Eggeling and Morton Boyd.

The wide range and depth of practical experience and knowledge accumulated benefited many other scientists and organisations internationally (Holdgate 1999). John Berry in 1954 played a key role in setting up the

IUCN Commission on Ecology and was responsible for the organisation of the IUCN (then IUPN) General Assembly held in Edinburgh in 1956. Other NC staff made significant contributions to numerous wide-ranging activities: Max Nicholson and Barton Worthington to the International Biological Program and the UNESCO Man and the Biosphere Program; to the development of Conventions, such as David Jenkins on Wetlands (RAMSAR) and Duncan Poore on Endangered Species (CITES); and to the 1972 Stockholm Conference; and, later, myself to the future of Antarctica.

Scientists and administrators from NC and its successors have held for several decades positions of leadership in numerous international organisations, influencing policies and action in IUCN, the Council of Europe and European Union, and numerous specialist environmental bodies world-wide. Some of these achievements have never been recognised, because they were initiated abroad to overcome frustrations in the UK.

Many international activities continue, both by serving staff and former members enjoying retirement. Norman Moore is a classic example of the 'Active Elder', attending IUCN specialist groups around the world. And Martin Holdgate, another 'Third Ager', most significantly in the past decade took on the challenging post of Director General of IUCN and thoroughly refuted the assertion by some that it was 'ungovernable', leaving it after six years firmly established as the leading global union of conservation.

RELATIONSHIPS

It was difficult, in the early years, for members, associates and staff of the NC to grasp the vast extent and number of relationships which action for nature conservation would demand. Obviously, the scientific community and landed interests loomed large, but political interests and those of a proliferating number of land users – ramblers, sportsmen, naturalists and so on – soon necessitated thorough consideration. Local government and statutory agencies, major and local sectors of industry and commerce and a host of other economic activities were soon involved. The voluntary bodies, especially over sites, birds and pesticides (notably the RSPB), and other groupings such as the County Naturalists' Trusts and the Council for Nature and bodies such as Friends of the Earth and Greenpeace were becoming highly important in anything related to the environment.

One of the most important set of relationships was, however, 'in-house'. By the late '50s, the diverse talents, experience, and knowledge of the staff – many scientific disciplines, land agency, administration, public relations – had melded into quite a unique capacity. Mutual training sessions and projects ensured a fast-learning curve from activities all over the country, achieving a

recognition which impelled training specialists from the Treasury to participate.

The corpus of knowledge thus commanded by the NC and its successors
led to a 'language of conservation' applicable from the formality of Whitehall
to the reality of the day-to-day work of landowners, farmers, lawyers,
volunteer experts and so on. This was reflected in numerous ways: with
members of the Association of British Manufacturers of Agricultural Chemicals (ABMAC); with providers of electricity and gas and sand and gravel;
with the Association (and in Scotland, Federation) of Country Landowners;
with the Farmers' Unions; with the National Trusts; and with most sectors of
economic life.

More widely, the NC developed liaison with the National Federation of
Women's Institutes and Townswomen Guilds, with Rotary Clubs and, of
course, with numerous environmental voluntary bodies and, importantly,
with educational institutions. One of the NC's great successes was mobilising
at Keele University in 1965 (under the '1970' Movement) some 60, mainly
national, organisations involved in all levels of education, including the then
Minister of State for Education. Much of the content focussed on *Science out
of Doors* – a book produced by a group Chaired by Max Nicholson with Tom
Pritchard as Scientific Secretary. If only this and Keele had been followed up
by the teaching profession!

Unfortunately, within the scientific community there were some still not
persuaded of the strength, as scientific disciplines, of the various sciences,
particularly ecology, crucial to the underpinning of conservation, nor, in some
cases, of the value of the aims and activities for nature conservation. Their
views often surfaced, most notably in the various reviews leading to the setting
up of NERC in 1965 and later in the 'split' of 1973 (see Sheail 1998).
However, a greater awareness of the sciences underpinning nature conservation was provided in June 1976 with the Royal Society's discussion on
'Scientific Aspects of Nature Conservation in Great Britain'. There was no
challenge then to the statement in my concluding remarks on 'the need to use
and extend our scientific understanding in order to retain what is best in our
natural environment and to create new quality in it'.

CAMPAIGNING

Nearly all the relationships in nature conservation involved some element or
sense of campaigning for 'a cause'. It took many forms, of which perhaps the
most important were the personal one-to-one contacts of staff from the
regions and research stations giving numerous and frequent talks, lectures,
papers and so on, to a wide variety of audiences. The core of this 'campaign-

ing' was not propaganda (in the unpopular usage), but the constant need to initiate explanation and to enthuse others to join in achieving specific goals. A classic case was that of staff from the NC and the RSPB achieving a high quality of rapport with representatives of ABMAC over pesticides, often out-flanking the policies and preferences of MAFF.

Some staff trod delicately in dual roles in the organisation and as leaders in voluntary bodies. Regular liaison with the RSPB, Society for the Promotion of Nature Conservation (SPNC) and the Council for Nature became increasingly fruitful. In 1963, the first National Nature Week Exhibition in the Royal Horticultural Society's halls in London contained a major dramatic exhibit on the deterioration of the countryside prepared by Brian Grimes, Head of NC's technical staff. This was the spur to HRH The Duke of Edinburgh to invite Max Nicholson to 'do something' and led to the initiative of The Countryside in 1970. At its first Conference in 1963, some 150 types of impacts on the countryside were identified. For eight years it involved directly around 1,000 representatives of 330 organisations.

This activity further changed the scale and scope of the environmental movement, involving policy makers and people in all walks of life and the burgeoning membership of voluntary bodies. It made a major contribution to the vast shift in public attitudes and support emerging from the numerous brilliant and popular TV programmes and prize-winning films, such as 'The Living Pattern' by National Benzole and films on leisure by Shell and pollution by BP. A new generation, informed and influenced in the late '50s and early '60s, was becoming conscious of its inheritance and as these took up positions in the professions and industry and government so the terms of reference everywhere started to change in favour of the environment.

All this was also of personal benefit to me. The contacts I developed with many organisations and leaders at home and abroad were a source of confidence and knowledge for my book *Man and Environment* (Arvill, 1967) and its five editions from 1967 to 1983. This, in turn, materially influenced the aims and activities I pursued as Secretary to '1970' and as Chairman of the main Committee and Vice President of the European Conference in the European Conservation Year (ECY). The last named was five years in the planning and was initiated and led from the NC. It comprised several specialist groups and numerous activities in over twenty countries. Its main focus was the first European Conservation Conference in February 1970, which appraised the impacts on the environment of urbanism, industry, agriculture and forestry and leisure and produced a 'Declaration on the Management of the Natural Environment'. The Conference was attended by Royalty and Prime Ministers and leaders from near thirty countries, including East Europe and the Soviet Union, Japan and the USA.

Some of today's critical issues would still benefit, I believe, from a reading of my Review for the Third '1970' Conference and from follow-up to the ECY Conference Declaration on the management of Europe's environment, now reflected in an excellent strategy drafted a few years ago for the Council of Europe by Dick Steele (my successor as Director General, NCC). Sadly, this is inadequately known and acted upon; if the 'past is a foreign country', then that of much of conservation terrain (e.g. toxic chemicals) seems rarely visited!

But campaigning of the kind inherent in nature conservation and parti-cularly in '1970' and ECY was considered inappropriate by some members of the formal scientific establishment, as well as by key Whitehall departments. Consequently, when the NC became part of NERC its staff were enjoined not to get involved in policy issues and certainly not to campaign. Unavoidably, the exception had to be made for the '1970' and ECY activities because they had by then already acquired high-level sponsors. But this did not stop pressure from certain departments and NERC to curtail my activities, though my colleagues and I still carried out our NC work. I was, therefore, particularly grateful to Duncan Poore (then Director of the NC in NERC) for the support and protection he gave to enable us – in his words – 'to get on with the job'.

But the failure to understand that value judgements and policy issues are inherent in nature conservation was a key factor in the 'split' of 1973. The task of proving this to NERC and others (in particular, the Chief Scientist in the Cabinet office) was shouldered by Duncan Poore, backed by the majority of the Nature Conservancy Committee. This led inevitably to the 'split' and, of great importance, the emergence of the NCC – all now an essential part of conservation history.

In sum, the distinctive and unique qualities of the NC – its interweaving of research and conservation management, its wide-ranging and diverse relation-ships with an ever-present element of campaigning – created and accumulated a wealth of experience which led many to leadership internationally.

For myself, although nothing can overshadow memories of my activities for UK '1970' and ECY '70, my proudest specific recollection of campaigning for a great environmental cause is that of my contribution to the governance of Antarctica. As Martin Holdgate records (1999, pp. 160–1, 168), the activity I was involved in (after retirement from NCC) from May 1980 to late 1982 'defined the Union's (IUCN) Antarctic policy for many years to come'. It ensured an ecological basis for the Convention on the Conservation of the Marine and Living Resources of Antarctica and 'paved the way for the Antarctic Conservation Strategy' of IUCN.

APPRAISAL

All of these 'impressions of an era' and much other activity of the pioneers in environmental management offer lessons for the twenty-first century. But their application will be affected by many massive shifts in the bases of modern society. Two of these – the ageing of society and the scale and depth of intercommunication – merit very special consideration by all concerned to evaluate the economic, environmental, social and political elements governing all life on this planet.

Turning again to the specific impressions, what lessons can be briefly noted at this stage? Immediately, it is worth quoting the view expressed by Sir Robert May – Government Chief Scientific Adviser – in the 1998 Annual Report of The Institute of Zoology, 'better understanding, and better public awareness, of our imperilled heritage of biological diversity' is 'the greatest challenge of our time'.

Survival can be put in question by mergers and re-organisation. These may blur aims and blunt the edge of purpose. And survival is always on the agenda when failure to have advice accepted becomes too frequent. This may further be imperilled by the complexity and fragmentation both of issues and of policies and structures to respond to them. One longs for the prophetic clarity of the rare Treasury official who wrote in 1948 – re the NC – of 'the value (for the Government) of having better warning of the problems likely to arise from the 'degree and direction of man's interference with nature' ' (Sheail 1998, p. 32).

Reserves, SSSIs and other key areas continue to be threatened by pressures on coast and the wider countryside – which have been so much affected in recent decades. It is ironic that after near four decades of including clauses in much legislation 'to have regard to' conservation/environment, the Government finds it necessary to include in a recent strategy document (Department of the Environment, 1999, p. 30) that the 'creation of all new bodies to *include consideration* of specific remit on sustainable development'. Such considerations will be subject, inexorably, to changes, such as those in the Common Agricultural Policy with the entry into world markets of the East European countries, and the advent of new technologies, such as genetically modified products with the control vested in multi-national concerns. Vigilance is more vital than ever before.

Research can suffer – and often does – from inadequate resources and, sadly, from time to time, the lack of true independence and freedom – the mainsprings of enquiry and scholarship, more vital today than ever before as demonstrated in recent years in several countries within the European Union. New systems, such as 'blind trusts', need to be devised so that the activity of scientists may be increasingly governed less by the providers of finance (whether government or industry) and more by codes of guidance on ethical and professional issues and, as always, by the appraisal of their scientific peers.

And as for *campaigning and relationships*, as illustrated in this paper, these will always be central to a balance between short- and long-term goals, as we aspire to achieve a healthy mind, in a healthy body, in a healthy environment. The voluntary bodies and other environmental activists are vital to this endeavour. They must ensure that their aims are well-founded on facts, clearly focussed and achievable in well-set target times. Their task in informing, educating and mobilising public awareness and concern is formidable, as they face much competition for public attention and much cynicism from many people about the trustworthiness of those in positions of authority. So sustainability of effort must also prevail in the policies and programmes of these leaders in custodianship of the environment.

CONCLUSION

Today we find that the practical responses of many people to caring for and sharing our environment are based more and more on a renewed quest – ethical, moral, religious, humanitarian – for a sense of purpose in life. And nature conservationists, in particular, have shown that their blend of these qualities has proven to be a valuable form of long-range realism. But constant vigilance is required to ensure that the fundamentals are maintained – whatever key words (such as sustainability, biodiversity) are operable at any given time.

Overall, the first thirty years of the NC and its successors have been blessed with numerous challenges and opportunities which have led now to generations much concerned about wildlife and their habitats and, increasingly, the quality of the biosphere, as a recognition both of their obligations to posterity and the survival of mankind.

REFERENCES

Arvill, R. (1967). *Man and Environment. The Strategy of Choice.* Penguin – A Pelican Original. Harmondsworth. Five editions to 1983.

Department of the Environment, Transport and the Regions (1999). A Strategy for Sustainable Development in the UK. Cmd. 4345. Stationery Office.

Holdgate, M. (1999). *The Green Web. Fifty Years of IUCN.* Earthscan.

Sheail, J. (1998). *Nature Conservation in Britain. The Formative Years.* Stationery Office.

Sheail, J. (1985). *Persticides and Nature Conservation. The British Experience.* Clarendon Press, Oxford.

3

Toxic Chemicals and Wildlife: Raising Awareness and Reducing Damage

Norman W. Moore

CONSERVATION IS ABOUT the future, as I said twelve years ago in the opening sentence of my book *The Bird of Time* (Moore 1987). Celebration of the past fifty years can surely be fully justified if it helps us make a better future. Therefore in this contribution I shall first describe how we studied the effects of pesticides on wildlife so that we could reduce their harmful side effects, and then suggest ways in which the experiences of the 1960s can help us tackle tomorrow's problems.

Our work at Monks Wood in the 1960s must be seen in its historical perspective, which has been so admirably described by John Sheail (1976, 1985). It was a very different world from today's. The environment was rarely in the news once people had lost interest in the myxomatosis problem. In the 1950s most people had not even heard of the Nature Conservancy. In 1955 only three Wildlife Trusts existed. To those who were concerned, the main threats to wildlife seemed to come from urbanisation, planting conifers in unsuitable places and the persecution of rare species. There was extraordinarily little interest in agriculture and the wildlife that depended upon it; hedges were taken for granted and were not talked about or written about. However, by the end of the 1950s all this began to change. Those living in areas where arable farming predominated came across large numbers of dead birds and mammals, apparently killed by pesticides. Attention became focussed on agriculture. Those in charge of the overall policy of the Nature Conservancy, most notably Bob Boote (Chapter 2 above), Max Nicholson and Barton Worthington, saw that the organisation must do something about the growing challenge to wildlife on farmland. Accordingly Monks Wood was planned in 1959 and the Toxic Chemicals and Wildlife Section started work in 1960, incidentally two years before the publication of Rachel Carson's book *Silent Spring*. We moved in to the new Experimental Station in 1962.

I had been working in South West England in the 1950s and had not realised the scale and seriousness of the pesticide problem till I saw what was happening in East Anglia with my own eyes. Clearly the problem was extremely complicated; a large range of pesticides was already being used and they varied not only in toxicity but also apparently in their effects. Some organisms seemed little affected, others were clearly suffering huge losses. As the head of the newly established Toxic Chemicals and Wildlife Section, I had to make decisions about our lines of attack and hence about recruitment, laboratory equipment and experimental land requirements. In particular, I had to make decisions about which pesticides to study, and to assess which species appeared to be most threatened and which therefore should be studied intensively. I had to decide how far we should go in determining toxicological and ecological mechanisms, and the extent to which we should study other factors in the countryside which could also be affecting wildlife.

Forewarned by what Hunt and Bischoff (1960) had discovered at Clear Lake in California I decided that persistence of pesticides was probably more important than their toxicity, and that we must attack the pesticide problem both in the laboratory and the field. I also decided that the destruction of hedges was on such a huge scale that we must assess the amount lost and assess its implications. So, we took a broad view of hazards to wildlife in the countryside. I soon realised that our work might appear negatively anti-pesticide, therefore we also worked on projects to discover whether some herbicides might not be useful tools for conservationists in habitat management.

Quite early on we developed an hypothesis which could explain the avian casualties which we, the RSPB, the BTO and the Game Conservancy were observing in the field. It was this. The seed-eating birds were dying because they ate corn dressed with the very toxic persistent organochlorine insecticides aldrin, dieldrin and heptachlor. Birds of prey, foxes and badgers were dying from eating the seed-eating birds which had built up considerable residues of these chemicals or their metabolites in their fat. Sub-lethal doses of the much less toxic DDT were affecting the egg shell thickness of birds of prey. Thus the catastrophic declines of Peregrine, Sparrowhawk and Kestrel were due to a combination of both lethal and sub-lethal doses of persistent organochlorine insecticides. To date only a few species appeared to be seriously threatened by these chemicals but their increasing use in arable farming, horticulture and animal husbandry was likely to affect a growing number of species, including economically important fish which bred in coastal waters. We felt that the evidence collected in the early 1960s justified the country taking precautionary action by banning or greatly restricting the use of the persistent organochlorine insecticides.

Restrictions on these pesticides could only be implemented through the Pesticide Safety Precautions Scheme, which by agreement with the chemical industry controlled the use of pesticides in the United Kingdom. As the only environmentalist on the Scientific Subcommittee of the Advisory Committee on Pesticides, I had a difficult task in trying to persuade my colleagues to act on circumstantial evidence. To a field biologist the circumstantial evidence seemed very good. No alternative hypothesis held water: there was no evidence of disease affecting the stricken species and none of them had ever shown sudden declines as part of natural population cycles in the past. The bodies of birds of prey found dead rarely showed signs of starvation. The only really new factor was the introduction of the pesticides. The amounts of the pesticides found in the bodies of birds found dead indicated that the birds had been killed by the pesticides.

My colleagues in the regulatory committees wanted experimental evidence to support our hypothesis, but conclusive experimental evidence was impossible to provide. Peregrines were too rare to be used in toxicological experiments, and at that time it was not known how to breed them in captivity. Field trials covering hundreds of square miles on a widely dispersed declining species were clearly out of the question. In practice we had to rely on toxicological evidence obtained from Bengalese Finches, and on comparisons of the success of birds of prey in areas where few pesticides were used with that in areas where they were widely used. While industry and the PSPS were happy to rely on toxicological experiments on rats to assess the risks of pesticides to human beings, they appeared not to accept experiments on Bengalese Finches when assessing risks to Peregrines!

The underlying problem was that the suspect pesticides were extremely valuable to farmers, and their sales produced large profits for their manufacturers at home and abroad. No one wanted to hear anything against the use of DDT which had saved countless lives at the end of the Second World War and afterwards.

Persistent organochlorine insecticide residues having been discovered in the bodies of sea birds and their eggs (Moore and Tatton 1965) and in the bodies of Antarctic birds (George and Frear 1966) we had no doubt that environmental contamination by pesticides was a global problem. There was growing evidence that other persistent toxic chemicals, notably PCBs, were also widely dispersed. In those days the idea of pollution on a global scale was novel. We thought it was so important that we ought to alert the public to it. Therefore we took opportunities to discuss the issue on TV, radio and in the press. We took great care to be as accurate as possible and to make it clear we were not anti-pesticide as such. Sometimes we were not helped by the media and others making false claims, for example on the harmfulness of DDT to humans. The scientific credibility of those demanding restrictions on the persistent organochlorine insecticides was crucial. There is little doubt that the public debate did force Government, Industry and PSPS to take the results of our research at Monks Wood and our recommendations more seriously.

The use of aldrin, dieldrin and heptachlor as a cereal seed dressing at spring sowing was the most obviously dangerous use of these chemicals. It was phased out quite quickly. It took several years before the other uses of these chemicals were withdrawn, but eventually they were. The bans on them could at last put our hypothesis to the test. As we had predicted, the populations of Peregrine, Sparrowhawk and Kestrel recovered as the persistent organochlorine insecticides disappeared from the environment. That particular threat to wildlife in Britain had been removed and, in reducing damage, we had raised awareness of the worldwide problem of environmental pollution.

I believe it is important today to analyse why we were generally speaking successful. First, I believe that the composition of the Toxic Chemicals and Wildlife Section was crucial. It was multidisciplinary. It contained good field workers who were in close touch with what was actually happening on the ground. It contained good chemists whose chemical analyses could be trusted and good toxicologists who could relate what they were doing with what was being observed in the field. We worked side by side as a team and believed what we were doing was important.

Secondly, thanks to the philosophy and, I suspect, actions of our headquarters and of Kenneth Mellanby, the Director of Monks Wood, we had total independence and freedom from interference from our own organisation, other Government bodies and the chemical industry. While we had a continuous dialogue with the PSPS committees, ABMAC and individual chemical firms, pressure was never put on us to keep quiet. In fact we had good relations with several chemical firms and even did joint research projects with them. Non-interference seemed to have full Government backing. I well remember a cabinet minister reminding us that since the Nature Conservancy was a Quango it must be free to criticise Government policy when it felt it should do so. During the 1960s and early 1970s our work interested many scientists and conservation bodies overseas. I was frequently asked to visit other countries and international organisations to describe what we were doing. The thing that most impressed conservationists overseas was that the Nature Conservancy had its own totally independent research branch. Thus our independence had international as well as national support.

Thirdly our efforts to alert the public to the dangers of environmental contamination by pesticides and PCBs and to the losses of hedgerows gained us widespread public support. We were seen to be at the cutting edge of conservation. Also it prevented us in the Nature Conservancy from living in a scientific ivory tower remote from public concerns.

The events I have been describing took place thirty to forty years ago. The situation is very different today. The Nature Conservancy has been divided up into four agencies and part of a Research Council. Most of the research work of the agencies has to be done through contracts. However, information is more readily available, there are more observers in the field and there is much more interest in conservation. Despite these differences I believe our experiences in the 1960s have considerable relevance today.

First, do we still need something equivalent to the Toxic Chemicals and Wildlife Section? In other words do we still need a research unit which keeps an eye out for trouble, which assesses the risks of new technologies to wildlife and seeks solutions to the problems which have been discovered? It is excellent that English Nature is demanding proper testing of the effects of genetically modified crops, but much time might have been saved if warnings had been given earlier, as undoubtedly they would have been if a watchdog unit had been in operation in recent years. Trade becomes globalised and information technology develops apace. As a result, technological developments which affect the land and the sea produce new problems more quickly. Experience shows that all developments have side effects, and many side effects are deleterious and unforeseen. The need for a watchdog unit to identify and to study them seems to have increased rather than diminished since the 1960s.

The extent to which a watchdog unit should itself carry out research on the problems it unearths is a technical one depending on the problems encountered. They are likely to be so diverse that it is probable that the unit would have to give contracts for the study of many, if not most of them. The important conclusion is that some body, headed and staffed by independent scientists, should be made responsible for systematically looking for environmental trouble and giving advice on how harmful side effects should be reduced.

My second conclusion is a more general one and concerns the conservation agencies of which the watchdog unit would be a part. It concerns the relationship between the agencies and conservation bodies and the wider public in England, Scotland and Wales today. In the 1960s those of us working on the problems which arose from new agricultural technologies learnt that constructive contact with the NGOs and the general public was immensely important. To gain support we had to convince everyone that we were wholly independent and totally committed to conservation, while demonstrating to everyone, and especially the scientific community, that we were being objective and fair in our judgements.

The need for good relationships between the agencies on the one hand and the NGOs and general public on the other is even greater today. Therefore it is not surprising that the agencies put so much emphasis on Public Relations and Partnerships. As one of the founders of the Farming and Wildlife Advisory Group (FWAG) I know the value of partnership with those whose interests often conflict with ours. But there is a danger that the need to maintain partnership can lead to seeking consensus at all costs. By papering over the cracks we can give the impression that we are not being whole-hearted advocates of conservation. (I say 'we' because although long retired I still identify myself with my past employers!) Sometimes it can look as if we are putting ourselves above the battle and are acting in a judgmental role. When we appear to accept compromises which are clearly unacceptable from the conservation point of view it alienates grass roots support. Once that occurs it is only a matter of time before we lose the support of the general public.

However good the PR and the partnerships, we cannot avoid conflict altogether. Some conflict between conservation and other interests is inevitable because it is built in to nearly every situation. This is because we cannot help competing with other interests for resources, notably land. Conservation is not an extra which one adds if possible when other demands have been met. It is an essential ingredient of modern life: our future depends upon it. We in the agencies have a duty to defend and promote it robustly on behalf of the nation, no less than farmers and foresters defend their interests.

In some conflicts there is no doubt to all concerned that conservation should prevail, and it does. However, in many conflicts a compromise must be sought. Sometimes we will be defeated when we should not be. I believe that how we react to that situation is crucial. We must, of course, accept the verdict of Parliament, the Inquiry Inspector etc., as is required by law. But at the same time we must make it clear that we believe the verdict is wrong. It is only by doing this that we deserve our independence and retain the support of the whole conservation movement.

Some of you may think that I am making too much of this delicate balance between pragmatic and necessary compromise and transparent dedication to the cause of conservation. It may look like splitting hairs, but the numerous discussions I have had with members of staff of the agencies and of NGOs convince me that it is not. It was probably easier for us in the 1960s, but I believe that we did get the balance better then than we do today. To sum up, I would like to see the agencies celebrate our fifty years by setting up a watchdog unit and by a renewed, more overt and robust support of conservation values in the coming years, confidently based on good science.

REFERENCES

George, J.L. and Frear, D.E.H. (1966). Pesticides in the Antarctic in *Pesticides in the Environment and their Effects on Wildlife* (ed. N.W. Moore) supplement to volume 3 of the *Journal of Applied Ecology*. 155–167.

Hunt, E.G. and Bischoff, A.I. (1960). Inimical effects on wildlife of periodic DDD applications to Clear Lake. *California Fish and Game* 46. 91–106.

Moore, N.W. (1987). *The Bird of Time. The Science and Politics of Nature Conservation.* Cambridge University Press, Cambridge. 290pp.

Moore, N.W. and Tatton, J.O'G. (1965). Organochlorine insecticide residues in the eggs of sea birds. *Nature* 207, No. 4992. 42–3.

Sheail, J. (1976). *Nature in Trust. The History of Nature Conservation in Britain*. Blackie, Glasgow and London. 270pp.

Sheail, J. (1985). *Pesticides and Nature Conservation. The British Experience 1950–1975*. Clarendon Press, Oxford. 276pp.

4

New Pressures on the Land: Recreation

Michael Dower

THIS IS A story covering forty years of social change, which in turn contributed to a new perspective on the relations between people and the land. My focus is on recreation, and particularly the demands of city-dwellers for recreation in the countryside. These demands played a major role in the origins of the National Parks Act of 1949. Popular desire for access to the countryside had fuelled in the late nineteenth century the growth of access organisations and the early attempts by Bryce and others to secure access to mountains through legislation.

Thus the Dower and Hobhouse reports, and the 1949 Act itself, had a strong element of provision for recreation. Their main emphasis was upon the needs of ramblers. My father's view was that the National Parks authority should take direct responsibility for meeting those needs:

> What is asked and what must substantially be given if the insistent claims of all ramblers' organisations and of the large and growing army of individual walkers are to be at all satisfied, may be simply stated: *(a)* as regards all 'uncultivated' land, *i.e.* mountains, moors, hill grazings, heaths, clifflands, etc. that the public shall have the right to wander at will over their whole extent, subject only to a minimum of regulations to prevent abuse and to a minimum of excepted areas where such wandering would clearly be incompatible with some other publicly necessary use of the land; and *(b)* as regards all 'cultivated' farmland and woodland, that the public shall have assured right to use an ample provision of footpaths and other ways through it.
>
> (Dower, 1945, p.28)

One may remark immediately that, fifty years later, these simple answers to 'insistent claims' have still not been fully achieved.

Space for rambling was, however, only part of what the Dower and Hobhouse reports called for, in order to meet the phrase in my father's definition of a National Park, that 'areas and facilities for public open-air enjoyment (should) be amply provided'. The reports called for ample and varied holiday accommodation; space for specialist activities (Hobhouse charmingly called them 'country contentments') such as rock-climbing, cycling, canoeing, boating, sailing, riding, fishing and the study of natural beauty; facilities for motorists, though on a basis of segregated use of roads in a manner that we would today call 'traffic management'; and guidance to visitors through warden services, public information and the creation of National Park centres. (Dower, 1945: National Parks Committee, 1947).

A striking point about the two reports, as we look back on them after fifty years, is their optimism about the compatibility between the different purposes of, or activities within, the National Parks. My father's report notes that: '. . . generally speaking the interests of agriculture and of landscape beauty are at one . . . Agriculture, landscape preservation and recreational provisions must march together' and again 'between rambling and farming there is no major conflict of interest, nor in practice any serious amount of trouble'. Being himself a rambler and a grouse shooter, he dismissed the concept that these two activities might be incompatible (a point to which I will return).

However, the pioneers of the National Parks did recognise that there were forms of recreation that did not fit well into National Parks. My father stated that:

> . . . those who come to National Parks should be such as wish to enjoy and cherish the beauty and quietude of unspoilt country and to take their recreation, active or passive, in ways that do not impair the beauty or quietude, nor spoil the enjoyment of them by others. For all who want to spend their holidays gregariously, and to enjoy the facilities – so well provided by the resorts – of cinemas, music-halls, dance-cafés, bathing pools, pleasure parks, promenades, shopping-centres and the like, National Parks are not the place.
>
> (Dower, 1945, p.23)

The Hobhouse report, in its turn, said that national parks should be managed so as to:

> . . . ensure the peace and beauty of the countryside and the rightful interests of the resident population are not menaced by an excessive concentration of visitors, or disturbed by incongruous pursuits.
>
> (National Parks Committee, 1947, p.9)

These phrases foreshadow the comments about 'quiet enjoyment' in the Edwards Report of 1991. (National Parks Review Panel, 1991, p.34 et seq.)

The creation of the ten National Parks during the 1950s coincided with a period of post-war austerity and then of gradually-rising prosperity. The demands for open-air recreation rose, but a pace which did not place severe pressure on the Parks. In the Country Life book on *Britain's National Parks*, published in 1959, Harold Abrahams recorded that:

> . . . the Parks are very young (but the) first steps have been firmly taken. Properties in the Lake District and on the Pembrokeshire Coast have been acquired to provide hotel and hostel accommodation; many new car parks and lay-bys have been provided throughout the National Parks; new camping and caravan sites laid out and in use; new footpaths created; . . . and land acquired to give public access, or to make parking facilities when money is more plentiful. Facilities for public access for recreation to open country in the National Parks are on the whole satisfactory, by the goodwill of landowners, and so far only in the Peak District has it proved necessary to secure major changes in the *de facto* position. There, by agreements made from 1954 onwards, access has been secured to some 24,000 acres of Kinder and Bleaklow plateaux.
>
> (Abrahams, 1959, pp. 116–117)

However, writing (in the same book) on 'The future of National Parks', Pauline Dower foreshadowed the threat to the Parks represented by the rise in ownership and use of cars:

> The majority of tourists come by car to National Parks and may be expected to do so in future. Car drivers are prone to like good motor roads and the opening of the new motorways will encourage some to expect that roads throughout the country will be improved to accommodate faster motor traffic. But a country road is part and parcel of the landscape through which it runs, and to alter such a road to suit fast motor traffic is no part of the purpose of National Parks.
>
> (Abrahams, 1959, p.129)

By the early 1960s, the growth in demand for leisure activities, including countryside recreation, was becoming very evident. The demands were new, not in kind but in quantity and in their penetration of the countryside. They arose because of the growth in personal incomes, leisure time, car ownership and related factors. There was a formidable growth in the volume of recreational visits to the countryside by British people, and particularly in visits by car. Tourism also grew rapidly, with a strong component of countryside visits. The activities pursued became more varied and sophisticated, for example in the trend towards air, water and motor sports.

Delegates to the first Countryside in 1970 Conference, held in 1963, recognised that the provision that was being made by national park committees and by local authorities under the 1949 Act was not sufficient to cope with this rising demand. It was clear that demand was being frustrated, and that recreation and tourism were having adverse impact on the countryside. Calls were made for more vigorous action on rights of way, for more access to open land, for legislation to secure sound management of common land, for warden and information services, for outdoor education, for traffic management and zoning systems in national parks, and for increased recreational use of forests, reservoirs and inland waters (The Nature Conservancy, 1964, pp.30–35).

The emphasis, in fact, was shifting from the national parks onto the broader countryside, including the areas near the cities. Speaking at the Annual Conference of the National Playing Fields Association in 1963, the Duke of Edinburgh said:

> We are on threshold of the age of leisure, and the problem is no longer academic. There are stark and immediate problems facing us. The queues for playing fields are getting longer; the pressure on general sports and recreation clubs of all sorts is increasing. Swimming pools and sailing clubs are getting crowded, and recreational users of water are beginning to run into each other.
>
> It is no longer a question of encouraging people to take part; from now on we have to concentrate on providing facilities of the right sort and in the right place, and properly organised.
>
> (Quoted in Civic Trust, 1964, p.13)

The implications which this 'age of leisure' might have for countryside recreation had been set out the year before on the other side of the Atlantic. The U.S. Outdoor Recreation Resources Review Commission, reporting in 1962 on the basis of extensive research, showed that active use of leisure went up as personal income rose: that growing mobility was putting heavy pressure on recreation resources never used before; that widespread education not only released more youngsters on holiday but changed their attitudes towards leisure, the better educated being more active; and that older people were remarkably keen on the less vigorous outdoor activities, such as walking, driving, sight-seeing, fishing. The broad conclusion of the American report was that their population might double, but the demand for outdoor recreation would treble, by the year 2000. They pointed to the need for a National Outdoor Recreation Policy, in which the States should play a pivotal role, local governments should expand their effort to provide space and recreation areas, and private enterprise should be an important force (Outdoor Recreation Resources Review Commission, 1962, pp.3–10).

These American conclusions affected the thinking of the Civic Trust team, led by Leslie Lane, which in 1963–4 prepared the proposals for creation of a regional park in the Lee valley, in north-east London. As a member of that team, I spent a happy year tramping the tracks and derelict lands in the 20–

mile length of the valley, and meeting everybody who mattered in the fields of sport and leisure provision. We created a vision for a highly versatile playground for Londoners, providing for a wide variety of sport, informal recreation and entertainment – a vision which has in large part been realised by the Lee Valley Regional Park Authority (Civic Trust, 1964).

That experience, in turn, provided the stimulus to my own report of 1965, *Fourth Wave: the Challenge of Leisure.* I showed how in Britain the population, personal income, car-ownership and educational levels had all risen over the previous decade; the length of the basic working week had fallen; the number of retired people had increased – and how these trends appeared set to continue. I commented that:

> . . . the flood gates which have opened in America are beginning to open here, and it seems likely that our own surge of leisure will be more dramatic than the Americans' in proportion to population. Until the vital study of leisure growth has been made, we must assume that demand for active leisure in Britain may well treble within this century.

> This growth will put enormous pressure on the face of Britain. Already the weekend multitudes are congesting our roads, fouling our downs and commons with litter and soiling our lay-bys: their chalets and caravans threaten all parts of our coast, their cars and motorboats echo in quiet valleys and lakes. Yet the very leisure that brings this onslaught could permit that widening of life, of human pleasure and achievement, which the Greeks understood and which 'generous-hearted men have dreamed of for long generations'. Can we enhance the lives of our people without ruining the island they live upon? This is the new acute challenge to architects and planners.

> (Dower, 1965, p.123)

I spelt out the implications of this challenge at the level of the city, the region and the nation. I noted that:

> The National Parks Commission now intends to take a 'second look' at all the national parks to see what further recreation could and should be placed within them. There is a danger that the sheer weight of recreation already pressing upon the parks may force the commission to accept denser use than the parks can take. The 'second look' *must* therefore be put into the context of the whole leisure needs and resources of the nation. The best way to achieve this would be to give the National Parks Commission the power and the staff to do a real national job.

> (Dower, 1965, p. 175)

I concluded my report by recommending (*inter alia*) that:

> The Government should initiate, possibly through an enlarged National Parks Commission, an assessment of national demand for leisure facilities, and should formulate broad principles for satisfying this demand.

> In consultation with the Central Council of Physical Recreation, the Arts Council and other bodies, the Government should also initiate research into standards of provision for buildings and other facilities for leisure in urban areas.

> Government agencies, statutory bodies and private landowners, including the Forestry Commission, National Trust, British Waterways and Railways Boards and managers of common lands, should be encouraged to consider provision for leisure as a major or secondary use of land or buildings they control.

(Dower, 1965, p.189)

That report was published in 1965; and the same year saw the creation of the Sports Council, as the first of a series of Government responses to the growth of popular demand for leisure activity. The following years saw the creation of the Countryside Commissions and the Tourist Boards; and enhanced responsibilities in the recreational field for the British Waterways Board, the Forestry Commission and local authorities.

In relation to the heritage of the 1949 Act, the most significant of these initiatives was the creation of the Countryside Commissions. In England and Wales, the Commission replaced, and subsumed the duties of, the National Parks Commission, but was given wider responsibilities related to protection of the natural beauty of the whole of the countryside and to provision of facilities for public enjoyment of it. The Commission's powers included the ability to designate, and to grant-aid, country parks and picnic sites proposed by local authorities and other bodies. The Countryside Act of 1968 enabled local authorities to make provision, in these and other ways, for countryside recreation.

The Countryside Commission came into existence in August 1968. Inheriting the staff of the National Parks Commission, it was able to get quickly into stride. The recreational clauses of the Countryside Act attracted an active response among local authorities and other bodies. The powers to propose country parks and picnic sites were used, in some places, to extend the facilities and to improve the management of sites already open to the public; and elsewhere to create new public facilities.

Within 10 years of the passing of the Act, the Commission had designated a total of 154 country parks (129 sponsored by local authorities, 25 by other bodies) and 193 picnic sites (173 by local authorities and 20 by other bodies). Very many of these country parks and picnic sites were located in the south and east of England, in regions which had no national parks. But in the north and west of England, and in Wales, country parks were in some areas deliberately used by local authorities to serve recreational needs which might otherwise have fallen on the National Parks.

This was in line with a recommendation of the National Parks Policies Review Committee, which had been set up in 1971 under the chairmanship of Lord Sandford. This Committee noted the adverse impact upon the national parks of private cars, which had grown in number from 2.4 million when the first national parks were created in 1951 to 12.1 million in 1971. The Committee called for more country parks to be set up near centres of population to help siphon some of the pressures off the national parks. They proposed a zoning approach to the planning and management of recreation pressures on the national parks. They argued that caravan and camping provision should be made at the periphery of the parks. They suggested that more use could be made of traffic management schemes and public transport to diminish the destructive force of the car (National Parks Policies Review Committee, 1974).

Through the creation of country parks and other facilities in the early 1970s, the public sector came more fully into the field of leisure provision; and recreation became a significant secondary – and in some areas the primary – use of many areas of land or water in National Parks and in the rest of the countryside. The prospect was of continued formidable growth in recreational demands. The House of Lords' Select Committee on Sport and Leisure, reporting in 1973, said that:

> The Committee are convinced that the demand for facilities for participation in sport and in the enjoyment of leisure out-of-doors has increased greatly and will continue to do so . . . there is particularly vigorous growth in outdoor recreation. Urgent action must be taken to meet the heavy pressure which is building up on the countryside, on waterspace and on sport facilities, or the well-being of the community and the conservation of the countryside will suffer.

> A change in emphasis in countryside facilities is recommended, to concentrate sites for day-trippers on the urban fringe in preference to the heart of the countryside . . . the committee call for a campaign to bring into existence new schemes like that in the Lee Valley. (Select Committee of the House of Lords on Sport and Leisure, 1973, pp. cxxvii-cxxviii).

The House of Lords' Committee recommended a national recognition of the slogan 'Recreation for All'. The irony is that that report was published in the very year of the war between Israel and the Arab states, followed by the use of oil price as a weapon, the consequent effect in inflation, and later the lead-in to depression. The result was that the assumptions on which predictions of continued growth in recreational demand had been based were shattered. It became clear that the national economy was not going to grow in a way that would bring the poorest and least mobile into the 'leisure society' enjoyed by the majority. Many countryside sites experienced a fall, rather than a continuing rise, in the number of visitors.

There followed the recessions of the early 1980s; the impact of Conservative policies from 1979 onwards; growing pessimism about the world; and a rapid rise in environmental concerns. These factors had a major impact upon the trends that we had foreseen in the mid 1960s. They contributed to a slowing-down, then a halt, in the rise of population in Britain; to slower than predicted growths in personal incomes; to stabilising, rather than the predicted sharp fall, in the length of the working week - these being three of the key factors which cause growth in leisure demand. Another key result of these changes was the rise in unemployment, a form of enforced leisure which is seldom accompanied by the financial means or the morale to permit the full enjoyment of that leisure.

The effect of these trends was to polarise the public reaction to, or demand for, countryside recreation. On the one hand, those who had the means and the personal mobility to get out into the countryside were using it in an increasingly varied way. Recreation activities became very diverse, often depending upon expensive or sophisticated equipment - for example ski-ing, water ski-ing, sailing, hang-gliding, para-scending, potholing, climbing, and the motorised forms of transport across the countryside, with the potential that they have for damage or disturbance to other countryside users.

Moreover, recreation was increasingly penetrating the whole countryside. What the Countryside Acts in the earlier era had set in train was a defensive mechanism, that is the Country Parks, places where recreation could be brought into managed areas, set aside from the general countryside, with minimum impact upon the residents of the countryside. But people aren't so easily bid! It became clear that people really do want to get out into the general countryside, and penetrate it - in walking, in riding, in cycling, in sight-seeing and in the other diverse activities which I have described. As a result, there has been an increase in the impact of recreation activity upon the countryside.

On the other hand, there was a large part of the population who still could not take part in this type of countryside recreation. Their position was

described in the report *Leisure Policy for the Future*, published in 1980 by The
Chairmen's Policy Group:

> There are still large numbers of people who are short of money or of
> other resources or who are affected by ill-health or other disability, so
> that their leisure is severely constrained. They include the low-paid,
> many of the growing millions of pensioners, the disabled and the
> handicapped, and those who are unemployed . . .
>
> The fall in real personal incomes and the rise in unemployment draw
> attention strongly to those who – through poverty or personal con-
> straints – are unable to take a full part in a leisured society . . .
>
> Many people have health problems: these may inhibit their leisure
> activity, or may be a reason for such activity. Nearly one million people
> are registered as disabled; their needs pose a challenge for leisure
> provision. Many others are affected by personal constraints of other
> kinds.
>   (The Chairmen's Policy Group, 1983, pp.3–4)

The Chairmen's Policy Group concluded that in these ways millions of people
were constrained in their leisure activity; and said:

> Their needs present a major challenge . . .
>
> Particular effort is needed to connect with many in those groups who are
> most at risk of low quality of life – for example, mothers of young
> children; single parents and their families; the divorced, separated and
> widowed; the elderly and the housebound; and those in low incomes.
>
> For many of these people, the prime emphasis may be on activity in or
> near the home; on local facilities, with ready access and a welcoming
> atmosphere; on help to overcome problems of mobility or other
> constraints; and on holidays or other opportunities for a change or
> rest, possibly assisted by subsidies.'
>   (The Chairmen's Policy Group, 1983, p.9)

I have to say that this message was *not* well received by the Government. The
Minister of Sport, Neil Macfarlane, declined to take any action on it. That
does not reduce my own belief that the message was right.

These two trends – variety and penetrating use of the countryside by the
majority, constraints experienced by a large minority - help to explain the
changing emphasis in countryside recreation during the 1980s. The emphasis

moved further away from the National Parks onto the general countryside, with a particular focus on the countryside around the cities; and also, to some degree, away from capital investment onto the 'software' which would help to connect people to the existing provision.

In the *Recreation 2000* documents of the mid-1980s, the Countryside Commission placed the focus strongly on connecting with people. They urged that leisure providers should understand people and their needs, and seek to reflect that in what they do. The needs and aspirations of people could very often by met by what had already been provided, if they knew about it. So, there was a strong focus in the *Recreation 2000* reports on informing people about the available recreation resources. There was also emphasis on provision of 'access for all' – for example through further access to open lands and commons – and on the effective deployment, maintenance, signposting and interpretation of the footpath system.

The concept of access for all also helps to explain the strong emphasis on the countryside near the towns, expressed in a succession of initiatives – the urban fringe experiments and the Groundwork Trusts, in England; and the Scottish Central Woodland, and the Countryside around Towns initiatives, in Scotland.

Meanwhile, the National Parks had developed and diversified their role. With strengthened administration from 1974, and gradually growing re-sources, they were increasingly recognised as offering what Anne and Malcolm MacEwen, in their second book on National Parks, called *Greenprints for the Countryside* (MacEwen, 1987). With strong teams of rangers and other countryside staff, they were able to undertake intensive management of open lands and of footpaths and other systems, and gradually to bring into effect the schemes of traffic management which had been first mooted in the 1950s. Acquisition of land by the Park authorities themselves, and by the National Trust and others, led to a gradual increase in the area of land open to the public. A major initiative of the 1980s, the Common Land Forum, appeared to offer a solution to the long-standing unfinished business of common land management, including a remarkable consensus on the principle of public access to common land. However, this consensus was broken by the emergence of, and effective lobbying by, the Moorlands Association, repre-senting the owners of the grouse moors. They persuaded the government not to pursue a new round of common land legislation. In subsequent elections, the Conservative manifesto at first included a commitment to such legislation, and then dropped that commitment.

The Moorlands Association played a significant part also in the difficult process, through the late 1980s, of re-negotiation of the access agreements on moorlands in the Peak District. The owners of the grouse moors covered by the agreements claimed that public access was depressing the value of the shooting; and that the compensation paid by the National Park authority on the renewed access agreements should be far higher than the roughly 50p per acre per year that was then being paid.

While this negotiation was in train, the situation on the grouse moors became fraught because of the action of those who oppose blood sports. The access agreements provided that each grouse moor could be closed to public access for up to fourteen days per year, for purposes of shooting, provided that these days were publicised in advance so that would-be ramblers could know they should walk elsewhere. This publicity alerted the blood-sport saboteurs to the planned shoots, and they began to disrupt shoots by 'driving' the moors in the early morning and then standing in front of the butts during the shoot. The moorland owners asked the National Park authority to control the saboteurs. We in the park authority refused to do this, on grounds of neutrality: the most that we would do was to station rangers on the edge of the moor and advise people to keep off the moor. The moorland owners reacted by refusing to publicise the closed days, which carried the risk that walker could enter the moors during shoots and wander into the line of fire. When I left the Peak Park in 1992, this situation – and the re-negotiation of the access agreements – remained unresolved.

CONCLUSION

Reflecting on the situation as it was in 1990, I am proud of the National Parks in England and Wales, for reasons which echo some of the points made earlier in the Conference. The Parks are run by enthusiasts, both board members and officers. Their teams are multi-disciplinary – including (for example) ecologists, archaeologists, architects, planners, land agents, rangers, information officers, teachers and many other skills. They work in increasingly close and effective partnerships with a wide range of bodies: this partnership is expressed in many formal agreements and in the policies published in the National Park Plans. The Park authorities set an example to other landowners through the sustainable management of their own lands.

The National Park Plans, and the day-to-day action of the park authorities, are increasingly based upon a concept which is more sophisticated than the assumptions of the 1940s or the 1970s. I refer to the concept of *inter-dependence* between the three main purposes of the National Parks – conservation, recreation and the well-being of local residents. This idea of inter-dependence replaces the assumption of the 1940s about the simple compatibility of these purposes, or of the 1970s that conflicts between them might have to be reconciled. Nowadays, the assumption is that – with deliberate planning and management – we can achieve the three purposes together. In terms of the focus of my paper, this implies that recreation is seen as capable of bringing benefits to the visitors *and* in the conservation of the resource *and* for the well-being of those who live in the Parks.

This theme of inter-dependence figures strongly in the report which I prepared last year, for Scottish Natural Heritage, on the socio-economic benefits of national parks and protected areas in Europe. (Dower *et al.*, 1998). I am pleased that Scotland is now moving towards the creation of National Parks, with a remit which is broader than that of the Parks in England and Wales and which is based upon inter-dependence between conservation, recreation, rural well-being and the principles of sustainable development.

REFERENCES

Abrahams, Harold (ed.) (1959). *Britain's National Parks.* Country Life Limited, London.
Civic Trust (1964). *A Lea Valley Regional Park.* Civic Trust, London.
Dower, John (1945). *National Parks in England and Wales.* HMSO, London.
Dower, Michael (1965). Fourth Wave: the Challenge of Leisure. Reprint from the *Architects' Journal,* Civic Trust, London .
Dower, M., Buller, H. and Asamer-Handler M. (1998). *Socio-economic Benefits of National Parks and Protected Areas in Europe.* Scottish Natural Heritage, Edinburgh.
MacEwen, Ann and Malcom (1987). *Greenprints for the Countryside?: the Story of Britain's National Parks.* Allen and Unwin, London.
National Parks Committee (1947). *National Parks in England and Wales.* HMSO, London.
National Parks Policies Review Committee (1974). *Review of National Park Policies.* HMSO, London.
National Parks Review Panel (1991). *Fit for the Future.* Countryside Commission, Cheltenham.
Outdoor Recreation Resources Review Commission (1962). *Outdoor Recreation for America.* ORRRC, Washington D.C.
Select Committee of the House of Lords on Sport and Leisure (1973). *Second Report of the Select Committee.* HMSO, London.
The Chairmen's Policy Group (1983). *Leisure Policy for the Future.* Sports Council, London.
The Nature Conservancy (1964). *The Countryside in 1970: Proceedings of the Study Conference November 1963.* HMSO, London.

5

The Rise of the
Environmental Movement, 1970–1990

Robin Grove-White

IN THE TWO decades between 1970 and 1990, environmentalism came of age in Britain. This paper reflects on why.

The issue has considerable contemporary urgency, viewed from the present perspective. Though striking advances have been made in addressing many specific environmental problems over the past decade, it continues to be hard to be optimistic about industrial societies' capacity to contain some of the deeper difficulties. Anthropogenically-induced climate change is now upon us, at a time when, perversely, the immediate price advantages of increasing fossil fuel dependency have rarely been more favourable. Society's commitment to the car, and to evermore subtle and pervasive patterns of new chemicals, generates mounting social and environmental burdens. And the ingenuity of science harnessed to industrial innovation, for example in the biosciences, is confronting an increasingly globalised world with ever-more complex problems of governance – a foretaste of which Europe experienced in the remarkable 1999 brouhahas surrounding genetically modified crops and foods.

Clearly, though much has been learnt over the past thirty years about the handling of that class of issues we have learnt to call 'environmental', there is a long way to go – and, perhaps, not much time in which to do it. I want to argue that an urgent necessary condition for grappling with such issues is now a richer understanding of their deeper cultural dynamics. By which I mean that environmental issues need to be seen not simply as objective scientifically specifiable problems arising from humankind's relationship with the natural world – but also as expressions of historically embedded tensions and faultlines in contemporary ('late-modern') ways of understanding the world and ourselves.

This thought (to which many others have contributed) points to an urgent need to unravel some of the factors underpinning the emergence of environmentalism in its formative period between 1970 and 1990, in order to understand better its component parts. Indeed, equipped with such a richer cultural and historical appreciation of how environmental issues and problems have come to be constituted, fresh ways of engaging with them in future may become apparent – of particular relevance to the problems of political authority now facing our institutions in a 'globalising' world. So in a spirit of *reculer pour mieux sauter*, here are some observations on the period 1970– 1990 in Britain, through two rather different prisms.

AN `ORTHODOX´ PRISM

Consider first a perspective familiar to most of us who were active in the environmental politics and science of the period.

Early days

On this account, the emergence of environmentalism in Britain, as elsewhere, reflected increasingly widespread international recognition of the pollution and degradation of air, water, and soils and of depletion of wildlife through the 1960s. In such a context, the Torrey Canyon oil pollution disaster of 1967 became the catalyst for new forms of political response in Britain – most notably the creation of the standing Royal Commission on Environmental Pollution and the world's first Department of the Environment in 1970. Shadowing such events were a host of wider developments – the launch of a British chapter of Friends of the Earth, the publication of The Ecologist's *Blueprint for Survival* and the Club of Rome's *Limits to Growth*, and the embryonic reinvigoration of the established NGO conservation movement through the 'Countryside in 1970' conferences.

Emergence of an environmental 'politics'

Such processes – the largely familiar account runs – then took on their own wider momentum. The 1972 UN Stockholm Conference on the Environment, spearheaded intellectually by the Ward/Dubos book *Only One Earth*, spawned the United National Environment Programme (and, in the 1980s, the Brundtland Commission) – whilst closer to home a new popular politics of the environment gained increasing momentum as the 1970s progressed, focusing most conspicuously on energy (particularly nuclear) developments, motorway-based transport policies, and intensive agriculture. Paralleling these developments, British accession to the European Union (then the 'European Economic Community') led to fresh forms of intellectual cross-fertilisation on ways of addressing environmental problems – both official and unofficial. Nigel Haigh (1987) has shown how British official attitudes towards historically-unchallenged regulatory approaches underwent steady change as a result of EU negotiation pressures in the '70s and '80s. And in parallel, through the educative processes of involvement in the European Environmental Bureau, UK NGOs also became progressively more attuned to the opportunities for new patterns of political pressure (as well as to new forms of constraint) arising from greater engagement in Europe.

Momentum of the 1980s

Indeed, it is a piece of UK legislation prompted by Britain's wider EEC obligations – the 1981 Wildlife and Countryside Act – which is often argued to have constituted the key catalytic event in the emergence of a co-ordinated contemporary environmental NGO movement in Britain. Coming at the same time as Marion Shoard's seminal book *The Theft of the Countryside* (1970), and reports by the Nature Conservancy Council and others highlighting the destructive impacts on wildlife and landscape of the forms of industrialised agriculture being promoted by the Common Agricultural Policy, the controversies around the Act's passage helped to crystallise a new confidence and momentum in the political emergence of environmentalism. Building on such experience in the mid-1980s, NGOs such as Friends of the Earth, RSPB and CPRE – and in a dramatically different register, Greenpeace – catalysed a succession of environmental campaigns with increasing public resonance, on emblematic issues from nuclear pollution to Green Belts.

The accumulated effect of these campaigns – coupled to wider international developments such as the publication in 1985 of the UN-inspired Brundtland Commission report, *Our Common Future* and mounting scientific concern about anthropogenically-induced changes to the ozone layer and global climate – was to provide an unavoidable stimulus for a succession of mainstream political responses in the late 1980s. The most striking of these was Mrs. Thatcher's September 1988 speech to the Royal Society, which gave unprecedented prime Ministerial legitimacy to the idea that environmental concerns – particularly global concerns, such as climate change and the depletion of wild nature – now required new forms of co-ordinated political action. *De facto* endorsement from such a quarter had an immediate and striking impact on public support for the country's environmental NGOs. Their memberships shot up and their relationships with government began to change – particularly after the Euro-elections of May 1989, when the Green Party attracted a massive 15% of the vote.

Hence by 1990, environmentalism had come in from the cold, to become acknowledged, rhetorically at least, as a central concern of contemporary government. Optimism was in the air. The Cold War was also at an end, and a new era of international co-operation in prospect. The stage was set for the emergence of 'sustainable development' as an expected focus for fresh forms of negotiation and partnership around a shared environmental agenda, with the 1992 Rio Earth Summit, twenty years after Stockholm, providing a high profile context.

An orthodoxy?
It seems to me that something like this brief account of the emergence of environmentalism in Britain would be endorsed by many people working in government agencies, the NGOs, academia and the media: a combination of scientific insights (frequently from within official agencies), popular pressures crystallised by increasingly confident NGOs, and 'orthodox' political processes, induced governments to respond increasingly – in the process generating widespread recognition of environmental issues as concerns of central significance for late-twentieth-century societies.

But let me point to some of what is missing from such an account.

AN 'ALTERNATIVE' PRISM

Environmentalism has emerged not only as a response to increasingly evident physical problems, but also as an emergent expression of a new stage in Western culture. Understandably, this reality has often been obscured from the view of those working most actively to address the immediate problems in the two decades with which this paper is concerned. But consider the following:

A new cultural turn
Environmentalism since the 1960s has been reaching far beyond any inherited notions of 'conservation'. It has embodied a dawning sense of limits in industrial society. This has involved, indeed continues to involve, processes of collecting *groping* – an uneven reaching-out for new philosophical ordering principles for humankind's relations with 'nature'. None of us knows quite what this may turn out to mean. We are all involved in the same overall process, though without knowing quite how our own bit relates to the rest (like the blind man and the elephant).

Multiple intellectual influences
It would be invidious for any one discipline – or prophet – to claim intellectual primacy in identifying what is at stake in 'environmental' issues. The pioneers of ecological understanding and scientifically-based conservation – Tansley, Rachel Carson, Max Nicholson, Frank Fraser Darling – vital though their role has been, constitute only one important strand of the story. The same is true of the pioneers of land use planning, from Ebenezer Howard to Patrick Abercrombie.

There have been a host of wider influences. The 1960s and 1970s were a period of increasingly articulate concern about the implications of trends in technological society for human agency and well-being – by Lewis Mumford,

Jacques Ellul, Ivan Illich, Theodore Roszak, and others. This paralleled the
waning of socialism as a source of creative political optimism. It is no
coincidence that the grass-roots emergence of environmentalism in the
1970s and 1980s was contemporaneous with the exhaustion of left-wing
Marxisant political drives in the industrialised world. Much of the raw
political energy of the student movements of the 1960s found more creative
and appropriate forms of expression in the development of environmentalism
than in involvement in established patterns of radical political organisation.

Nor is it chance that the emergence of environmentalism has coincided
with the continuing fragility of support for established Western forms of
religious praxis. The increasing take-up of Eastern traditions such as Bud-
dhism, Yoga and the martial arts, has both influenced and reflected the
emergence of new 'ontological' sensibilities in countries like Britain – with the
pursuit of more integrated human/nature attunements a central focus. So a
host of influences beyond science and ecology helped constitute environmentalism intellectually and morally from the late 1960s onwards.

Tensions and hopes within late industrialism
Paradoxically, environmentalism has been simultaneously a vehicle for both
optimism and pessimism about the future. It might even be interpreted as a
realistic corrective to naïve doctrines of 'progress' embedded in ideologies as
different as Marxism and utilitarianism. Its pessimism reflects concern that
events may now be running chronically out of control, contemporary society
in the grip of 'organised irresponsibility', as Ulrich Beck (1992) has put it. By
contrast, environmentalism's optimism is evident in the fresh creative pos-
sibilities to which it has been contributing in civil society – a burgeoning
reinvention of active energy and citizenship, in the circumstances of 'late-
modern' polities.

New social movements and changing social identities
All of this underlines the reality that the 1970s and 1980s were a period of
rapid social, cultural and economic change. Particularly striking in the present
context was the proliferation in countries like Britain of new self-help and
NGO movements. These developments have arisen in a context of wider
social fragmentation and reconstitution, as sociologists like Giddens (1990)
and Albrow (1996) have shown – processes entailing a dislocation of
established social identities for many. But in parallel, reconfigured patterns
of collective action have been emerging in novel forms. Environmentalism can
be pictured as one such form – indeed, with feminism, perhaps the most
successful yet to have crystallised.

The constraints of orthodox politics

A corollary has been the waning of deference towards institutionalised patterns of 'professional' expertise, also conspicuous in the 1970s and 1980s. Repeated social surveys have confirmed the continuing attrition of trust in and uncritical respect for politicians and established political institutions. Environmentalism can be seen as having colonised some of the new political spaces being opened up by this harder-eyed public sense of the limitations of 'orthodox' inherited politics. In the 1970s and 1980s, NGOs contributed fresh imagination to the business of making governments more responsive on issues outside the familiar patterns of party politics.

'Technology as legislation'

Moreover, in industrial society, it is increasingly *technological developments* and their commercial diffusion which structure the routine conditions of everyday human existence. Yet society's commitments to the longer-term trajectories of such developments lie largely outside accessible frameworks of strategic political discussion or control. Think of our collective experience with the car, the television, the internet, or the new gene technologies.

Following Ellul and Mumford, the American political scientist Langdon Winner (1977) has argued that contemporary technologies need to be seen as having 'a distinctly political form', in that increasingly the shapes they take prescribe the very ground rules within which government itself is then required to function. Initiatives aimed at strategic political anticipation and oversight in the Anglo-Saxon world – the now defunct US Office of Technology Assessment, the UK's exiguously funded Parliamentary Office of Science and Technology (POST) and Technology 'Foresight' programmes – have proved strikingly ineffectual so far. Environmentalism can be seen as one form of social response – from below, as it were – to the resulting *lacunae*. The 1999 crisis around genetically modified crops and foods – and the role of environmental organisations, statutory and NGO, as critical watchdogs – has highlighted the continuing seriousness of these dynamics.

The Politics of Symbols

Responding to such emerging realities, environmental bodies were drawn through trial and error in the '70s and '80s towards new forms of interaction with public opinion and political institutions – emphasising graphic single issues (Windscale/Sellafield, the rate of national hedgerow loss, the plight of the great whales . . .) as ways of dramatising wider generic concerns. This involved symbiotic relationships with the media, entailing a reification of more 'visible' issues – arguably at the expense of official attention to more opaque background relationships. This underlies the fact that the emergence of environmentalism coincided with a period of rapid evolution of contemporary communications technologies – with continuing implications for the patterns of representation of 'issues' which emerged subsequently.

The many faces of science
The same period also saw the creeping emergence of public ambivalence towards the role of science in relation to government and industry. Environmentalism can itself be seen as something of a harbinger of such ambivalence – now widespread at the end of the twentieth century.

Environmentalist concerns about (for example) nuclear power, air and water pollution, and the ecological impacts of intensive agriculture were both dependent on, and highly critical of, then-dominant scientific orthodoxies in such spheres. Science was needed to help clarify and correct what was at issue. But it had also helped create the problems in the first place. As the biologist Lord Ashby, first Chairman of the Royal Commission on Environmental Pollution, pointed out in 1978, it was scientists who in the post-war period first articulated an 'I - Thou' relationship with nature on society's behalf. But at the same time, continuing shifts in patterns of research funding in countries like the UK were creating uncomfortably close relationships between scientific innovation and dominant interests in government and industry. This issue has now developed to become of major current concern. Its contours emerged initially through some of the key environmental controversies of the 1970s and 1980s.

'Nature' and Human Nature
This reminds us again that environmentalism has emerged as an expression of mounting concern about certain dominant ways of *knowing*, in modern industrial societies. The history of ideas will show the extent to which many environmental controversies in the period under discussion reflected emerging social unease at limitations in the reductionist technical knowledge paradigms dominant in official *risk assessment* practices – and particularly, the inadequate official acknowledgement of *uncertainty* and *ignorance* in spheres of long-term environmental significance.

In this sense, environmentalism can itself be seen as a cultural *symptom*, a signal of urgent new attempts to embed more intelligent and accurate ways of understanding humankind's relationship to the wider order of things. Epistemologically, the primary focus has been on *'nature'* – reflecting, perhaps, the success of our currently dominant secular modes of ontological understanding. But whatever the new guise, the central question is ultimately an old and familiar one: How are humans to understand themselves and their responsibilities to creation?

I have offered two versions of the emergence of environmentalism in the 1970s and 1980s. These should not be seen as mutually exclusive. Rather, the two are inextricably linked. The first ('Orthodox') prism has highlighted the overt political manifestations in Britain of some of the underlying cultural drives and forces which impelled the emergence of environmentalism, as clarified through the second ('Alternative') prism.

And what is the contemporary relevance of such an exercise? Simply this. As the new century begins, society's scientific understanding of the scope and contours of key environmental problems is now more than adequate to justified enhanced action in many spheres. The outstanding difficulties are rather social, political, and institutional – reflecting a need to generate more authoritative shared *meanings* and social processes, adequate to give political legitimacy to more vigorous responses.

So the key issues now concern *people*. Social and organisational innovation needs to be designed to go with the grain of human needs and aspirations, *properly understood.* Analysis of the early history of modern environmentalism can throw important light on such matters, which, for most of the 1990s, may have been obscured by the politically beguiling (but I regret, ultimately pyhrric) hope of unproblematic social consensus around the notion of 'sustainable development'.

The current crisis of legitimacy within the World Trade Organisation and parallel vigorous social debates about 'science and society' create the opportunity for looking again at such matters with fresh urgency. And it is to the cultural domain that we should now be turning, for clues as to how to move things forward.

REFERENCES AND FURTHER READING

Albrow, M. (1996). *The Global Age.* Cambridge, Polity.
Ashby, E. (1978). *Reconciling Man with the Environment.* Cambridge, CUP.
Beck, U. (1992). *Risk Society: towards a New modernity.* Lonodn, Sage.
Giddens, A. (1990). *The Consequences of Modernity.* Cambridge, Polity.
Haigh, N. (1987). *EEC Environmental Policy in Britain.* London, Longman.
Hajer, M. (1995). *The Politics of Environmental Discourse, Ecological Modernisation and the Policy Process.* Oxford, Clarnedon.
Lash, S., Szerszynski, B., & Wynne, B. (eds.) (1996). *Risk, Environment and Modernity: Towards a New Ecology.* London, Sage.
Macnaughten, P. & Urry, J. (1998). *Contested Natures.* London, Sage.
Shoard, M. (1970). *The Theft of the Countryside.* London, Temple Smith.
Ward, B. & Dubos, R. (1972). *Only One Earth: the care and maintenance of a small planet.* New York, Penguin.
Winner, L. (1977). *Autonomous Technology: Technics-out-of-control as a Theme in Political Thought.* Cambridge, Mass. & London, MIT Press.

6

Managing the Countryside in a Period of Change – 1970–1990

Adrian Phillips

THIS PAPER TRACES the changing context in which countryside issues were debated and acted upon in the period 1970–1990. October 1970 marked the last of the three 'Countryside in 1970' Conferences. 1990 saw the passing of the Environmental Protection Act that broke up the Nature Conservancy Council and split the Countryside Commission; it was also the year in which the first Environment White Paper was published. These two decades were themselves divided by the political watershed of 1979.

1970 THE YEAR OF THE COUNTRYSIDE

Between 26 and 28 October 1970, over a thousand people from more than 330 organisations in Britain gathered at the Guildhall, London, for the last of the three 'Countryside in 1970' Conferences. It is a fascinating experience to re-open the report of this event (R.E. Boote, 1970). At first sight the themes appear familiar enough – the threats to the countryside, the need to raise awareness of environmental and countryside issues in the public mind and on the political agenda, the importance of getting the right institutional and legal frameworks, and so forth. But on closer reading, it is a report from a very different world. No one foresaw the huge impact on the countryside of EC membership (entry came within three years) – and the word 'computer' does not appear in the entire conference report, nor does anyone advocate a Parliament in Scotland (or a Welsh Assembly). While it is easy to be wise with the benefit of hindsight, the 1970 Conference is an excellent reference point to measure how far and fast things were to change over the ensuing twenty years, often in ways which could not be foreseen at the time.

The 'Countryside in 1970' movement gives an excellent insight into the state of environmental politics in Britain thirty years ago. It was a high profile, seven years campaign begun in 1963 to raise awareness of countryside and environmental issues. Its principal architect for much of the time was the energetic Bob Boote, the Secretary to the movement after 1966, and Deputy Director (Conservation and Management) of the then Nature Conservancy.

There were other important links to that organisation, including the influence of the ever-youthful Max Nicholson; also the conservancy provided the secretariat for the conference. Even the choice of the President for the 'Countryside in 1970' movement, the Duke of Edinburgh, was someone with strong nature conservation credentials. In taking the lead in this way, the Nature Conservancy was at the pinnacle of its influence – after twenty years, this institution had achieved, in Dudley Stamp's words, 'a quite remarkable success story' (Stamp, 1969). Almost certainly, its standing was never quite so high again, nor could it ever lay claim to such a broad agenda. Some might have argued that its status, from 1965, as part of the Natural Environment Research Council, had already begun to clip its wings. A further threat to its central position came with the creation of the Countryside Commission for Scotland in 1967, and that for England and Wales in 1968, both successes of earlier efforts of the 'Countryside in 1970' movement. It would have been inconceivable a few years later that the Countryside Commissions would have permitted the Nature Conservancy, or its successor, the Nature Conservancy Council, to have taken copyright over the term 'countryside', or to have played such an unchallenged role of leadership.

The Guildhall conference tells us a lot, too, about how the forces in the countryside saw themselves in 1970. Speakers from across the conservation spectrum declared their concern over the impacts of the accelerating rate of agricultural change on the wildlife and scenery of rural Britain. While David Lea of the RSPB reported that the 1969 Silsoe Conference had shown that 'a reconciliation with agriculture was possible' (Boote, p. 45), the spokesman of the National Farmer's Union, Michael Darke, gave little ground: 'The first obligation placed upon the agricultural industry by society is the responsibility to produce food . . . The second obligation . . . is the welfare of those people living in predominantly rural areas who are dependent upon the prosperity of agriculture for their livelihoods.' Concern for the environment came a very poor third in this analysis. There were numerous warnings from Michael Darke (all very accurate) that further large-scale change would occur in the countryside; indeed he told 'amenity societies and planners' to 'revise their attitudes towards change in the countryside' (Boote, pp. 48–49). It was uncompromising stuff, derived from what the late Gerald Wibberley called 'agricultural fundamentalism'. This is 'the belief that any person who is actively engaged in agricultural processes and who is living and working amongst natural forces and with natural fauna and flora, develops traits of character which are different to those developed by people living in towns', and that these characteristics are 'somehow vital to the development of a healthy nation' (Davidson and Wibberley, 1977, pp. 12–13). Such a belief can easily become contempt for those who have different values or have a mainly urban experience.

Agricultural fundamentalism lives on. In a recent letter to the *North Devon Journal*, a local farmer is quoted thus: 'I can proudly say that on my farm, that employs not only my family, but also four outside workers, there are no badgers, no rabbits, no mice, no snakes, no lizards, no rodents, and if I could stop the birds from flying over I would. My farm produces food, not fluffy little animals. I am farmer, not a zoo keeper' (*Private Eye*, May 1999).

Another feature of the 1970 conference is confidence in the power of science. As in politics, so in the almost unquestioning respect for science, the post-war consensus still reigned. But it was already being challenged. Duncan Poore was among a number of people who pleaded for a more explicit recognition of the cultural values of nature (Boote, p. 41). And Ruth Harrison dared to argue that a concern for animal welfare should be part of the countryside agenda for a civilised people (*ibid.* p. 114).

There was unquestioning confidence too in the role of public agencies as deliverers of conservation and recreation services in the countryside; voluntary bodies were viewed as supporters of public initiatives, not as an arm of civil society in their own right. Funding for countryside care was expected to come from government (no lottery or EC funding in 1970). 'Industry' in the 'Countryside in 1970' movement tended to mean large nationalised under-takings, with just a handful of the major petro-chemical companies and major manufacturers; most other sectors – retailers, the media, hotels, airlines and banks, for example – were absent.

The conference was launched as a contribution to European Conservation Year. This was an initiative of the Council of Europe, not of the European Community. Indeed the absence from the debate of references to the then Common Market is surprising. It was not even mentioned by the Prime Minister, Ted Heath, when he addressed the conference at the closing session and looked forward to the 1972 United Nations Stockholm Conference on the Human Environment. Reading the report now, one is left with the impression that, while its organisers did understand that the global and European context was the big picture into which the UK countryside and environmental movement would need to fit, rather few of the participants could clearly see those connections.

THE PERIOD TO THE 1979 WATERSHED

For the countryside, the years 1970–1979 were, in general, still dominated by the attitudes and power structures so evident in 1970. Four broad trends can be identified over this period which are a dominant feature of annual reports from the agencies and which also received their fair share of debate and funding:

- Responding to the new demands for recreation in the countryside,
- Discovering the potential of countryside management,
- Faith in planning, and renewed faith in the national parks, and
- Facing up to the increasingly unacceptable nature of un-regulated, heavily subsidised farming.

The two new Countryside Commissions were given powers in 1967 and 1968 to help set up country parks and picnic sites to meet the pressures on the countryside from an increasingly mobile and leisured public. Such places were established mainly by local government and bodies like the National Trust (though there were also some private sector country parks) with up to 75% grants from the Commission. Identified by their distinctive logo, country parks became almost the hallmark of the Commissions, especially that in England and Wales. By 1974, 111 such country parks had been set up or recognised with support from the Countryside Commission, including a large number of premier countryside sites, such as Box Hill, Lyme Park and the Seven Sisters (Countryside Commission, 1975); additional sites were being added at a rate of 20–30 a year. In that year, the Commission was given more flexible powers to support countryside schemes of all kinds, and it began to switch some of its recreational concerns and funding away from site-specific projects towards support for rights of way, countryside management and ranger service schemes. But if country parks were a little less in favour by the early 1980s, a considerable investment had been made through them in the enjoyment of the countryside. When separate statistics were last reported on (in 1984) there were 171 local authority country parks and 29 run by non-public bodies; the equivalent picnic site figures were 214 and 23. Total grants paid to country parks and picnic sites were by then running at about £1 million annually (Countryside Commission 1985).

The Commissions were not, of course, the only public agencies involved in dealing with the new pressures for recreation in the countryside. This was a period in which 'a wide range of public-sector leisure facilities (became) accepted parts of the range of basic services to be provided or supported by various levels of government' (A.J. Veal, in Glyptis, 1993, p. 86). Local authorities took the lead: some counties, such as Hampshire or East Sussex, built up impressive teams of professional staff in leisure, estates and planning departments. In the same period, the Forestry Commission, the still publicly-owned water authorities and the British Waterways Board all gave a higher profile to the recreation potential of the forest, other land and water in their ownership. The National Trust began to get to grips in a more professional way in the management of its land for recreation and public access (Phillips, in Newby, 1995). By the end of the period, provision for recreation in the countryside involved a wide range of public, private and voluntary managers of owners of land – and had become a recognised area of public policy.

Through the country park and other programmes, many thousand of hectares of land were either managed for countryside recreation and conservation for the first time, or managed far better than hitherto. This called for the development of people-management and nature-management expertise, and for the promotion of interpretative and design skills. A whole profession of rangers and countryside managers came into being on the back of the country parks programme, and applied their expertise in countryside and coastal sites around Britain. In Scotland, the Countryside Commission for Scotland (CCS) added its own distinctive contribution by developing an open-air display centre at its headquarters at Battleby at which countryside 'furniture', suitable for country parks and elsewhere, was promoted as part of its strong training profile. Meanwhile in England, in 1974 the Countryside Commission imported a team of US interpretative experts to work on two National Trust owned country parks, Tatton Park and Clumber Park, with a view to promoting higher standards in this area (Countryside Commission, 1976). And over and above the development of professional expertise, the countryside recreation programmes of the 1970s meant that a generation of people, many first time car-owners, had somewhere to go to enjoy the countryside and learn of its attractions without the danger of a hostile encounter with a farmer – or a bull.

If country parks was one project associated with the Countryside Commission, the other was countryside management, a concept for which the Commission's first Director, Reg Hookway, should be given much of the credit. He saw a niche for the Commission in promoting the idea of area-based management, made up of numerous small tasks that lie outside the scope of the planning system. Speaking towards the end of his time at the Commission, he told an American audience how the Commission had begun experimenting with these ideas in the Lake District and Snowdonia (the pioneer upland management experiments) before 1970. It had then applied the same ideas in coastal areas (the three pilot heritage coast schemes in Suffolk, Dorset and Glamorgan) and in the urban fringe, in the Bollin Valley south of Manchester (now sadly partly buried under the new airport runway). Hookway laid great stress on the quality of the project manager, who needed 'special personal qualities – needing to know about the countryside and . . . about farming . . . Project officers of the right type and personality quickly become identified with the area in which they work and with the people. They can reduce conflicts . . . and get things done on the ground'. With small sums of money, a great deal could be achieved by this approach, bringing together landowners, farmers, community and conservation groups, local people and so forth – this was Local Agenda 21 in operation ahead of its time. By 1979 there were 39 area-based countryside management schemes underway throughout England and Wales, covering mountain, moor, coast, river valley and urban fringe (Hookway, in Stipe ed. 1980).

The reliance on public sector provision for leisure and recreation in the 1970s sat well beside confidence in public sector planning. Following the Town and Country Planning Act of 1968, local authorities embarked on a major programme – interrupted by the reforms of local government in 1974 – to prepare structure and local plans. A great deal of effort was spent by statutory agencies and NGOs in influencing the process, which was opened up much more to public consultation and became more responsive to the demands of pressure groups. But it was individual, highly controversial schemes affecting national parks which caused the most excitement – the improvements to the A66 through the Lake District or potash mining in the North York Moors for example.

Concern about the outcome of such cases, and of the vulnerability of the national parks, led to the appointment of Lord Sandford's committee (National Park Policies Review Committee, 1974). The committee's report, which called for strengthened policies for protection and visitor management, was published at the same time as the national park measures in the Local Government Act of 1972 came into effect. Until then, the parks (apart from the Peak District and the Lake District which had been governed by boards since they were established) were administered as largely ineffective, minor departments of the relevant county councils, with a complex structure of committees where more than one county were involved. Now they would all be run by boards or by single, strengthened committees. They were also to have designated staff, a statutory management plan and 75% exchequer funding. As a result the parks were ready to take up the challenge of planning and management over the 9.6% of England and Wales within their boundaries, engaging much more seriously with the farmers and landowners in tackling conservation and recreation issues. Far less attention was given in the period to Areas of Outstanding Natural Beauty (AONBs).

The Countryside Commission for Scotland embarked on the development of its own proposals for a 'park system for Scotland' (CCS, 1974). This report contained two sets of inter-related proposals, one for recreation provision and one for landscape conservation. The Government acted upon the Commission's proposals for the establishment of regional parks and for national scenic areas: less successful were its proposals for 'Special Parks'. Whilst avoiding the term 'national park' (words which caused a lot of friction in some quarters), the CCS recommended Special Parks in the Cairngorms, Loch Lomond/ Trossachs and Ben Nevis/Glen Coe. These 'displayed characteristics not dissimilar to National Parks in England and Wales (especially the Peak District), (and) it is likely that they would have been referred to as Scotland's National Parks' (Moir, 1991 pp.64).

The final theme of this first period concerned farming. The 1970s saw the UK entry to Europe and the impact of the CAP. These were boom times for farming: European entry brought with it generous subsidies (Richard Body, 1982, estimated these at £3.35 billion annually), surpluses were not yet a reality and the public relations standing of farmers and farming was still high. But the damage done to the rural environment was becoming a central concern of environmental bodies in the public and voluntary sectors. Documenting the loss of habitats fell mostly to the Chief Scientist's Team at the Nature Conservancy Council (NCC) (e.g. NCC, 1977). The NCC had replaced the former Nature Conservancy on its removal from NERC (less some of its research functions) in 1973, a development which perhaps enabled it to speak out more freely on such matters. Few conservation events or publications of this period were complete without quoting from stark figures which catalogued the loss of wetlands, flower-rich hay meadows, chalk downland and so forth. The data fuelled the polemic, and writers such as Marion Shoard attacked farming head on:

> A new agricultural revolution is under way. If allowed to proceed unhindered, it will transform the face of England. Already a quarter of hedgerows, 24 million hedgerow trees, thousands of acres of down and heathland, a third of our woods and hundred upon hundred of ponds, streams, marshes and flower rich meadows have disappeared. They have been systematically eliminated by farmers seeking to profit from a complex web of economic and technological change.
>
> (Shoard, 1980)

The concern aroused by these trends, and the public outcry which followed, created a rather confused response among both farmers and conservation bodies. At first farmers' interests groups argued that since farmers had always created a working landscape, the outcry was misplaced: providing farmers could earn a decent living, a healthy landscape would result (see Leonard and Stoakes in Davidson and Lloyd, 1977). Henry Plumb had expressed this view as an article of faith: 'well-farmed land is naturally beautiful' (Boote, p. 39). But in face of the mounting evidence, a more realistic and sympathetic response emerged, typified by the growth of the Farming and Wildlife Advisory Groups (FWAGs). These were set up at county-level, with the support of enlightened leaders in the farming community, to encourage voluntary action by farmers to care for the countryside; after 1980, the

Countryside Commission helped to fund FWAGs. Indeed the Commission had a strong belief in the value of education, demonstration and awareness raising in informing the countryside and agriculture debate. Its New Agricultural Landscapes programme, launched in 1974, was 'looking at the changes in lowland Britain to discover whether modern agriculture will result in the destruction of a familiar landscape, or whether a new landscape will be created which, though completely different, is as interesting and varied as that which it replaces' (Countryside Commission, 1975, p. 17). With hindsight, these comments look rather innocent. The Commission was confronted with a harsher reality in its bruising encounters over the future of Exmoor's moorland, where cherished national parks landscapes were being ploughed up and re-seeded. This was one of the triggers which led, via the Porchester Inquiry of 1977, to new countryside legislation by the end of the decade. Lord Porchester fastened onto the willingness of some farmers on Exmoor to accept the principle that certain farming activities should be restricted if the price paid was sufficient. He proposed Moorland Conservation Orders, binding in perpetuity and backed by a one-off compensation payment for landowners (MacEwen and MacEwen, 1982).

Porchester's report seemed to point the way ahead for SSSIs, national parks and other threatened habitats and landscapes. The Labour Government introduced countryside legislation in 1978 which, while emphasising the value of management agreements between conservation bodies and landowners, included a fall-back power for the Minister to make conservation orders. In the event, the bill fell with the defeat of the Government in 1979. Although the concept of compensation for not being able to maximise the economic potential of the land was eventually included in the measures to protect SSSIs in the Wildlife and Countryside Act of 1981, the centrepiece of the new legislation was to be the voluntary principle.

1979 A WATERSHED IN THE HISTORY OF THE COUNTRYSIDE

Margaret Thatcher expressed her lack of interest in the environment when she addressed Scottish Tories at the height of the Falklands conflict in these terms:

> When you have spent half your political life dealing with humdrum issues like the environment, it's exciting to have a real crisis on your hands.
>
> (Young, 1991, pp. 273)

Nonetheless, the 1980s were in a number of ways a more encouraging period for the countryside than the decade before. Five broad trends can be detected:

- Re-writing the countryside recreation agenda,
- Popularisation and democratisation of the conservation movement,
- Searching for common ground between agriculture and conservation,
- The impact of environmental concerns on the countryside debate, and
- The 'countryfication' of the conservation agencies.

In the early days of the recreation and access movement, the ideal was the sturdy rambler bent on climbing mountains and striding over the moors. The 1967 and 1968 Countryside Acts addressed the requirements of car-borne families. But society's needs of the countryside moved on again during the 1970s. While people were certainly more mobile, many visitors to the countryside wanted more than a visit to a country park, and were looking for contact with the real countryside, buying and reading maps, travelling further afield and so forth. On the other hand, there were other groups in society who were not able to make use of the countryside at all, such as inner-city communities and other under-privileged sectors. There was also a growing number of overseas visitors to the UK countryside.

For an increasingly diverse and discriminating clientele, an increasingly varied strategy of provision was called for. In 1986 and 1987, the Countryside Commission, which had been given a more independent status under the 1981 Act, encouraged a debate to help rethink countryside recreation policy and practice. The new policy, launched in 1987, included the target of putting the 135,000 miles of the rights of way network into order by the end of the century (Countryside Commission, 1987). This was a response to new trends in countryside recreation and it caught the public imagination. However, the emphasis in that policy was as much on 'people' as on 'place'. This was a revolutionary concept: it meant that recreation policy was not just about responding to demand as hitherto, but also about raising awareness and understanding, and improving public confidence and ability to use the countryside. As well as new emphasis on the network of rights of way, the content of people-related access policies included:

- a rethink of country parks as 'gateways' to the countryside (literally and metaphorically) rather than as an end in themselves, so that people can use them as stepping off points for a deeper countryside experience,
- programmes directed at ethnic minorities, those with physical disabilities and others would otherwise have little confidence or ability to use the countryside,
- developing countryside information centres in city high streets (taking the countryside to the towns), and producing more materials in the languages of visitors to Britain,

- providing users of the countryside with a range of information sources, such as the Country Code and the Countryside Access Charter so that rights can be exercised with confidence and responsibility,
- encouraging public transport as a means to help the 40% of the urban population who lack access to their own cars get to the countryside, and
- supporting simple, cheap accommodation, by adding camping barns and bunkhouse barns, for example, to the established service provided by youth hostels, camping and caravanning.

(Countryside Commission, 1989)

While the Commission was leading these policy initiatives, the wider political processes of deregulation and privatisation, and reductions in local authority budgets, were pervading influences in the provision for countryside recreation. Local authorities were less able, and less inclined, to see themselves as providers in the area of countryside conservation and recreation, and more as enablers. This gave a further boost to the concept of countryside management, even though local authority funds for ranger services etc. were hard stretched. In parallel with this, there was a trend towards the 'commodification' of the countryside: entrepreneurial landowners exploiting the earning potential of countryside resources in their ownership. Paul Cloke has described this as the 'pay-as-you-enter' or 'pay as-you-use' approach (in Glyptis ed., 1993). He points out that there were two forces at work here. There was a state-led response to the farming crisis, in which farmers were actively encouraged to diversify their incomes; and a market-driven approach in which the farmers, landowners and owners of attractions served up a 'countryside experience' to a more environmentally aware public. Whatever the reason, the development of countryside attractions based on previously unrecognised assets – through experiences as varied as watching red kites feeding, making your own charcoal and visiting farm open days – became an important feature of the British countryside in the 1980s.

The 1980s also saw a marked change in the nature of the environmental movement, and thus in the political context in which the fate of the countryside was debated. There were several aspect of this:

- growth in numbers
- growth in influence
- greater variety in types of bodies
- forging of alliances

Though a steep take-off in the increase of membership of some environmental organisations can be traced back to about 1970 (the National Trust for example), the 1980s were a period of still greater expansion. By 1990, conservation and environmental groups claimed a combined membership of 4 million, twice the number of ten years earlier (Secretary of State for the Environment *et al.*, 1990, p. 235). Between 1980 and 1993, some groups, such as the Worldwide Fund for Nature (WWF), whose membership rose from 60,000 to 270,000, Friends of the Earth (18,000 to 230,00) and above all Greenpeace (30,000 to 408,000) enjoyed dramatic rates of growth (HMSO, 1994). As politicians were frequently reminded, this was a larger army than that which the political parties could muster, and it demanded respect from the countryside and conservation agencies. The patronising term 'voly. bods' fell out of use; in its place came 'NGO partner'. The agencies themselves played a part in encouraging this growth of numbers by supporting projects to strengthen the effectiveness of their 'client' NGOs. An example is the NCC's support for running of the County Wildlife Trusts, rising from £15,500 in 1976/7 to £418,700 in 1988/9 (Dwyer and Hodge, 1996).

The voluntary sector also became much more diverse. Thus the Ground-work Trusts were set up with Government support so as to build on experience gained in the 1970s in urban fringe management but reflecting also the 1980s approach of involving the private sector in the delivery of public services. The local distinctiveness movement emerged at the other end of the spectrum, with bodies such as Common Ground promoting commu-nity-based action. Other bodies which flourished in the 1980s included BTCV, which marshalled practical volunteer effort, the Woodland Trust, which developed a national programme to save and manage woodlands, and the FWAGs (see above). The Countryside Commission supported the development of many such organisations. The 1980s also saw the develop-ment of powerful NGO alliances in the environmental field. Rural Voice was set up in 1980 to bring together a range of countryside campaign and user groups to promote a vision of what we would now call a 'sustainable countryside'. Wildlife and Countryside Links were set up to provide a focus for conservation NGOs to influence government policy, countryside legisla-tion, and the policies and practices of the statutory agencies. By the end of the 1980s, the influence and access to government of some NGOs, such as the RSPB with its formidable research and policy capacity, began to rival that of the agencies themselves.

A driving force behind much NGO effort was still the nexus of farming and the environment. While the countryside at the end of the decade showed even more serious signs of environmental crisis than in 1980, with falling water tables, catastrophic declines in the populations of some previously common birds, and the same with some species of flowers, the debate had become markedly different. The Ministry of Agriculture was no longer the undisputed master of the rural house; for example, Environment Minister William Waldegrave felt able to describe MAFF as the 'engine of destruction' (Pye-Smith and Hall, 1987, p. 102). The sudden arrival of milk quotas in 1984 was a sign that the days of surpluses had arrived and that European and national agricultural policy would now be increasingly directed to cutting production. The conservation bodies received much media coverage when they rang the alarm bells; farmers' leaders who, ten years ago could brush conservation concerns aside, now found that they had to deal with them seriously. High profile disputes, like the threatened 'arabalisation' of the Halvergate marshes in the Norfolk Broads, or the draining of the Somerset Levels, helped to change attitudes and, in the case of Halvergate at any rate, spurred the search for solutions.

From the Halvergate dispute emerged the prototype Environmentally Sensitive Area (ESA), the Broads Grazing Marshes Scheme. This was pioneered by the Broads Authority, the Countryside Commission and (an initially reluctant) MAFF, using the Commission's experimental powers under the Countryside Act of 1968 to support traditional grazing on marshes. The idea of supporting traditional farming systems because they are good for the environment was subsequently incorporated into an EC regulation (Article 19 of EC Regulation 797/85). 'Article 19' was then widely applied throughout the EC to reconcile conservation and agricultural interests in areas designated as environmentally sensitive. Within the UK, the countryside and conservation agencies advised Agricultural Departments on the identification of these areas and on suitable regimes for supporting traditional systems of farming in them. Prescriptions and payment rates for farmers were developed to ensure the protection of wildlife, scenery and archaeology; later ESA schemes included access as well. Thus the agencies throughout Britain became partners in seeking practical solutions to the difficult problems posed by modern farming.

The work was taken further in 1988 with the Countryside Premium Scheme, a demonstration scheme for environmental use of set-aside land; this was set up by the Commission because MAFF was unwilling to run such a scheme themselves. The Environment White Paper of 1990, announced that the Commission had been asked by the Secretary of State for the Environment, Chris Patten, to pioneer a country-wide scheme for environmentally sensitive land management, Countryside Stewardship. Though this too was at first resisted by MAFF as a rival to their own ESA programme, Countryside Stewardship (and its Welsh counterpart, Tir Cymen) went on to become an established part of the battery of agri-environmental programmes available to government.

The countryside debate became increasingly influenced by environmental concerns during the 1980s, many of which were driven from the international level. But things did not begin auspiciously with the disappointment of the Conservation and Development Programme for the UK (WWF/UK et al, 1983). This was the product of a very large investment of time and energy by agencies and NGOs in response to the launch in 1980 of the World Conservation Strategy (WCS) by IUCN, UNEP and WWF. The programme was a conscious effort to link conservation and development policy in the UK to the emerging international idea of sustainable development (which first surfaced in the WCS). It included a formidable analysis of the need for a new approach to countryside policy prepared by Prof. Tim O'Riordan, 'Putting Trust in the Countryside'. But the day chosen to launch the work happened to be the day of Mrs. Thatcher's post-Falklands triumphant re-election in 1983. The exercise made minimal impact.

Although the universal use of terms like 'sustainable development' and 'biodiversity conservation' did not occur until the Rio Conference in 1992 (the Earth Summit), these ideas had nonetheless begun to appear in debates about the environment some years earlier. Their progress may have been spurred by a reaction to the open hostility of Nicholas Ridley (Environment Secretary 1987–1989) to the planning system and to environmental lobby groups, especially over North Sea pollution and the development of the Habitats Directive. In any case, a green backlash developed. Mrs. Thatcher's Royal Society speech, late in 1988, marked the environmental coming of age of the political establishment in London. At the 1988 European elections, the Green Party won 15% of the vote.

The higher political profile given to environmental issues had a bearing on countryside policy and practice. It helped to promote two complementary ideas: that the whole countryside was in need of care, not just the special places; and that environmental considerations needed to be integrated with economic and social ones across the whole of rural Britain.

To some extent, the idea that the countryside needed to be addressed in its entirety, not just the special places, had motivated the passing of the Countryside Acts of 1967 and 1968, which had created two Countryside Commissions with a mandate for the *whole* countryside. But public policy – especially agricultural and planning policy – was slow to catch up with that notion. So throughout the 1980s, conservation agencies and NGOs argued *both* for better protection of outstanding sites *and* for the lessons learnt to be applied more widely, advocating new and strengthened designations as part of a more integrated approach to countryside planning and management. There were several strands to this campaign: focusing more attention on the 'Cinderella' designation of AONBs, establishing the Broads as a quasi-national park, remedying the deficiencies in SSSI protection under the 1981 Act, strengthening the national parks of England and Wales; and – in Scotland – creating them.

Progress was made with AONBs: the designation cycle was effectively complete by the end of the 1980s, and the management of some such areas was put on a firmer footing. The Broads became in effect the eleventh national park by legislation in 1988. The CCS's proposals (CCS, 1990) to set up national parks in Scotland put the topic back on the agenda – where it has stayed to this day despite the lukewarm government response at the time. Towards the end of the 1980s, some of the countryside designations, such as national parks and AONBs, began to be seen as 'greenprints' for the countryside as a whole (MacEwen and MacEwen, 1987) and also to attract international interest as models of sustainable development (Countryside Commission, 1989a). The panel under Prof. Ron Edwards, set up in 1990 by the Countryside Commission to look afresh at the national parks, carried these ideas forward; it reported in 1991 (National Parks Review Panel, 1991), and its key proposals came into law in 1995.

Though emphasis was on the stronger protection of places of high environmental value, there was also growing interest in targeting environmental recovery programmes on neglected areas. Examples are schemes for a National Forest in the Midlands, for twelve Community Forests around English cities, and for a new forest in Central Scotland.

In contrast, the local distinctiveness movement stressed the value of the countryside beyond the formally designated areas: its proponents claimed that 'everywhere is special, and special is everywhere' (King and Clifford, 1985). It was reflected too in the Countryside Stewardship scheme, which in principle made grants available across entire landscape types wherever they might occur, such as river valleys, chalk and limestone grasslands or old orchards. A 'whole countryside' approach was advocated in the Countryside Commission's uplands recommendations (Countryside Commission, 1984) and in the CCS mountain areas (CCS, 1990) proposals. In today's language, this was sustainable rural development: environmental considerations informing the planning and management of the entire countryside, alongside economic and social considerations.

In these various ways, the debate on the countryside of Britain came to be seen as part of a broader international discourse around the concept of sustainability. This was clearly the case with the CAP and agricultural issues, but during the later 1980s, other aspects of sustainability, relating to energy, transport, water and minerals for example, had also moved centre stage for the countryside agencies and NGOs, alongside their traditional pre-occupation with planning, agriculture, recreation and forestry. In 1990, the first Environment White Paper placed the conservation of the wildlife, scenic and historic heritage of the British countryside into its global environmental context, and recognised how the efforts of the agencies contributed to achieving the UK's global environmental objectives (Secretary of State for Environment et al, 1990).

The Thatcher government stood strongly for a centralised approach and in general did as little as possible to accommodate to the pressures for greater autonomy in Scotland and Wales. Yet in the field of countryside protection and nature conservation it seemed to show itself sympathetic to these forces. In July 1989, it announced plans to break up the NCC, abolish the CCS, split the Countryside Commission and establish separate conservation agencies in Scotland and Wales. It brought these proposals forward in 1990 in the Environmental Protection Bill. The Government's action to devolve policy may have been ahead of its time, but if the changes had not been made then, it is certain that this would have been one of the early consequences of devolution in the late 1990s. How did it come about that the Thatcher Government acted so out of character?

We are too near the event for government records to be opened and so to be sure what happened. However, it is evident that – in pursuit of what it saw as its statutory duties in Scotland, and especially in seeking to protect the Flow Country from afforestation – the NCC had alienated too many landowners and other influential people (Bishop, 1997). There was resentment, too, in Scotland at what was seen as the remote hand of Peterborough. On the other hand, Nicholas Ridley was no friend of quangos. His attitude is summed up in his autobiography. He dismissed all conservation experts, EC officials, pressure groups, quangos and other greens contemptuously, claiming that 'countrymen' (amongst whom he counted himself) 'in Britain know more about preserving wildlife than the lot of them put together' (Ridley, 1992, p. 114). Given these preconceptions, he was understandably sometimes critical of the way that the NCC had fulfilled its responsibilities. Moreover, he felt it was constitutionally wrong that he, an English Minister, should be drawn into determining a series of controversial conservation and planning issues in Scotland. So the Department of the Environment and the Scottish Office both saw advantage in breaking up a UK-run NCC. Having taken the decision in principle to create a free-standing Scottish conservation body, it was logical to add the Countryside Commission for Scotland so as to make an effective new body in that country. The follow-through in Wales was an inevitable consequence (Reynolds and Sheate, in Howarth and Rodgers, 1993). As an incidental result of the break-up of the NCC, and of the ensuing 'countryfication' of the agency arrangements, responsibilities in Scotland and Wales for landscape protection and countryside enjoyment on the one hand

and nature conservation on the other, were merged. These strands had of course been separate ever since the 1949 Act, but their merger was never a motive behind the changes.

If this analysis is correct, and the cause of the problem was at least in part the NCC doing its job, then it is interesting to consider whether the NCC was perhaps the wrong model for the 1980s. With its executive powers to designate SSSIs and own land, and with a large staff (built up even more following the SSSI re-notification exercise after the 1981 Act), the NCC was not naturally suited to the political values of the 1980s. It was perhaps too inflexible for the times. In this, it contrasted with the Countryside Commission. The Commission had far fewer staff and no executive powers, but was able to thrive through the Thatcher years. Since it had no choice but to work through others (often supporting them financially), the Commission developed strong and basically positive relationships with influential organisations, who saw it as a supporter, not as a rival. While it may have been a relatively weak body when established in 1968, it developed an approach to work that was well suited to the straitened times of the 1980s. It put emphasis on working through others because its small staff gave it no choice; it used financial incentives to encourage land owners and managers because it had no executive powers to instruct or prohibit them; and it was more flexible because it could use its funding to support innovation, rather than having it tied down in staff salaries and SSSI payments. The Commission was caught up in the 'backwash' of the break-up of the NCC, of course, since it lost its Welsh operations to the new Countryside Council for Wales. But by comparison with the NCC it emerged fairly unscathed from the reorganisations of 1990 (Phillips, in Gilg, 1993). Thus the relative abilities of the Countryside Commission, the Countryside Commission for Scotland and the Nature Conservancy Council to adapt to the forces at work in the 1980s account for the rather different fates which awaited them in 1990.

CONCLUSIONS

'Managing the countryside' is a shared activity, in which landowners, communities and public agencies at local and national levels play a part, within a broader political framework. It is where public policy and private objectives converge, and sometimes collide. The period 1970–1990 was one of great change in the context in which this activity took place.

These twenty years mark the transition from the post war consensus that still prevailed in 1970 to the radically different world with which we are now familiar in the late 1990s. In 1970, it was still generally assumed that:

- public agencies delivered services for, and to the public, and country-side conservation and enjoyment were no exception to this,
- environmental matters were very secondary in public policy to economic and social concerns, and could usually be assumed to be in conflict with these ('jobs before beauty'),
- the environmental changes wrought by farming had to be accepted, and in any case were not a cause of serious public concern, and
- in the environmental field at any rate, Britain really did not need to worry too much about the rest of the world.

By 1990, all these assumptions had been thrown overboard. The role of the public sector had been fundamentally reassessed through the Thatcher years. Market forces were seen as dominant and public services privatised wherever possible. At the same time, many organisations within civil society were no longer prepared to accept a form of governance in which public agencies acted in a top-down manner: consultation had to give way to participation; partnership between governed and governing became the norm. Sustainable development had become the mantra by which it was believed social, economic and environmental agendas could be reconciled. Agriculture was largely dethroned in public and political esteem and many of its environ-mental impacts regarded as unacceptable. And the outside world was making itself felt in every aspect of UK countryside policy and practice. The family of British conservation and countryside agencies which was created in 1949 (or in 1967 in the case of the Countryside Commission for Scotland) was itself part of that post war consensus. All these agencies had to adjust mightily to the changed circumstances, and emerged into the 1990s as very different animals.

REFERENCES

Bishop K. (1997). *The Challenge of Convergence – Countryside Conservation and Enjoyment in Scotland and Wales in Nationality and Planning in Scotland and Wales* (Macdonald and Turner eds.). University of Wales Press, Cardiff.

Body R. (1982). *Agriculture – the Triumph and the Shame.* pp.1–25. Maurice Temple Smith, London.

Boote R.E. – The Secretary to the Standing Committee of 'The Countryside in 1970' (1970). *Proceedings of the Third Conference, October 1970.* Royal Society of the Arts, London.

Countryside Commission (1975). *Seventh Annual Report of the Countryside Commission (1973–1974).* HMSO, London

Countryside Commission (1984). *A Better Future for the Uplands.* Countryside Commission, Cheltenham.

Countryside Commission (1985). *Eighteenth Annual Report of the Countryside Commission (1984–1985).* Countryside Commission, Cheltenham.

Countryside Commission (1987). *Enjoying the Countryside: Priorities for Action.* Countryside Commission, Cheltenham.

Countryside Commission (1989). *Policies for Enjoying the Countryside.* Countryside Commission, Cheltenham.

Countryside Commission (1989a). *Sustainable Development in National Parks.* (CCD 61) Countryside Commission (1989).

Countryside Commission for Scotland (CCS) (1974). *A Park System for Scotland.* CCS, Battleby.

Countryside Commission for Scotland (CCS) (1990). *The Mountain Areas of Scotland.* CCS, Battleby.

Davidson J. and Lloyd R. (1977). *Conservation and Agriculture.* Wiley, Chichester.

Davidson J. and Wibberley G. (1977). *Planning and the Rural Environment.* Pergamon Press, Oxford.

Dwyer J. and Hodge I. (1996). *Countryside in Trust.* Wiley, London.

Gilg A. ed. (1993). *Progress in Rural Policy and Planning.* Belhaven, London.

Glyptis S. ed. (1993). *Leisure and the Environment.* Belhaven, London.

HMSO (1994). *Social Trends 24.* HMSO, London.

Howarth W. and Rodgers C. eds. (1993). *Agriculture, Conservation and Land Use.* University of Wales Press, Cardiff.

King A. and Clifford S. (1985). *Holding your Ground.* Temple Smith, Hounslow.

MacEwen A. and MacEwen M. (1982). *National Parks – conservation or cosmetics?* George Allen and Unwin, London.

MacEwen A. and MacEwen M. (1987). *Greenprints for the Countryside? The Story of Britain's National Parks.* Allen and Unwin, London.

Moir J. (1991). *National Parks: North of the Border* in *Planning Outlook,* 34.2.

National Park Policies Review Committee (1974). *Report of the National Parks Policies Review Committee.* HMSO, London.

National Parks Review Panel (1991). *Fit for the Future.* Countryside Commission, Cheltenham.

Nature Conservancy Council (1977). *Nature Conservation and Agriculture.* NCC, London.

Newby H. ed. (1995). *The National Trust – the Next Hundred Years.* The National Trust, London.

Pye-Smith C. and Hall C, (1987). *The Countryside we Want.* Green Books, Bideford.

Ridley N. (1992). *My Kind of Government.* Fontana Books, London.

Secretary of State for the Environment et al (1990). *This Common Inheritance – Britain's Environmental Strategy.* (Cmd. 1200). HMSO, London.

Shoard. M. (1980). *The Theft of the Countryside.* Temple Smith, London.

Stamp D. (1969). *Nature Conservation in Britain.* Collins, London.

Stipe R. ed. (1980). *New Directions in Rural Preservation.* US Department of the Interior, Washington DC.

WWF/UK *et al* (1983). *Conservation and Development Programme for the UK – a Response to the World Conservation Strategy.* Kogan Page, London (2 volumes).

Young H. (1991). *One of us.* Macmillan, Basingstoke.

7

Post-War Changes in
Forest Practices and their Effects

William E. S. Mutch

IT IS EVIDENT that forestry has made one of the principal impacts on nature and rural landscape in Britain since 1945. The direction of the development of forestry in this half-century was not casual or market-driven but was largely the product of decisions by Parliament and Treasury.

A review of the changes of forest practice requires first a position-statement of forestry at the starting date, against which the changes may be set. H.M.Steven (1954) provides a useful contemporary critique but, because trees are long-lived, the determinants of the 1945 condition were some decades earlier.

As the world's leading industrial and trading nation in the nineteenth century, Britain had imported magnificent coniferous and hardwood timbers, principally from the opening of North America but also from the East, all from the destructive exploitation of forests mistakenly thought to be in-exhaustible. These high quality timbers were sold in Britain at such low prices that home-grown produce could not compete and, from around 1870, home cutting virtually stopped; therefore replanting stopped and the indigenous forestry expertise and activity decayed. The neglected woodlands stood until the 1914–18 war when most were felled. The implications of long neglect and the devastation of woodland in the war were considered in 1917 by the parliamentary Acland Committee. Parliament then decided on the creation of a state forest service, the Forestry Commission, and on the funding of a vigorous national programme of re-forestation.

In the two inter-war decades, the Forestry Commission had been active and successful in buying land, re-planting and afforesting on a large scale, promoting private forestry and beginning research. Three aspects of silvicul-ture of the inter-war period were notable in determining the 1945 position. The choice of species for lowland planting tried closely to match the soil conditions on each site (Anderson, 1950), resulting in a diverse mosaic of tree stands, somewhat expensive to manage. Second, British foresters perfected earlier Belgian techniques of planting trees upon hand-cut upturned turves on peatland and found that spruces could be established in afforestation of upland peats (Maxwell, 1929); as a result, the extensive peatland plantings at Keilder, Argyll and elsewhere began. Third, foresters, following the experience of nineteenth-century arboriculturists, made much use of exotic conifers. Britain has only one native conifer of commercial value but the awkward fact is that the great bulk of market demand was and is for coniferous wood, for construction timbers, pulp and (still crucially important in 1945) for pit-props and sawn mining timber.

Two important papers were produced by the Forestry Commission just prior to 1945: *Post-war Forest Policy* (Cmd 6447, 1943) and the *Supplementary Report on Private Woodlands* (Cmd 6500, 1944). The former set long-term targets for afforestation and the latter dealt with the proposed Dedication Scheme. This was a strategic concept, similar to the present Countryside Stewardship scheme, whereby the nation, through the Forestry Commission, undertook to provide continuing financial support for defined areas of woodland and to protect them from bureaucracy in exchange for a covenant by the owner that the land would not be alienated from forestry and would be managed in approved silvicultural practice. It is regrettable that, for legalistic reasons (briefly, that one cannot irrevocably bind one's successors), the scheme was fatally weakened twenty-five years later. It provided the foundation for private forestry in the first half of the period under review.

In 1945, as it had been since 1919, a central element of forest policy was that a three-year standing reserve of timber should be created as a national security in case of war. This was abandoned only after the report of the National Resources (Technical) Committee in 1957 (Zuckermann Committee, 1957) which questioned the usefulness of a three-year supply of timber in the context of nuclear war. The fundamental problem was then already apparent of how to keep in being a biological resource which would continue to grow and age. After 1959 the Forestry Commission wisely steered national policy towards the sustainable management of a renewable natural resource for multiple objectives.

It is well to point out that, until 1949 and in the absence of a national conservation agency, nature conservation in Britain was strongly sustained by foresters and by the Forestry Commission in particular. Many Commission publications were autecological monographs concerned with woodland wildlife, and individual foresters showed their commitment to conservation and the ecological basis of silviculture, for example Anderson (1950, 1953), Steven (1927) (both Forestry Commission research officers before their academic appointments), and, within the Commission, Chard (1953), Edlin (1947) and many others. Especially noteworthy in this regard are the guides to the national forest parks; Argyll was established in 1935, Dean in 1938, Glen Trool and Hardknott in 1945 (Forestry Commission 1938, 1947, 1949a, 1949b etc.).

The most far-reaching change in post-war forestry practice was undoubtedly the introduction of ploughing as the general land preparation technique for afforestation. Ploughing before tree planting had been done on a small scale as early as 1800 and research on its effect had been done by the Forestry Commission before the war but it was the development of wide-track crawler tractors and heavy draining ploughs in the period 1948 to 1953 that made the techniques commercially feasible.

Silviculturally the impact of ploughing was massively to simplify the resultant forest structure. It was no longer necessary closely to match the tree species to minor changes in topography and soil: plough cultivation and the application of small amounts of phosphatic fertiliser (about 55g basic slag per plant) created sufficient site homogeneity to allow a uniform tree stand to be established over a wide area. From the economic standpoint this appeared highly desirable, simplifying management and, above all, timber marketing.

Three types of plough evolved: deep-draining ploughs designed to cut open drains in peat, to intercept surface water; shallow ploughs to create local planting sites for trees, mechanically mimicking the hand-cut inverted turves; and tine ploughs with shallow mould-boards to cultivate glacially compacted soils and iron-pan podzols (Forestry Commission, 1968). By the use of these machines land became plantable which previously had been technically or economically impossible.

Some reference to the finance and economics of post-war forestry is essential. Throughout the period 1919 to 1959, grants-in-aid were made by Parliament to the Forestry Commission and to each annual grant was attached the current Treasury borrowing rate, like a fixed-rate mortgage. The crucial fact is that, throughout that 40–year period, the Treasury borrowing rate was around 2 percent per annum. In 1959 Britain suddenly abandoned this 'cheap money' policy in favour of rates of 8 or 10 percent per annum or higher and these were attached to the Forestry Commission's grants-in-aid. Those rates were far beyond the sustainable yield of any tree-based production system but the Treasury accountants continued to demand their yield return, which forced the cheapening of forest practice.

The plough had made afforestation technically possible on peat uplands, land which was cheap. Treasury pressure made it inevitable, if the required national programme was to be achieved, that this land should be purchased and planted in preference to areas which would have been better for woodland management: that is, more productive, more accessible and less prone to severe wind damage.

Planting at Inverliever in Argyll at the beginning of the century and at Corrour (Maxwell, 1929) had demonstrated the capacity of Sitka spruce to grow well on superficially drained peat. Given minimal nutrition, either from surface mineral water or by fertiliser application (Taylor, 1991), and the avoidance of heavy Calluna stands where mycorrhyzal antagonism can cause the growth of spruces to stagnate ('go into check'), Sitka spruce grows better than any other tree on upland peats and it was planted widely, especially between 1960 and 1980.

Later, the shortcomings of ploughing became evident, especially on peat land exposed to severe wind. Trees planted on spaced upturned turves tend to develop radially balanced root architecture, whereas those on ribbons of ploughed peat develop strongly linear root systems, ill-equipped to resist wind pressure at right angles to the direction of ploughing. In exposed uplands, stands of Sitka spruce on ploughed peat might be expected to suffer severe windthrow when the trees attained a height of about 20m, say at age 35 years. Since thinning does not significantly improve stability, and indeed may impair it if it is delayed, a new practice emerged during the 1970s, with some exposed areas treated as 'non-thin stands', that is, established with normal early tending but no thinning, to be clear-felled around age 35 years or shortly before the expected onset of extensive windblow. Incidentally such practice may offer some benefits for wildlife management, since it allows large areas of forest to be completely undisturbed by man for some thirty years.

Forest practice has recently moved substantially away from ploughing and, for both afforestation and regeneration, machines such as bucket excavators and scarifiers are now used which allow each tree to grow a radially balanced root system. Through the period, forest practice has benefited from the national programme of soil mapping and better understanding of the restriction on tree growth imposed by the complex called 'exposure'. Soil, topography, exposure, existing land use and institutional considerations have been combined in the preparation of land capability surveys which provide a guide to afforestation proposals and forest management (Bibby *et al*, 1988; Miller, 1985; Dry & Hipkin, 1989; etc.).

Throughout the period from 1945 to date, the Forestry Commission has consistently led the industry technically, setting the standards of forest practice, acting as the innovator and research leader. During the 1950s the Commission also planted more land each year than the private sector. Later this changed. In 1917 the Acland Committee had recommended that, to encourage private landowners to replant, taxpayers should be allowed to treat the capital cost of planting and replanting as a deduction from other income before the assessment of income tax. Since the highest marginal rate of income taxation in the post-war period was around 95 percent, this Schedule D regulation provided a huge incentive to forestry investment, in effect allowing a top-rate taxpayer to acquire a £100 asset for £5 net. Surprisingly little advantage was taken of this provision until after 1960 when several management companies emerged to provide city investors with the necessary land and services to promote afforestation. Scrutinised closely by the Labour Government in 1966 and declared to be in the national interest, the system continued until its cancellation in the 1988 Finance Act. Its demise then was due more to press attack on particular personalities investing heavily in forestry and concern at afforestation of the Caithness flow country than to reasoned criticism of the investment system itself.

The tax mechanism proved to be a powerful lever for inducing private land use to change in accord with national policy, as the scale of private sector afforestation achieved under Schedule D income tax demonstrated. This was especially true for land owned by very rich individuals. The operation of the Wild Land Tax of British Columbia provided a similar example of the strength of a fiscal mechanism.

Through the half-century there has been progressively greater attention to the structural design of forests, beginning with the advocacy by Anderson (1951, 1953) of group selection structure for upland forests in Scotland to promote their non-productive influences. Twenty-five years later landscape design was formally incorporated in forest practice (Crowe, 1978), for reasons of visual amenity and of topographic influence on landscape ecology.

The period has been marked by strong development of tree improvement and applied genetic science, first by simple identification of *plus trees* for seed collection, then as selected parents for controlled crossing, coupled with the cloning of the progeny to form new plantations (Rook, 1992) and lately in isozyme research and molecular biology. There is increased concern at substantial importation from elsewhere in Europe of seed and plants of species indigenous to Britain, thus compromising their genetic integrity. The Forestry Commission has recently issued draft guidelines on acceptable seed origins for planting stock of indigenous species for different parts of Great Britain.

Thinning practice has undergone cyclic change, thus continuing the pattern noted by Steven (1954). In the immediate post-war period, low thinning was normal practice. In the mid-1950s a form of crown thinning was introduced in South Scotland. In the decade after 1960 close-planted stands were 're-spaced' by pre-commercial cutting. The unprofitability of the early thinnings and pressure to reduce the initial establishment costs led to the practice of planting fewer trees per unit area. Plant spacing increased from around 1.25m post-war to 2.5m or 3m by 1980, but recently the trend has reversed. Current practice for fast-growing conifers is to plant at 2m by 2m spacing in order to reduce the formation of juvenile wood in the most valuable butt logs which should be destined for the production of building construction timbers. Regrettably much broadleaved tree planting (including oak) in the past twenty years has been done at a spacing of 3m by 3m, which is likely to provide little timber of good quality. It appears that the policy of accepting such wide spaced planting for the payment of grants (and hence of encouraging it) has been misguided, however politically convenient in increasing the area of so-called 'natural woodland'.

A turning point in forest practice was the *Broadleaves in Britain* symposium (Malcolm *et al*, 1982), following which the proportion of broadleaved trees planted and the attention to broadleaved silviculture have both markedly increased.

In the late 1980s the uniform coniferous stands produced by extensive afforestation began to be 're-structured' and their diversity markedly enhanced in both age and species. The process combines the reality of windthrow risk with the achievement of a balance between timber production and environmental enhancement. The proportion of broadleaved trees is greatly increased, particularly in ecologically key areas such as along watercourses. The age range of stands is widened by deliberately cutting some early, while holding adjacent ones well beyond the rotation of highest financial return (McIntosh, 1991). The diversity of the upland plantings was bound to increase in successive rotations, irrespective of this action; although the plantings were largely even-aged, their growth was not uniform, owing to differences of soil and micro-topography, some areas being windblown, others stable. The practice of re-structuring has accelerated and managed a process that was inevitable. Nevertheless diversification is not costless, at least in the rotation in which it is first imposed.

Since 1990 there has been increasing pressure by the Forestry Authority to ensure that all forest management, both state and private, conforms to best practice in regard to wildlife conservation, visual amenity and stand diversity. The best practices are codified in continually updated publications (Forestry Commission, 1990) which reflect and conform to the obligations of the Rio Convention and the Helsinki Accord. They also made possible the recent agreements which guarantee that the timber sold from the designated forests is from an ecologically sustainable system.

Forest practice in harvesting has changed radically in this half-century. In 1950 most trees were felled by two-man cross-cut saw; branches were trimmed by axe; much timber was hauled by horses and logs were commonly sawn in local or estate mills. Until 1960 large amounts of timber were sold to the coal mining industry for pit-props, chockwood and sawn mining timber, and more was sold to the railways for sleepers and wagon building. All these markets have now gone.

As the volume of timber from British woodlands has increased, so mechanisation has become possible, mostly following Scandinavian practice.

Tree cutting and trimming moved first to the petrol power-saw and now to the harvester-processor machine capable of felling, trimming and cross-cutting up to 100 trees per hour. The extraction of timber from the stand is achieved by tractor skidding, by forwarder or by wire ropeway. The road haulage of logs is now by 38–tonne truck, which obliges the grower to build forest roads to a very high specification. Finally the old estate sawmills have been replaced nationally by a small number of large factories, for sawing, pulping or board manufacture, with close integration of processes; from a particular operation there may be a wood residue but there is now no wood waste. As wood processing has become more intensive, the influence of the end use industry on forest practice has increased, particularly in coniferous stands, by putting large financial premiums on species, stem straightness and log size in a narrow range of diameter. At the same time the forest manager tries to adopt practices to increase stand diversity, allow public access and achieve good conservation of woodland wildlife.

The mechanisation of harvesting, the intensified processing and the large investment involved even in a single mill all result in market pressure towards large scale forest management: larger, more uniform forest stands, highly productive and, if possible, concentrated close to the factory site in order to minimise haulage costs. In the future this trend may evolve towards cutting systems further to increase the volume harvested, so-called 'whole-tree' harvesting or forest chipping, which could have important ecological implications by removing not simply more biomass from the land but nutritionally the most critical part.

Already there is a dichotomy in British forestry between the large forest areas and the small, affecting management style, silviculture, structure and marketing. The owner of small woods finds it increasingly difficult to sell produce into the supply of the few big processing mills. It may be that this difficulty will stimulate new small processors to emerge (and some revived processes), a development that will be essential for the future of the small woodlands which, because of their lowland location and their diversity, are vital for the maintenance of woodland wildlife habitats and for countryside recreation.

In the last few years there has been a marked increase in non-commercial planting which aims to simulate the native woodland destroyed in centuries of inappropriate land management. It is interesting that this is precisely what M.L.Anderson (1954) advocated in papers which were disregarded and even dismissed at the time as idealistic.

Opposed to the market economies of forest scale and uniformity, there is public, press and professional support for diversity within tree stands, for small woodlands rather than large forests and for the creation of non-commercial wildwood. Nevertheless it is well to reflect that, since Britain currently imports some 75 percent of our consumption, home timber prices are driven by world prices and that silvicultural diversity is more costly than uniformity. These costs must be carried. At the extreme, woodland that is entirely non-commercial has to be financially supported by public or private subvention, not merely at its creation but decade after decade. In the past, good examples of such support have been provided by landowners (including the Forestry Commission) who have sustained non-commercial activities with the proceeds of the financially profitable areas.

The question may arise whether there should be a formal separation of responsibility for large commercial timber forests from the multiple-objective woodlands. Subventions for isolated non-commercial activities are always highly tempting targets for an accountant or Chancellor looking for savings, so such isolated activities are particularly vulnerable. Non-market activities which are supported by income-earning ones in the same management, although never entirely secure, are at least less exposed. This is not merely an important merit but a clinching argument for multi-purpose forestry which is the current national policy, and for the practices by which it is implemented. Separation of commercial forestry from the duty of environmental enhancement would be a disastrous folly, as has been shown elsewhere in the world. It is a mistake we should not make here.

REFERENCES

Anderson, M.L. (1950). *The selection of tree species.* Oliver & Boyd, Edinburgh.
Anderson, M.L. (1951). Spaced group planting and irregularity of stand structure. *Empire Forestry Review* 30, 328–341.
Anderson, M.L. (1953). Plea for the adoption of the standing control or check in woodland management. *Scottish Forestry* 7, 38–47.
Anderson, M.L. (1954). Forest Policy in Scotland. *The Scotsman* December 1954. (Published anonymously as 'specially contributed').
Bibby, J.S., Heslop, R.E.F. and Hartnup, R. (1988). *Land capability classification for forestry in Britain.* Soil Survey Monograph. The Macaulay Land Use Research Institute, Aberdeen.
Chard, J.S.R. (1953). Highland birch. *Scottish Forestry* 7, 125.
Cmd 6447 (1943). *Post-war Forest Policy.* Forestry Commission, HMSO, London.
Cmd 6500 (1944). *Supplementary Report on Private Woodlands.* Forestry Commission, HMSO, London.
Crowe, S. (1978). *The landscape of forests and woods.* Forestry Commission Booklet 44. HMSO, London.
Dry, F.T. & Hipkin, J.A. (1989). *Land capability for forestry in south-east Scotland.* Forestry Commission and Macaulay Land Use Research Inst., Aberdeen.
Edlin, H.L. (1947). Forestry and woodland life. Batsford, London.
Forestry Commission (1933). *Forestry Practice.* Bulletin 14. (11th edition, ed. B.G.Hibberd, published as Forestry Commission Handbook 6, 1991). HMSO, London.
Forestry Commission (1938). *Argyll: National Forest Park Guide.* HMSO, London.
Forestry Commission (1947). *Forest of Dean and Wye Valley: National Forest Park Guide.* HMSO, London.

Forestry Commission (1949a). *Glen Trool: National Forest Park Guide.* HMSO, London.
Forestry Commission (1949b). *Hardknott: National Forest Park Guide.* HMSO, London.
Forestry Commission (1968). *Ploughing practice in the Forestry Commission.* Forest Record 73. HMSO.
Forestry Commission (1990). *Forest nature conservation guidelines.* HMSO, London.
Malcolm, D.C., Evans, J. & Edwards, P.N. (eds.) (1982). *Broadleaves in Britain.* Proceedings of symposium by Forestry Commission and Instit. of Chartered Foresters. ISBN 0–907284–02–7.
Maxwell, Sir J.S. (1929). *Loch Ossian Plantations.* Privately printed.
McIntosh, R. (1991). Planning for the second rotation. In *Forest Practice,* ed B.G.Hibberd. Forestry Commission Handbook 6. HMSO, London, 211–222.
Miller, K.F. (1985). *Windthrow hazard classification.* Forestry Commission Leaflet 85. HMSO, London.
Rook, D.A. (ed.) (1992). *Super Sitka for the 90s.* Forestry Commission Bulletin 103. HMSO.
Steven, H.M. (1927). The silviculture of conifers in Great Britain. *Forestry* 1 (1), 6.
Steven, H.M. (1954). Changes in silvicultural practice in Scotland 1854–1953. *Scottish Forestry* 8, 48–61.
Taylor, C.M.A. (1991). *Forest fertilisation in Britain.* Forestry Commission Bulletin 95. HMSO, London.
Zuckermann Committee (1957). *Forestry, Agriculture and Marginal Land.* A Report by the National Resources (Technical) Committee, Office of the Lord President of the Council. HMSO, London.

8

Applying Ecology to Wildlife Conservation: Have Attitudes Changed?

Charles H. Gimingham and Michael B. Usher

I. INTRODUCTION: FOUNDATIONS IN RESEARCH

ECOLOGY AS A scientific discipline is almost exactly a century old. Solid foundations were laid in the first half of this period, but it is the last 50 years that have seen major strides as the subject built upon its descriptive base and blossomed into an analytical and experimental science. In terms of the development of new ideas in ecology, the two decades with which we are now particularly concerned, from 1970 to 1990, have been especially significant. At the same time the organisation and practice of nature conservation have been maturing in a context of an increasing public awareness of acute environmental problems. The questions addressed in this paper concern the extent to which ecological science has been able to inform the practice of nature conservation. Has nature conservation emerged from the immediacy of responding to threat and opportunity into a properly science-based procedure, designed to achieve long-term goals, and integrated with other environmentally-based disciplines?

We have selected a limited series of examples of advances in ecological science, in the 1970s and the 1980s, which we believe have helped to mould the evolution of attitudes and practice in nature conservation, but naturally all are rooted in research which began well before those two decades. To set the scene, therefore, brief mention must first be made of four areas of work, initiated prior to 1970, which significantly influenced both the subsequent development of the science and its applications in practical nature conservation.

In the first place, an important objective of much of the early work was to build up comprehensive and systematic surveys and descriptions of plants and animals, and their communities, and from these to provide firm foundations for the emerging science of ecology. The work of Tansley (1939), Elton (1949), Elton & Miller (1954) and McVean & Ratcliffe (1962), for example, on animal and plant communities, contributed to rapid progress in methods of description and classification of communities. This made possible the first comprehensive descriptive review of terrestrial and freshwater sites of conservation value throughout Britain (Ratcliffe, 1977), which was an essential prerequisite for a coherent policy for protection and management. The development of a similar descriptive basis for conservation in the marine environment has been substantially slower, and is only now being developed (e.g. Hiscock, 1996).

Second, a new emphasis on investigating the mechanisms at work in ecosystems was gaining ground. On the plant side, Watt's (1947) work on pattern and process in the plant community was a great stimulus, as was Harper's (1961) work on the dynamic interactions between species and individuals within communities. Animal ecologists interested in dynamic interactions found it necessary to work at the population level, which led to rapid developments in population theory (e.g. Andrewartha & Birch, 1954), quickly also taken up on the botanical side (Harper, 1964). These studies not only fed substantial advances in ecological theory and understanding, but had a marked influence on conservation practice, which took on board a new awareness that conservation management often involves control of plant succession or manipulation of population dynamics. It was increasingly realised that the effects of management practices such as grazing or burning must be understood in terms of the perpetuation of certain stages in an ecological process. Pattern or mosaic in vegetation, seen as a desirable source of biodiversity, is also the outcome of dynamic processes, and must be managed accordingly.

Third, the phenomena of biological invasions (Elton, 1958) captured the imagination of population ecologists who sought to discover the factors which initiate them and the processes governing their development. Research on these fundamental problems was especially relevant when such invasions had adverse effects on native populations, or created economic problems.

A fourth development of far-reaching importance was that of ecological genetics. A leader in this field was Bradshaw (1948), who studied the selection of heavy metal tolerance in certain grass species which enabled them to colonise the specialized habitats of mine waste. As a well-researched example of the evolution of physiological adaptation, and as a pointer to new ways of approaching re-vegetation of mine waste, this was of both scientific and practical value (Bradshaw & Chadwick, 1980). On the animal side, Berry's (1971) ideas, derived from research on the genetics of small mammal populations, particularly the genetical changes in island mouse populations (Berry, 1964), had a direct bearing on conservation practice.

These were all products of research driven by a desire to elucidate the ways in which vegetation and animal populations function, in the belief that such knowledge is important in understanding the way that the natural world functions. They were not primarily directed towards answering particular practical problems, but all of them soon had profound influence in that direction.

2. THE 1970S: A DECADE OF IDEAS

We have designated the first of our two decades as one of 'ideas', not because other periods were devoid of ideas but because, in the 1970s, a number of very significant trends of thought were being established. There is space to discuss only a few, and the following selection is inevitably rather eclectic. We have chosen

- global perspectives and biogeography in the development of ecological theory and conservation practice;
- the concept of 'adaptive strategies' in plants and animals; and
- diversification of multivariate methods of data analysis and their application in ecology.

2.1 Global perspectives and biogeography

The trend from basic descriptive work towards process-orientated research was being fostered in the years prior to 1970 by studies directed at the level of whole ecosystems. Strongly influenced by Odum (1975), these included quantification of energy flow through ecosystems and the cycling of water and nutrients, greatly facilitated by the development of methods of systems modelling. One outcome of this line of thought was an interest in comparative studies of ecosystem function in all the major biogeographical regions of the world, in an attempt to explain differences in productivity. This could only be achieved by means of wide international collaboration and standardization of methods, as developed by the International Biological Programme which took shape towards the end of the 1960s and culminated with publication of most of its results in the first half of the 1970s. Critics have taken the view that the practical value of much of this work was not commensurate with the effort devoted to it, but it did demonstrate the value of getting specialists from a wide range of disciplines to concentrate their efforts on selected sites so as to obtain a comprehensive picture of the processes at work. It also drew attention to the need for extension of the systems approach to the scale of the whole biosphere if impacts of human activities are to be understood.

These developments had their effect in stimulating a wider outlook on environmental management and conservation. In the 1970s, international collaboration in tackling environmental protection and wildlife conservation became more prominent, as instanced by the 1972 Stockholm Conference, and it is interesting to compare the attitudes expressed in the *Blueprint for*

Survival (Anonymous, 1972) with those of the *World Conservation Strategy* (IUCN, 1980). The former was of undoubted value in raising awareness of increasing damage to the global environment, but it was the latter which recognized that if conservation aims are to be realized they must be pursued hand-in-hand with 'sustainable development'.

The overall consequence of these developments was a growing effort to establish international collaboration on conservation issues, especially (as far as the UK was concerned) at the European level, as for example with the *Birds Directive* of 1979 and later the *Habitats Directive* of 1992. It was accepted that national conservation policies have to take account of responsibilities not only to sites regarded as of national importance but also to habitats and species listed as being of significance in a European context because of their rarity, or because of threats to their survival. Furthermore, such considerations stimulated revision of attitudes to site safeguard within our own country, because they increased awareness of the important regional variation in community composition and the need to ensure that site designations cover the full range of this biological variation. Progress in this field was subsequently enhanced and informed by an important scientific study which resulted in a new classification of 'Biogeographical Zones' in upland Scotland (Brown *et al.*, 1993a,b) and later by the use of huge datasets for Scotland as a whole (Usher & Balharry, 1996).

Other new ideas in biogeography also had input to conservation during the 1970s. For example, the theory of island biogeography (MacArthur & Wilson, 1967) was thought for a time to be capable of informing policy regarding the minimum viable size of nature reserves, and the effects of fragmentation of habitats. Certainly it focused attention on the adverse effects on species richness of 'insularization' (reductions in area, fragmentation and isolation of habitats). However, attempts to apply the theory to the establishment of rules of selection and management of nature reserves have had limited success, though the guidelines of Diamond (1975) have been widely quoted and have been extended (Fig. 1) by Usher & Keiller (1998). This is a subject in which more ecological research on the effects of insularization on plant and animal populations, and the potential value of buffer zones, habitat corridors and networks of reserves, might be fruitful (Spellerberg, 1991).

2.2 Species 'strategies'

Alongside the growing interest in ecosystem function, new ideas were emerging in the 1970s at the level of the properties of species which could be shown to be of selective advantage in particular environments. One of the pioneers in developing this concept of 'strategies' as a 'unifying approach to ecology' was Grime (1979), whose triangular model, based on the relative importance of

Figure 1. A diagrammatic representation of the conservation value of designed nature reserves, based on a study of macrolepidoptera in farm woodlands by Usher & Keiller (1998). Habitat remnants are shown as small black or white circles, and linear features (hedgerows in this case) by straight lines.

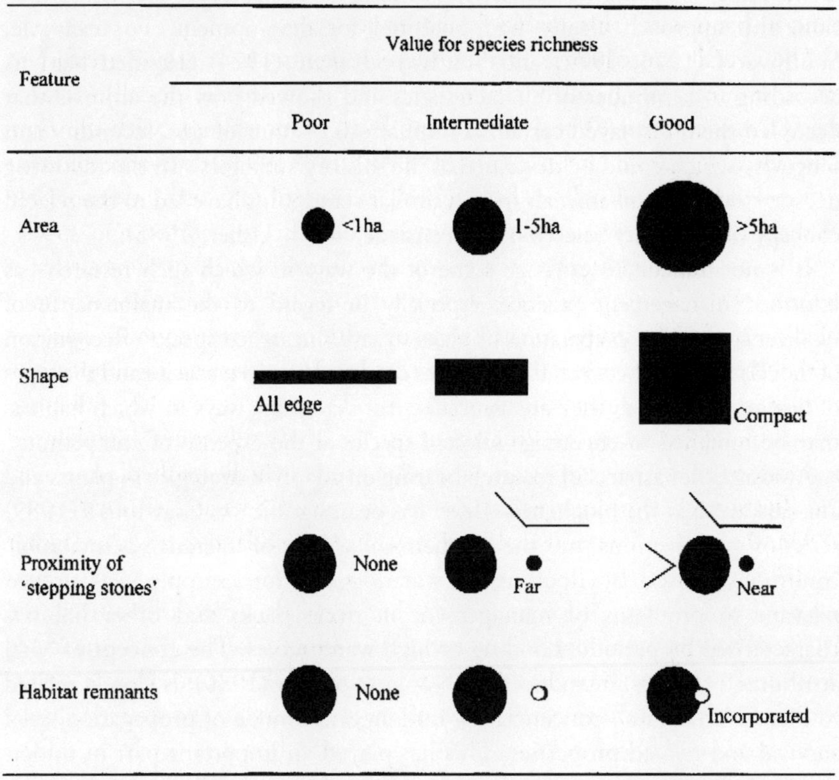

Feature	Value for species richness		
	Poor	Intermediate	Good
Area	● <1ha	● 1-5ha	● >5ha
Shape	▬ All edge	▬	■ Compact
Proximity of 'stepping stones'	● None	● • Far	● • Near
Habitat remnants	● None	● ○	● ○ Incorporated

competition, stress and disturbance as determinants of vegetation composition, has become very familiar (e.g. Bunce *et al.*, 1999). Plant species could be allocated places in this scheme according to the extent to which they display adaptive strategies to the environmental factor-complexes concerned. The life-history, relative growth rate, and physiological and reproductive characteristics of species were analysed as components of these strategies, conferring fitness in the spectrum of habitats defined by the triangle model. This research-based theory has significantly helped to establish the kinds of management required to conserve various types of plant species and communities, such as those which are intolerant of competition and hence may require certain sorts of disturbance or other stress in their environment for their survival.

Similar approaches were being applied in the study of ecological adaptation in animals. The *r* and *K* concept (Pianka, 1970) had suggested that contrasting types of environment could lead to selection of organisms displaying, on the one hand, smaller size, relatively short life-cycles and rapid reproduction (*r*-selection) or, on the other, larger size, longer life-span and fewer, larger offspring (*K*-selection). Although very much an over-simplification, this approach clearly had potential for development. For example, Southwood (1976, 1977) and Southwood *et al.* (1974) classified habitats according to a number of characteristics and showed how the animals that occupied them displayed certain combinations of traits of size, fecundity and longevity which could be described as 'life history strategies'. In the following decade studies of soil animals from a similar standpoint have led to the related concept of 'adversity selection' (Greenslade, 1983; Usher, 1985).

It is not difficult to envisage some of the ways in which such research has informed management practice, especially in regard to the maintenance of biodiversity and the preparation of plans to save threatened species. Recognition of the relationships between the strategies displayed by given species and the types of habitat with which they are associated can determine ways in which habitats may be modified to encourage selected species at the expense of competitors.

Among other aspects of research bearing on adaptive strategies in plants and animals, work at the biochemical level has been significant. Crawford's (1989) series of investigations into the biochemical aspects of tolerance of anaerobic conditions caused by flooding or waterlogging, for example, has proved relevant to problems of management in dune slacks and other habitats characterised by periodic flooding or high water tables. The concept of 'vital attributes' of plants, introduced by Noble & Slatyer (1980), is closely related to that of 'strategies', concentrating on longevity, mode of propagation, seed survival and related properties. This has played an important part in understanding plant responses to various causes of habitat perturbation such as fire.

2.3 The diversification of multivariate methods
At the community level of organization, ideas developed rapidly in the 1970s, partly as a result of the availability of new tools for handling and analysing large bodies of data. In particular, methods of multivariate analysis, introduced in earlier years, were being refined, extended and elaborated.

The application of multivariate methods to the ordination and classification of plant and animal communities not only improved understanding of the interactions between environmental factor-complexes and species representation, but also began to give an entirely new slant to community classification. By introducing more objective, data-based systems of classification, procedures were freed from the limitations of subjective judgement, and from the constraints of rigid theoretical frameworks. Especially noteworthy in this respect was the development of computer programmes, based on reciprocal averaging, such as TWINSPAN (Hill, 1979). These served a very evident need in conservation circles for efficient and universally applicable community classification and recognition, for purposes of site surveys, recording, comparison and evaluation. The acceptance and wide application of these approaches paved the way for the National Vegetation Classification, the first complete phytosociological classification of British plant communities, based on extensive sampling largely analysed by the use of TWINSPAN. Work on this project began in 1975 and culminated in the publication of five volumes of *British Plant Communities* between 1992 and 1999 (Rodwell, 1992a,b; 1993a,b; 2000).

The accelerating rate of change in landscape patterns and systems of land use underlined the parallel need for survey on the scale of broad vegetation categories. This was tackled during the 1970s by the Institute of Terrestrial Ecology, which produced its own classification of land classes, and undertook an England-wide sampling programme (Bunce *et al.*, 1981). At the same time the rapid improvement in remote sensing, from both aircraft and satellites, as well as the associated computer software, made available a powerful tool for this purpose. This also played a large part in the parallel Scottish *National Countryside Monitoring Scheme* (Mackey *et al.*, 1998). These projects have had their own practical value, but have also contributed to a change of attitude and outlook in conservation bodies. While the detailed recording and evaluation of habitat and species distributions remained important for purposes of site-safeguard, much attention has been paid in recent years to the problems of habitat loss and changes in land cover leading to the fragmentation and isolation of patches of semi-natural vegetation. There is now greater consciousness of a need to establish which kinds of habitat mosaic are most desirable in different parts of our country and what policies and mechanisms are required to achieve the necessary change.

2.4 The 1970s: a postscript.

As shown by these examples, the 1970s were a decade in which ecological science was exploring a range of ideas, which in themselves spawned subsequent research in both pure and applied ecology. This has led to quite substantial changes of outlook among both managers and conservationists, and has sown seeds which are still influencing attitudes to conservation today.

3. THE 1980S: A DECADE OF QUESTIONS

We have designated the second of our two decades as one of 'questions'. Ecologists have always had questions, but after a flourishing of ideas it appears to us that there were numerous questions to address. In many cases, the questions that exercise us today have their origins in the 1980s, or arose from concerns expressed at that time. Again space permits only a rather eclectic selection, but we have chosen to address the following three questions.

- How do we know if a population of plants or animals will persist into the future,
- why are there so many problems with non-native species in so many parts of the world, and do they matter, and
- what effects are humans having on the environment, in terms of pollution (especially acidification and eutrophication), and on our climate?

3.1 Questions about population persistence

Studies of population dynamics and studies of ecological genetics came together in attempts to ask questions about whether populations were viable. There was a feeling that there should be some lower limit, the *minimum viable population size* (MVP), below which a population was doomed to eventual extinction, and above which it was likely to persist. The work of Soulé (1987) is closely associated with the MVP concept, though he did not advocate a definitive MVP; he asked the question 'What are the minimum conditions for the long-term persistence and adaptation of a species or population in a given place?' (Soulé, 1987, p. 1).

This raises some interesting concepts. First, it is geographically referenced. This means that the conditions for persistence may vary from place to place. Second, what is meant by 'long-term'? Clearly no species or population persists for ever, and so 'long-term' evidently has to imply a time horizon. For much of the modelling of the 1990s this is arbitrarily taken as 100 years. Third, what is meant by 'minimum'? Should nature conservation management accept a 'minimum', or should there be some kind of 'insurance effect', recognising that populations are variable in time and that catastrophic events can happen?

These concerns have led to concepts of risk assessment. Examples exist of large populations that have gone extinct (the passenger pigeon, *Ectopistes migratorius*, of North America is frequently quoted), and of small populations that have survived and expanded so that they are no longer endangered (Usher (1998) quotes examples of these). It therefore appears that no population or species is 100% secure, and equally that very few are 100% doomed to extinction. The development of the concepts of risk assessment is well explained by Burgman *et al.* (1993). The population dynamic models that originated in the 1940s (such as the Leslie matrix model; Leslie (1945)) and that were developed in the 1970s (e.g. Usher's (1972) work on applying the Leslie matrix model to managed mammal populations and forests), have been incorporated into risk assessments based on introducing elements of stochasticity.

The links are also strong with the development of *population viability analysis* (PVA), which is a comprehensive investigation of all of the factors that might cause the extinction of a species (Gilpin & Soulé, 1986; Shaffer, 1990). Theoretical approaches are brought to bear on individual species, traditionally ones whose populations are declining. Whilst the techniques have, as yet, had little application to declining species in the UK, they have been used, for example, to explore the viability of species of plants in North America (e.g. Damman & Cain, 1998), birds in the Antipodes (e.g. Brook *et al.*, (1997) and marine mammals in Finland (e.g. Kokko *et al.*, (1997). In the majority of cases they have been used to explore the question 'how viable is this declining population?', and to assist in devising methods of managing the population so as to reduce its risk of extinction.

In Scotland, we have recently been turning these studies around to explore increasing populations, especially those of geese (Pettifor *et al.*, 1999a,b). The term *maximum tolerable population size* (MTP) has slipped into our vocabulary, denoting a socio-economic rather than a scientific concept (Usher, 1998). If conservation management is successful, at what point is the population sufficiently viable, or when is the risk of extinction sufficiently small, for strict protection to be no longer necessary? Whilst there is a dilemma for many species that are declining in numbers and distribution, there is also a 'dilemma of conservation success' for a few species that have recovered and are reaching 'pest' status.

3.2 Questions about non-native species
As mentioned earlier, Elton's (1958) book stimulated an interest in the invasion of plants and animals from one geographical area into another. In many instances it is clear which species were native to an area, and which species, aided by humans, are now invaders. However, in the UK where people have been coming and going for at least two millennia, the distinction between native and non-native species is not always obvious. To address such questions, Webb (1985) asked what criteria could be used. We think it true to say that there is no definitive, universally applicable criterion, but on the basis of Webb's eight criteria, and a ninth introduced by Preston (1986), a balance of probability towards native or non-native status can be established.

There is no doubt that invasion by non-native species can have a negative effect on biodiversity. In the 1980s the Scientific Committee on Problems of the Environment (SCOPE) inaugurated a programme of study on the ecological effects of biological invasions. The specific aims of the programme were to answer the following three questions (Drake *et al.*, 1989, p. xxiii).

- 'What are the factors that determine whether a species will be an invader or not?
- What are the site properties that determine whether an ecological system will be relatively prone to, or resistant to, invasion?
- How should management systems be developed using the knowledge gained from answering these questions?'

The programme was therefore focused on gaining knowledge of species and ecosystems, essentially searching for common patterns of invasiveness or invasion, and then applying this in management. Unfortunately, the synthesis of the programme (Drake *et al.*, 1989) failed to determine robust common patterns of invasiveness and invasion. Even where the programme concentrated specifically on invasions into nature reserves (Usher, 1988), it failed to produce generalisations, other than demonstrating a positive correlation between the numbers of visitors to a protected area and the number of non-native species occurring in that area. Williamson (1996) incorporated these and other findings in his conceptual framework, stating that all [ecological] communities are invasible, perhaps some more than others; a species' ecology in its native range is often irrelevant to its invasion success (which probably implies that prediction is impossible); and spread can be at any speed, in any direction, and at any time following establishment (again making prediction difficult). There appear to be some ecological questions that cannot be answered!

On a pragmatic basis, Scottish Natural Heritage has recently accepted that six categories of species can be recognised for practical nature conservation purposes. These are set out in Table 1, but it has to be noted that the categories are not mutually exclusive. They provide a framework within which management strategies can be devised.

Table 1. A practical classification of species on the basis of their nativeness or non-nativeness. In the 'Application' column, B relates to the overall use of the group name in the British Isles, whilst L relates to its use in a local part of the British Isles.

Group name	Application	Comments
Native	B, L	The main focus of biodiversity conservation management.
Formerly native	B, L	The species used to occur, but is now extinct due to environmental change or human activity.
Locally non-native	L	The species is native in some parts of the British Isles, but not locally.
Recently arrived	B, L	The species has only recently been 'discovered', and an assessment has yet to be made of whether its arrival is human assisted or 'natural'.
Long-established	B, L	The species has been present for centuries or millennia, and has become an integral part of the food chain.
Non-native	B	Possibly could become invasive and hence problematic.

3.3 Questions about a changing environment

During the 1980s there was increasing realisation that there were major anthropogenic influences acting on the global environment of the planet. Although in many ways these are linked, there are four categories of questions, namely

- why are surface waters and soils becoming more acidic,
- what has caused the ozone holes over the polar regions,
- how is the increasing CO_2 content of the air affecting the global climate, and
- are nitrogen oxides inevitably leading to increased eutrophication?

All of these are essentially aspects of pollution, resulting from the release to the atmosphere of oxides of sulphur, nitrogen and carbon, as well as the release of a suite of other (often synthetic) gases.

The problems of acidification in Sweden were summarised in 1990 (Anonymous, 1990). Acidification affects both land and water. Studying the uplands of Snowdonia, Kuylenstierna & Chadwick (1991) demonstrated that soils had become about one pH unit more acid over a 33–year period from 1957 to 1990. The more acid soils in 1957 had been least affected, with a pH drop of only about half a unit, whilst the least acid soils had been most affected. This is potentially serious for soil ecosystem processes, including both decomposition and nutrient cycling, since the soils were unlikely in their acidified state to be able to continue to support populations of earthworms.

In the aquatic environment the loss of wildlife in Swedish lakes led to investigations of causes and ameliorating treatments. Bernes (1991) traced the development of awareness of the problems of acidification from its beginning in the late 1960s, through the environmental conferences of the 1970s, to a fuller realisation in the 1980s. Sweden set about a programme of liming catchments, headwaters and/or directly into the lakes in an effort to counteract acidification and reinstate species of fish, invertebrates and plants. By the mid-1990s many lakes were showing the benefit of treatment, recognised by changes in water chemistry and by a biodiversity that was recovering (Bernes, 1991).

The problems of climate change have received much attention recently. Models have been developed for likely scenarios of temperature increase, precipitation change, change in mean annual wind speed, etc (DETR, 1998; Hill *et al.*, 1999). Ecologically, there is much work to do in interpreting these possible changes in climate in relation to impacts on species and habitats. How will each species react to an increase in temperature, to a change in precipitation, to reduced solar insolation, or to a doubling in CO_2 concentration? As habitats are essentially composed of collections of species, how will the differential effects on the individual species manifest themselves in changes to habitats? A preliminary, and in many ways speculative, analysis of the effects of environmental change on the species and habitats of nature conservation importance in Scotland has been undertaken by Hill *et al.* (1999).

Rather little is yet known about the effects of eutrophication, though, for example, nitrogen deposition is suspected of being responsible for the demise of the lowland heaths in the Netherlands (Smidt, 1995) and possibly also in south-east England. Although questions were being asked in the 1980s (e.g. papers in Whitby, 1992), there remains much ecological research still to be undertaken. Questions need to be asked about the effects of eutrophication, and about the interactions between eutrophication, acidification and climate change resulting from the increased CO_2 content of the atmosphere. Without doubt all of these influences on environmental change will affect the land cover (e.g. Mackey *et al.*, 1998) and the way that land use changes (Brouwer *et al.*, 1991; Whitby, 1992).

3.4 The 1980s: a postscript

The 1980s saw many questions being asked about fundamental issues in ecological science. The examples quoted in the preceding sections focus on research at the individual level, at the population level and at the global level. Between these there was increasing interest in landscape-scale processes, and advances in genetics and biochemistry meant that molecular ecology was poised to expand. The recognition of this hierarchy of processes, outlined by Allen & Starr (1982), has had profound impacts both on ecological research and on how we apply research findings to the management of populations and communities for nature conservation. The increasing use of mathematical models has meant that ecological science has been able to start moving away from its initial descriptive phase towards a more predictive phase, as outlined by Starfield & Bleloch (1986).

4. CHANGING ATTITUDES AND NEW DIRECTIONS

During the two decades under review, there has been an increasing realisation that communities of plants and animals are dynamic. Throughout the twentieth century, ecologists had argued about the most obvious of changes - ecological succession. Some saw it as a determinate and ordered process; others considered that it was essentially stochastic. Connell & Slatyer (1977) brought the many strands together, observing different pathways and developing a theory where determinism and stochasticity both had their place. This has had a profound effect on ecological thought, since in any changing ecosystem there is an element of determinism and an element of randomness. This is clearly seen in the post-fire development of Scottish heathlands, of which Gimingham (1987) said:

> While clearly a secondary succession, it was interpreted for many years as
> relay floristics . . . The commonly observed stages prior to the reasser-
> tion of *Calluna* dominance were viewed as a more or less deterministic
> sequence, but recent re-examination reveals far greater variability . . .
> (page 904).

If change is deterministic, then it could be predictable; if change is stochastic, then it is essentially not predictable. The challenge facing ecologists is to make the science of ecology more predictable. This is often achieved by modelling, as demonstrated by the model for predicting *Calluna* population dynamics described by Scandrett & Gimingham (1989), or the models predicting species richness, and the abundance of rare species, in less intensively surveyed parts of the world (McIntyre & Lavorel, 1994). Modelling for conservation biology is certainly not new, but it perhaps came of age with the publication of *Building Models for Conservation and Wildlife Management* (Starfield & Bleloch, 1986), though, as Policansky (1993) reminded us, ecologists will always have to deal with uncertainty.

Whilst the last few decades have seen a movement from descriptive ecology to the study of ecological change (Gimingham, 1997), in the last decade or so there has been a widening of interest both to smaller scales, with the incorporation of genetic and molecular approaches, and to larger scales, with an increasing interest in how different ecosystems interact with each other at the landscape scale. But what roles do 'molecular ecology' and 'landscape ecology' play in the development of ecological science?

Caughley (1994) considered that conservation biology had two threads; one was the small population paradigm, dealing with the effect of smallness on the persistence of populations (the other is the declining population paradigm). The main developments of molecular techniques have found their application in this area of conservation biology (Dhondt, 1996). The number of known genetical problems faced by small populations continues to grow, with the papers in Tew *et al.* (1997) including both plants (e.g. Scottish primrose (*Primula scotica*) and Plymouth pear (*Pyrus cordata*)) and animals (e.g. red kite (*Milvus milvus*) and wild cat (*Felix sylvestris*)) in the UK. Understanding genetic diversity, and how to manage small populations to retain that diversity, is important, especially as the only natural process that can counteract loss of genetic diversity is mutation (Lande, 1995). Genetic biodiversity is an integral part of the biodiversity of any territory.

This genetic diversity resides in a species, which lives with other species in communities, one or more of which form an ecosystem, a number of which form the landscape. Species, the most frequent focus of conservation action, live in the landscape, and landscape-scale processes will inevitably affect those species. Understanding the dynamics of landscapes, more naturally those of ecological succession and anthropogenically those of land use, is going to be important in achieving the aims of many biodiversity action plans. Although the subject of 'landscape ecology' is now more than two decades old (e.g. Tjallingii & Veer, 1982), we believe that there is still considerable potential to develop its role in applied ecology. Not only is it important in understanding species responses (With & Crist, 1995), but it also integrates both biological and earth science (e.g. geomorphological and hydrological) processes.

Landscapes are composed of a series of individual ecosystems, and it is here that another instance of changing attitudes is evident. Following Tansley (1939), much of the conservation effort was focused on the so-called 'semi-natural' ecosystems. Greater understanding of the ubiquitous influence of human activities on ecological processes has led to acceptance of the value of a whole continuum of ecosystems. These range from those that are little modified by human activities (the 'natural' and 'near-natural' ecosystems) to those which are intensively managed and hence are essentially 'unnatural'. Ecosystems at any point on this continuum may be important in respect of their contribution to the biodiversity of the landscape.

There has been increasing attention focused on the conservation of this biodiversity, as for example the UK's *Biodiversity Action Plan* (Anonymous, 1994) and the series of detailed action plans for about 400 species and 40 habitats that have subsequently been published (Anonymous 1995, 1998a, 1998b, 1999a, 1999b). Implementation of this collection of plans will require a huge amount of ecological knowledge, as well as the instigation of some ecological research. This will require both 'pure' ecological research, developing the predictiveness of ecological science, as well as the much more 'applied' ecological research. All the signs of increased interest in applying ecological knowledge are in evidence, with four categories of research being outlined by Underwood (1995) as

- using available research for the needs of management,
- research about the consequences of management,
- new basic and strategic research, and
- research into the process of management.

In all of this work ecological theory must be developed and applied (Doak & Mills, 1994), though it must not be forgotten that there are limits to what ecological research can actually achieve (Hilborn & Ludwig, 1993).

In this review we characterized the period during the 1950s and 1960s, the first two decades following the *1949 National Parks and Access to the Countryside Act*, as being focused on descriptive ecology and laying the foundations for the management of species populations and ecosystems. We have focused on the

1970s as a decade of ideas and the 1980s as a decade of questions. We do not yet have hindsight, but we suspect that the 1990s will be a decade of biodiversity, a time when scientific, political and public awareness was being raised, with many nations preparing and starting to implement plans to conserve their biodiversity. Will the decade following 2000 be a decade of application of ecological knowledge? A dynamic and ever-changing nature - as opposed to a stable nature - must be the feature of the way that we view the conservation and management of our country's, and of the world's, biodiversity. Attitudes to nature conservation, and to the conservation of biodiversity that links both scientific and social goals, have certainly changed over the last 50 years. And that change must embrace the whole of the planet, not only the terrestrial ecosystems and the soil on which they depend, but also the freshwater and marine ecosystems and the wealth of the species that they support.

REFERENCES

Allen, T.F.H. & Starr, T.B. (1982). *Hierarchy: Perspectives for Ecological Complexity.* University of Chicago Press, Chicago.

Andrewartha, H.G. & Birch, L.C. (1954). *The Distribution and Abundance of Animals.* Chicago University Press, Chicago.

Anonymous (1972). A blueprint for survival. *The Ecologist,* 2, 1–40.

Anonymous (1990). New Swedish action plans on environment. *Enviro,* 10, 1–28.

Anonymous (1994). *Biodiversity: the UK Action Plan.* HMSO, London.

Anonymous (1995). *Biodiversity: the UK Steering Group Report.* HMSO, London.

Anonymous (1998a). *UK Biodiversity Group Tranche 2 Action Plans. Volume I - Vertebrates and Vascular Plants.* English Nature, Peterborough.

Anonymous (1998b). *UK Biodiversity Group Tranche 2 Action Plans. Volume II - Terrestrial and Freshwater Habitats.* English Nature, Peterborough.

Anonymous (1999a). *UK Biodiversity Group Tranche 2 Action Plans. Volume III - Plants and Fungi.* English Nature, Peterborough.

Anonymous (1999b). *UK Biodiversity Group Tranche 2 Action Plans. Volume IV - Invertebrates.* English Nature, Peterborough.

Bernes, C. (ed.) (1991). *Acidification and Liming of Swedish Freshwaters.* Swedish Environmental Protection Agency, Stockholm.

Berry, R.J. (1964). The evolution of an island population of house mouse. *Evolution,* 18, 478–483.

Berry, R.J. (1971). Conservation and the genetical constitution of populations. In *The Scientific Management of Animal and Plant Communities* (eds. E. Duffey & A.S. Watt). Blackwell, Oxford. pp. 177–206.

Bradshaw, A.D. (1948). Evolutionary significance of genetic variation between populations. In *Perspectives on Plant Population Ecology* (eds. R. Dirzo & J. Sarukhán). Sinauer, Massachusetts. pp. 213–228.

Bradshaw, A.D. & Chadwick, M.J. (1980). *The Restoration of Land.* Blackwell, Oxford.

Brouwer, F.M., Thomas, A.J. & Chadwick, M.J. (eds.) (1991). *Land Use Changes In Europe: Processes of Change, Environmental Transformations and Future Patterns.* Kluwer, Dordrecht.

Brook, B.W., Lim, L., Harden, R. & Frankham, R. (1997). Does population viability analysis software predict the behaviour of real populations? A retrospective study on the Lord Howe Island woodhen *Tricholimnas sylvestris* (Sclater). *Biological Conservation,* 82, 119–128.

Brown, A., Birks, H.J.B. & Thompson, D.B.A. (1993a). A new biogeographical classification of the Scottish uplands. II. Vegetation-environment relationships. *Journal of Ecology*, **81**, 231–251.

Brown, A., Horsfield, D. & Thompson, D.B.A. (1993b). A new biogeographical classification of the Scottish uplands. I. Descriptions of vegetation blocks and their spatial variation. *Journal of Ecology*, **81**, 207–230.

Bunce, R.G.H., Barr, C.J. & Whittaker, H.A. (1981). *Land Classes in Britain: Preliminary Descriptions of the Merlewood Method of Land Classification*. Institute of Terrestrial Ecology, Grange-over-Sands.

Bunce, R.G.H., Barr, C.J., Gillespie, M.K., Howard, D.C., Scott, W.A., Smart, S.M., van der Poll, H.M. & Watkins, J.W. (1999). *Vegetation of the British Countryside - the Countryside Vegetation System*. Department of the Environment, Transport and the Regions, London.

Burgman, M.A., Ferson, S. & Akçakaya, H.R. (1993). *Risk Assessment in Conservation Biology*. Chapman & Hall, London.

Caughley, G. (1994). Directions in conservation biology. *Journal of Animal Ecology*, **63**, 215–244.

Connell, J.H. & Slatyer, R.O. (1977). Mechanisms of succession in natural communities and their role in community stability and organization. *American Naturalist*, **111**, 1119–1144.

Crawford, R.M.M. (1989). *Studies in Plant Survival*. Blackwell, Oxford.

Damman, H. & Cain, M.J. (1998). Population growth and viability analyses of the clonal woodland herb, *Asarum canadense*. *Journal of Ecology*, **86**, 13–26.

DETR (1998). *Climate Change Impacts in the UK: the Agenda for Assessment and Action*. Department of the Environment, Transport and the Regions, London.

Dhondt, A.A. (1996). Molecular techniques in conservation and evolutionary biology: a quantum leap? *Trends in Ecology and Evolution*, **11**, 147–148.

Diamond, J.M. (1975). The island dilemma: lessons of modern biogeographic studies for the design of nature reserves. *Biological Conservation*, 7, 3–15.

Doak, D.F. & Mills, L.S. (1994). A useful role for theory in conservation. *Ecology*, 75, 615–626.

Drake, J.A., Mooney, H.A., Castri, F. di, Groves, R.H., Kruger, F.J., Rejmánek, M. & Williamson, M. (eds.) (1989). *SCOPE 37, Biological Invasions: a Global Perspective*. Wiley, Chichester.

Elton, C.S. (1949). Population interspersion, an essay on animal community patterns. *Journal of Ecology*. 37, 1–23.

Elton, C.S. (1958). *The Ecology of Invasions by Animals and Plants*. Methuen, London.

Elton, C.S. & Miller, R.S. (1954). The ecological survey of animal communities. *Journal of Ecology*, 42, 460–496.

Gilpin, M.E. & Soulé, M.E. (1986). Minimum viable populations: processes of species extinction. In *Conservation Biology: the Science of Scarcity and Diversity*, ed. by M.E. Soulé. Sinauer, Massachusetts. pp. 19–34.

Gimingham, C.H. (1987). Harnessing the winds of change: heathland ecology in retrospect and prospect. *Journal of Ecology*, 75, 895–914.

Gimingham, C.H. (1997). Opening address: 'Burnett, 1964' and after. *Botanical Journal of Scotland*, 49, 117–126.

Greenslade, P.J.M. (1983). Adversity selection and the habitat templet. *American Naturalist*, 122, 325–365.

Grime, J.P. (1979). *Plant Strategies and Vegetation Processes*. Wiley, Chichester.

Harper, J.L. (1961). Approaches to the study of plant competition. In *Mechanisms in Biological Competition* (ed. F.L. Milthorpe). Cambridge University Press, Cambridge. pp. 1–39.

Harper, J.L. (1964). The individual in the population. *Journal of Ecology*, 52 supplement, 149–158.

Hilborn, R. & Ludwig, D. (1993). The limits of applied ecological research. *Ecological Applications*, 3, 550–552.

Hill, M.O. (1979). *TWINSPAN - a FORTRAN Programme for Arranging Multivariate Data in an Ordered Two-Way Table by Classification of the Individuals and Attributes.* Cornell University Press, New York.

Hill, M.O., Downing, T.E., Berry, P.M., Coppins, B.J., Hammond, P.S., Marquiss, M., Roy, D.B., Telfer, M.G. & Welch, D. (1999). Climate Changes and Scotland's Natural Heritage: an Environmental Audit. *Scottish Natural Heritage Research, Survey and Monitoring Report No 132.*

Hiscock, K. (ed.) (1996). *Marine Nature Conservation Review: Rationale and Methods.* Joint Nature Conservation Committee, Peterborough.

International Union for Conservation of Nature and Natural Resources (IUCN). (1980). *World Conservation Strategy.* IUCN, Gland.

Kokko, H., Lindström, J. & Ranta, E. (1997). Risk analysis of hunting of seal populations in the Baltic. *Conservation Biology,* 11, 917–927.

Kuylenstierna, J.C.I. & Chadwick, M.J. (1991). Increases in soil acidity in north-west Wales between 1957 and 1990. Ambio, 20, 118–119.

Lande, R. (1995). Mutation and conservation. *Conservation Biology,* 9, 782–791.

Leslie, P.H. (1945). On the use of matrices in certain population mathematics. *Biometrika,* 35, 213–245.

MacArthur, R.H. & Wilson, E.O. (1967). *The Theory of Island Biogeography.* Princeton University Press, Princeton.

Mackey, E.C., Shewry, M.C. & Tudor, G.J. (1998). *Land Cover Change: Scotland from the 1940s to the 1980s.* The Stationery Office, Edinburgh.

McIntyre, S. & Lavorel, S. (1994). Predicting richness of native, rare, and exotic plants in response to habitat and disturbance variables across a variegated landscape. *Conservation Biology,* 8, 521–531.

McVean, D.N. & Ratcliffe, D.A. (1962). *Plant Communities of the Scottish Highlands.* HMSO, London.

Noble, I.R. & Slatyer, R.O. (1980). The use of vital attributes to predict successional changes in plant communities subject to recurrent disturbance. *Vegetatio,* 43, 131–140.

Odum, E.P. (1975). Diversity as a function of energy flow. In *Unifying Concepts in Ecology* (eds. W.H. van Dobben & R.H. Lowe-McConnell). W. Junk, The Hague. pp. 11–14.

Pettifor, R.A., Percival, S.M. & Rowcliffe, J.M. (1999a). Greenland population of the barnacle goose (*Branta leucopsis*) - the collation and statistical analysis of data and population viability analyses. *Scottish Natural Heritage Research, Survey & Monitoring Report* No. 137.

Pettifor, R.A., Fox, A.D. & Rowcliffe, J.M. (1999b). Greenland white-fronted goose (*Anser albifrons flavirostris*) - the collation and statistical analysis of data and population viability analyses. *Scottish Natural Heritage Research, Survey & Monitoring Report* No. 140.

Pianka, E.R. (1970). On *r*- and *K*-selection. *American Naturalist,* 104, 592–597.

Policansky, D. (1993). Uncertainty, knowledge, and resource management. *Ecological Applications,* 3, 583–584.

Preston, C.D. (1986). An additional criterion for assessing native status. *Watsonia,* 16, 83.

Ratcliffe, D.A. (Ed.) (1977). *A Nature Conservation Review.* Cambridge University Press, Cambridge.

Rodwell, J.S. (1992a). *British Plant Communities. Vol 1. Woodlands and Scrub.* Cambridge University Press, Cambridge.

Rodwell, J.S. (1992b). *British Plant Communities. Vol 2. Mires and Heaths.* Cambridge University Press, Cambridge.

Rodwell, J.S. (1993a). *British Plant Communities. Vol 3. Grasslands and Montane Vegetation.* Cambridge University Press, Cambridge.

Rodwell, J.S. (1993b). *British Plant Communities. Vol 4. Aquatic Communities, Swamps and Tall-Herb Fens.* Cambridge University Press, Cambridge.

Rodwell, J.S. (2000). *British Plant Communities. Vol 5. Maritime Communities and Vegetation of Open Habitats.* Cambridge University Press, Cambridge.

Scandrett, E. & Gimingham, C.H. (1989). A model of *Calluna* population dynamics; the effects of varying seed and vegetative regeneration. *Vegetatio*, **84**, 143–152.

Shaffer, M.L. (1990). Population viability analysis. *Conservation Biology*, **4**, 39–40.

Smidt, J.T. de (1995). The imminent destruction of north west European heaths due to atmospheric nitrogen deposition. In *Heaths and Moorland: Cultural Landscapes*, ed. by D.B.A. Thompson, A.J. Hester & M.B. Usher. HMSO, Edinburgh. pp. 206–217.

Soulé, M.E. (ed.) (1987). *Viable Populations for Conservation*. Cambridge University Press, Cambridge.

Southwood, T.R.E. (1976). Bionomic strategies and population parameters. In *Theoretical Ecology, Principles and Applications* (ed. R.M. May). Blackwell, Oxford. pp. 26–48.

Southwood, T.R.E. (1977). Habitat, the templet for ecological strategies. *Journal of Animal Ecology*, **46**, 337–365.

Southwood, T.R.E., May, R.M., Hassell, M.P. & Conway, G.R. (1974). Ecological strategies and population parameters. *American Naturalist*, **108**, 791–804.

Spellerberg, I.F. (1991). Biogeographical basis of conservation. In *The Scientific Management of Temperate Communities for Conservation* (eds. I.F. Spellerberg, F.B. Goldsmith & M.G. Morris). Blackwell, Oxford. pp. 293–322.

Starfield, A.M. & Bleloch, A.L. (1986). *Building Models for Conservation and Wildlife Management*. Collier Macmillan, London.

Tansley, A.G. (1939). *The British Isles and their Vegetation*. Cambridge University Press, Cambridge.

Tew, T.E., Crawford, T.J., Spencer, J.W., Stevens, D.P., Usher, M.B. & Warren, J. (eds.) (1997). *The Role of Genetics in Conserving Small Populations*. Joint Nature Conservation Committee, Peterborough.

Tjallingii, S.P. & Veer, A.A. de (eds.) (1982). *Perspectives in Landscape Ecology*. Centre for Agricultural Publishing and Documentation, Wageningen.

Underwood, A.J. (1995). Ecological research and (and research into) environmental management. *Ecological Applications*, **5**, 232–247.

Usher, M.B. (1972). Developments in the Leslie matrix model. In *Mathematical Models in Ecology*, ed. by J.N.R. Jeffers. Blackwell, Oxford. pp. 29–60.

Usher, M.B. (1985). Population and community dynamics in the soil ecosystem. In *Ecological Interactions in Soil* (eds. A.H. Fitter, D. Atkinson, D.J. Read & M.B. Usher). Blackwell, Oxford. pp. 243–266.

Usher, M.B. (1988). Biological invasions of nature reserves: a search for generalisations. *Biological Conservation*, **44**, 119–135.

Usher, M.B. (1998). Minimum viable population size, maximum tolerable population size, or the dilemma of conservation success. In *Ecology Today: an Anthology of Contemporary Ecological Research* (eds. B. Gopal, P.S. Pathak & K.G. Saxena). International Scientific Publications, New Delhi. pp. 135–144.

Usher, M.B. (2000). The nativeness and non-nativeness of species. *Watsonia*, **23**, 323–326.

Usher, M.B. & Balharry, D. (1996). *Biogeographical Zonation of Scotland*. Scottish Natural Heritage, Perth.

Usher, M.B. & Keiller, S.W.J. (1998). The macrolepidoptera of farm woodlands: determinants of diversity and community structure. *Biodiversity and Conservation*, 7, 725–748.

Watt, A.S. (1947). Pattern and process in the plant community. *Journal of Ecology*, **35**, 1–22.

Webb, D.A. (1985). What are the criteria for presuming native status? *Watsonia*, **15**, 231–236.

Whitby, M.C. (ed.) (1992). *Land Use Change: the Causes and Consequences*. HMSO, London.

Williamson, M. (1996). *Biological Invasions*. Chapman & Hall, London.

With, K.A. & Crist, T.O. (1995). Critical thresholds in species' responses to landscape structure. *Ecology*, **76**, 2446–2459.

9

Public Perceptions –
Have We Helped Them Over 50 Years?

Ian Mercer

IT IS DIFFICULT to generalise about public perception – despite polls and their statistical interpretation it is not clear to me whether any sampling produces a view that would hold good for the whole of the population. For one thing the content do not talk voluntarily about their contentment: the disgruntled on the other hand take the platform whenever they can, stir up quiescent disgruntlement among others, and claim that in support of their own particular stance. Despite the fact that urban man asked by a pollster will say of course he is in favour of national parks and nature reserves, more often than not when anything to do with either makes headlines, even small ones low down the page, then the news is about the anti-individual or anti-social effect of actions by conservators. We must analyse the disgruntled, I suppose, to come to any reasonable conclusion.

The 'we' of my title is, of course, all our colleagues in the industries involved and the academics who study these things without having to carry any can about them. But that 'we' is also a population extending over the fifty years and before that, and part of my contention is that whatever our conclusion about our own help for public perceptions over fifty years or whether we help them now, depends in part upon how all this began – how in fact the 1949 Act came to be constructed.

On the face of it, that splendid compendium of tools which we still use that is the National Parks and Access to the Countryside Act showed remarkable foresight. Its flaws were imperceptible then and are not readily perceived, even by some practitioners, now. One of the strangest things about the Act is that while it invented National Nature Reserves and separately Local Nature Reserves, Areas of Special Scientific Interest, access areas which could be made by agreement or order, National Parks, Definitive Maps of Public Rights of Way, long distance routes, and Areas of Outstanding Natural Beauty, no positive connection within the Act is made between any one of those things listed. There are some negative connections: that an Area of Outstanding Natural Beauty is one *not being* a National Park, an area of Special Scientific Interest is one *not being* a nature reserve. But, because there are no positive connections there is no system, and connected systems are more easily understood than disparate collections. The man who lives in a listed building with a long distance route running past his doorstep, inside a National Nature Reserve, which is itself inside a Site of Special Scientific Interest, all in a National Park, and belonging to the National Trust has a perception problem which all too many practitioners will readily complicate (and in case you don't believe the scenario, I was once that man). I contend therefore, among other things, that poor perception is encouraged and exacerbated by the lack of a system readily understandable by laymen.

Sadly, in the legislation that has followed during the fifty years we are considering, particularly in 1967, '68, '72, '73, '81, '85, '90, '91 and '95, still no real attempt has been made to create order out of the jumble. Those milestones have sometimes produced improvement among the parts but never grasped the real need to provide connections. Some of the effects have actually increased the wrong kind of perception. As a lot of us here know, bureaucrats learn early the defence of their own activity area. Proposed improvement is usually analysed by them first for its effect upon their own work and perhaps their own beliefs about that work. One of the significant side effects of that phenomenon is that it breeds a lack of trust in anyone else's ability to do what one does oneself, and this is manifested regularly across the countryside even now. This creates at least one public perception that there are too many cooks and that they *are* spoiling the broth.

It is also significant, having got to the 'cooks', that we recognise that the recruitment of the whole population of practitioners is bound to include some whose intense dedication is founded on, or generates a self-belief in, the rightness of what they do against any odds. Even their less intense colleagues will feel beleaguered in a philistine world and behave accordingly. In both cases an attitude is developed which is perceptible to the interested observer, and of course by those whose own aspirations cut across the necessary process of the conservator. The perception of the attitude becomes the perception of the organisation, and its policy and programme.

I will return to the occupational hazards of those practising the art and the science of conservation of quality in all its forms, but it is necessary first just to analyse the events that led up to the construction of the 1949 Act and the nature of that construction. For, as I noted above, I contend that a large part of the problem we have faced in arousing the right public perception is because of the way things were, and are still, set down for us, and in that sense there is still a very stingy nettle to grasp if we wish to improve things.

This is not the place to go into the detail of the thinking of the '40s. But we should remember that while our founding fathers were still debating how they should advise Parliament, Parliament itself created agriculture's defences that were to last for nearly fifty years and at the same time nationalised land use and called it town and country planning. The Agriculture Act of 1947 gave farmers the privilege that became the great threat to habitat and landscape in the middle of the fifty years we are considering, and the Town and Country Planning Act of the same year provided the main machine which conservators were expected to use from 1949 on.

Whatever had gone before, *our* real problem began when the Hobhouse Committee decided it could not cope with nature conservation, so it spawned the Huxley Committee and the effect was that two separate White Papers were produced, Cmd 7121 and 7122. Despite the divorce between landscape and nature conservation, there was some recognition of connections between them. There is that nice reference to the space which wildlife needs that can never be provided by nature reserves, and equally that wildlife and habitat are major components of natural beauty, if that is what you are expected to conserve. Nevertheless when the products of the two committees came together in the 1949 Act, the basis for misconception and for competition which has persisted for fifty years is revealed. The nature conservation lobby managed to get a Nature Conservancy created before the Act itself, although all its tools were to be in that Act. The National Parks Commission on the other hand was simply part of the Act. Despite that apparent scientific foresight, the argument was not deployed strongly enough for either parliamentary draughtsmen or Parliament to conceive of nature conservation as more than merely something that naturalists needed. Just reflect for a moment on the title 'National Parks and Access to the Countryside Act': no reference to nature conservation. When you come to look inside the Act you realise that parliamentarians were persuaded that nature was important to conserve because it was the interest of a large number of people: 'of Special Scientific *interest*' is still the phrase in use. 'Opportunities afforded for Nature Study' was still the parliamentary language in the Environment Act of 1990, coming straight from the 1949 Act (and there's another inhibition affecting the creation of real order still: the timidity of parliamentary draughtsman, leading to the innocence which repeats phrases already tested whether or not they really express the new intention). Naturalists, including professional ecologists, were indulging in a form of recreation as far as 1949 parliamentarians were concerned.

The deeper implication is that nature reserves were to be a form of land use which it was necessary to provide within the whole spectrum from mountain top to barley field in order that a particular sector of society should have its interests indulged and a space for its learning protected. In parallel, the apparent primacy of conserving the landscape under the titles 'Natural Beauty' and 'National Parks' had of course been achieved on the back of a demand for access to that natural beauty. I need not rehearse the tales of the mass trespass and the involvement of senior Labour Party members in those activities. But they did dominate the government of 1949, and parallel with 'opportunities afforded for nature study' so National Parks would be selected in part on the basis of the 'opportunities afforded for open-air recreation'. John Dower had actually rationalised the relationship in 1945 when he wrote that the whole of the conservation exercise was hardly to be afforded by society unless it (society) perceived an immediate benefit to itself, i.e. access to that which was to be conserved.

So, the apparently far-sighted legislators of 1949 have to be forgiven by us now for not perceiving that what they saw as a set of activities related to different social needs for land use change, would be understood in fifty years time as critical processes in the protection of the human species, through the protection of its whole environment: not just of systems of all the other species arranged in their habitats, but as a life support system for the planet and all its inhabitants. *We* cannot go on expecting similar forgiveness as the next century gets going.

Hindsight is of course a wonderful thing, but we did start off on the wrong foot, or the wrong feet. Our nervous and tentative modifications over fifty years have not produced a system, and they have certainly not produced something adequate for the present purpose. Some specialists among us will argue that they have a system of their own, but we must recognise that the systems' number and their separation, demonstrate a huge inadequacy. They are individually so inadequate that they are still the subject of protest by the disgruntled to whom I referred earlier, by those frustrated in their own development aspirations through not getting the planning permission they want, for those whose contentment cannot be protected by the planning system we have, by those who object fiercely to other people's aspirations and their potential acceptance. The media, in all its forms, sides as often as not with the disgruntled; bad news, drama and crisis sell newspapers, news bulletins and in the end advertising. As I noted earlier, the man-in-the-street stopped by the pollster will certainly say he is in favour of national parks and nature reserves, the man-in-the-field having direct experience of these things on the other hand may well not be. He may only wish to carry on the management his father indulged, he may even have attempted to conform to new advice only to find that he has stopped the management that sustained the 'interest' in the first place. It is to him also that the media will turn.

That this is the case when the fifty years in question have seen so much ecological research, greatly widening education horizons and an amazing throughput of students on environmental and related courses from the age of eleven, suggests to me, as must by now be obvious, that the problem of poor perception must lie with the process itself and its lack of order. Why with the startling development in communication technology over the same fifty years and the remarkable attraction of wildlife programmes on television, for instance, have we not got a voting majority in the democracy understanding the good that we do? Does the fact that we use the tools that were invented for the study of nature, the attempt to protect landscape and for encouraging ramblers, explain why we are regarded still as an elite operating force, or as a special interest group, or closer to animal rights campaigners and hunting saboteurs, than we would all find comfortable?

I must not neglect the contemporary excuses either. What society appears to be trying to do, or has appeared to be trying to do over fifty years is to impose management and protective systems upon a landscape cover that developed over 5000 years by steady human effort, attractive by accident, and upon a set of habitats with a population of species that has evolved over 10,000 years or more within that landscape cover and is still evolving. Development plans and development control on the one hand, creating nature reserves on the other, wildlife enhancement schemes, stewardship, and Biodiversity Action Plans are all instant, even knee-jerk, reactions compared with the length of time involved in the evolution of those things they are now meant to sustain.

We had better also recognise that, while society appears to have charged us with pursuing these protective aspirations, the public perception of the erosion of freedom involved is necessarily one of our occupational hazards. More specifically, the development planner should not really be expected suddenly to simulate settlements which individual whim, harsh discipline, and the economies of medieval space created. Equally, the nature conservator is inevitably struggling with the enormous fragmentation of quasi-natural habitat in a land-use pattern developed subject to similar factors.

Please remember that I am searching for the explanation of the poor public perception of our work that appears to persist. Indeed in the face of that perception, what has been achieved in fifty years is quite remarkable in many ways. And in that sense I am simply arguing that we might have achieved much more if public perception had been different. If you look at the significant modifications that have been made over the fifty years they have not all been for the best of reasons. It took nearly twenty years from the '49 Act for action to be taken to widen the potential for public enjoyment in the countryside in an attempt to reduce pressures in particular places. The Nature Conservancy was taken over by the Natural Environment Research Council and almost as quickly came out of it with its own Act of Parliament to become the Nature Conservancy Council.

The 1981 Act was a great mixture. The excuse that allowed it to happen was the need to bring species protection in line with European regulation. There flowed from it that massive exercise in re-notification of SSSIs, leading to charts on office walls measuring the pace and volume of re-notification, misinterpreted by third parties as a kind of stamp collecting exercise. 'Areas of search' for SSSIs for junior officers exacerbated the impression. (We all know that we probably haven't found all the justified ones yet, but the perception that we may have more than the purpose needs because of the methodology and human competition, is widespread, and sometimes reaches our pay-masters, as I know to CCW's historic cost.) The same Act did of course give us a better grip on agricultural change and extended the principle of management by agreement to a very wide field. But the demand for maps of moor and heath in National Parks that it was 'most important to conserve' was cobbled together on a bench outside the House of Commons itself, and within four years there had to be an amendment Act to put it right.

Then in 1988 and '89 things occurred which the process, the tools, the methodology, did not allow us to contain, like Terry Wogan's Sitka spruce in the Flow Country, and the peat on Islay competed for by geese, malt whisky men and David Bellamy, all of which led to the Rifkind/Thatcher break-up of the Nature Conservancy Council. In Scotland and in Wales we have claimed that advantage overcame disadvantage, and in any case had it not happened then, by 1999 it would almost certainly have been on the cards. But that late-in-the day afterthought, the Joint Nature Conservation Committee, took a long time to settle, and there are those here who know better than me how well it works now. Ironically, Mrs Thatcher, having dislocated the nature conservation operation in this small island, had already articulated the concern that the survival of our species on the planet was beginning to be at risk.

From that moment on, though you may have your own particular thresholds to identify, there was a remarkably swift development of public perception of that risk, clouded of course by academic debate about cause and effect in respect to climate change and whether or not we were still seeing only a wobble that had happened before. I remember teaching students in the sixties that we were not as far away from the last glaciation as halfway through the last interglacial, so I can understand the perception that the jury is still out on the matter. Nevertheless, the concern which produced the Rio meeting, and the European reactions to it, have helped to create a greater public interest in what ought to be our business. And we all know that the Biodiversity Convention has pushed our business higher up the political agenda than ever before.

But even given all that apparent assistance, it is not clear to me that a majority of the voting population yet connect what we are doing in their local space – getting in their way, restricting their development, stopping activities their predecessors indulged happily – with that global question. Even 'street corner to stratosphere' in that huge analysis, *Our Common Inheritance*, passed over the majority of heads. How sad that just then teachers started to be distracted from environmental things by the same government's attack on their so-called basics, otherwise we might have seen a sea-change in real environmental education.

It is now fairly obvious that wobbling weather patterns, floods and overnight coastal erosion have brought home to some sectors of society that natural change is afoot and that should create new respect for nature and our work for it. It may well be that in the next decade the effect of global markets on north-west European agriculture will bring home more readily the significance of land-use change to everyone. As the countryside deteriorates in some eyes, will our preoccupations and activities be recognised more readily for what their value really is? But are we ready for it when it comes? Will we then be able to 'go with the flow', capitalise on the new public realisation, and create better perceptions than, say, that wise concept 'managed retreat' in coastal areas did or has done so far.

The problem is encapsulated behind Porlock Bay shingle ridge in Somerset (SSSI in LFA and ESA , threaded by coastal National Trail, all in a National Park); no agency was ready for, or immediately capable of coping with, the effect of apparently permanent breach, and thus daily saline inundation, on conservation status, path diversion, compensation, citation change (scientific and agricultural), or even exploitation of new salt marsh, amazingly rapidly and extensively developed. We of all people know the natural dynamics, but are we dynamic enough in our own forward thinking?

We are still complicating the scene as far as potential perception is concerned. An Environment Agency emerges and 'environment' therefore becomes a word that is to do with health and pollution but not really to do with surroundings, the true and useful meaning of the word. Biodiversity may be good at Heads of Government convention level, but it is a pretty awful word for interpreting ecological values to laymen: it may even distract them from *ecological* understanding. Remember the 'stamp collecting' charge – 'biodiversity' risks it again.

I have already said that the Scots and the Welsh will claim advantage from their separation from England, whatever the illogic of three parties pursuing the protection of the wildlife of one island. But the fact that in those two countries, landscape and nature conservation were brought together has to be the basis for potential improvement in the operations that existed for forty years before they were joined. Perversely the junction was not carried forward in England because it was claimed the scale was wrong, and within a very few years the demonstration of the best reasons for a convergence was mounted. The Countryside Commission began to produce country character maps, at about the same time as English Nature began to produce natural area maps. They have brought these two things together, although they still appear to be used separately.

I quote the case because it underlines the fact that there are fundamental problems about public perception of the public service in our area which we continue to fail to address. It has something to do with 'too many cooks', as I mentioned earlier. In England, English Nature reigns alone, or intact, and is the national ecological authority. The Countryside Commission has become the Countryside Agency and is understandably preoccupied with socio-economic affairs in the countryside. The DETR and MAFF are discussing a potential Rural White Paper and its construction at the same time as something called the Performance and Innovation Unit in the Cabinet Office is discussing rural economies. The Welsh Assembly and the Scottish Executive are doubtless looking to reposition their agents. Bureaucratic defences are up all around me. The European Union, having created for itself a marvellous opportunity to do something more radical about the way land use is managed and to introduce the concept of environmental goods to the whole of the rural economy and maybe to all the urban observers too, fudged it in March 1999. The public (without any question) must be forgiven for their perception problems – and the conclusion must be that we never have helped, and still did not. I think we may well need most of the separate national 'authorities'. It is on the ground that there are perceivably too many cooks.

Let us drop our defences and be objective. We need to simplify the system and cause the convergence of all its parts. It would be perfectly easy to continue to use all the conservation units (or parts) that have been invented, but to construct from them a comprehensive Russian doll system. No bureaucrat need lose his or her status – the total labour force involved now is still not adequate but it could be deployed better. The national authorities for ecology, landscape, agriculture, architecture, archaeology, (even 'environment', O help us) would all still be needed both to designate and to develop, monitor, and thus keep a hand in, the protective management of that which is designated. Contracts between them and their local agents upheld by both sides could ensure an improvement in the present standard of conservation and the promotion of enjoyment without damage. In the biggest space, which we currently call a National Park, one agent would carry out the day to day total conservation process. Statutory responsibility *at local level* throughout the countryside for the delivery of the conservation of quality in natural landscape terms on behalf of a national agent could alter perceptions overnight throughout the rural voting population. Just as nature conservators have quite cleverly adapted the nature reserve and Area of Special Scientific Interest into a system, so in landscape terms Areas of Outstanding Natural Beauty or National Scenic Areas (as we are where we are), and National Parks could also become hierarchical – indeed SNH has proposed nearly the same thing. So AONB – NP – SSSI – NNR could become a set of concentric spheres of designation at once, each also capable of free-standing as necessary. Hobhouse and Huxley would concur, and we would have a proper, single, comprehensive and understandable conservation system.

And while we are at it, we could improve in one or two places the jargon we have invented or inherited so that the public perception is eased. The 1949 Act used the word 'area' not the word 'site' (except in the margin), when talking of special scientific interest, a 'site' to the layman couldn't possibly be 22,000 hectares, as the Northern Irish at least accept. Equally 'interest' could well be replaced by the word 'importance' with good statutory precedence. If we were really brave we might just look at the European terminology and adapt it to our purposes. Natura 2000 will consist of Special Areas for Conservation eventually – why were they not properly called 'Special Areas for Nature Conservation' and then we could carefully consider using them in this country as a critical unit of the hierarchy?

Public perception of our activity is not good enough for a democracy. That such poor perception extends upwards to ministers and their closer advisors is the fault of persistent narrow thinking, and faulty jargon, allied with a failure to connect principle to practice. It needs to be improved and I think that that behoves us all to look really critically at the ways in which we operate, recognise what they have bred in us, and how they inhibit what we need to do to be more effective at out job, which is the strongest possible fully informed popular support.

10

The Legalities and Perceptions of Marine Conservation

Lynda M. Warren

INTRODUCTION

AN ANALYSIS OF the law and policy of marine conservation provides a useful case study to illustrate changes in society's understanding of, and approach to, nature conservation over the last fifty years. The purpose of this paper is to describe legal developments for marine conservation and compare these with provisions for terrestrial conservation. The paper takes an historical perspective. It starts with some thoughts on why the marine environment was not considered in the National Parks and Access to the Countryside Act 1949. The following sections consider the shifts in perception since then and examine the changes in policies and legislation that have followed. The paper finishes with an assessment of the success of the legal provisions for marine conservation and attempts to explain why marine conservation remains the 'Cinderella' of the conservation world – a description used in the Nature Conservancy Council's *Great Britain Nature Conservation Strategy, 1984.*

MARINE CONSERVATION IN 1949

The National Parks etc. Act 1949 is silent on marine conservation. This oversight is easily explained if we look at the initiatives that led to the enactment of this legislation. The 1949 Act was part of a suite of new statutes (the others comprised the Town and Country Planning Act 1947 and the Agriculture Act 1947) designed to reform the law relating to land use. It gave effect to the recommendations of the committees set up to consider the case for national parks and was the direct result of many years of lobbying on the part of bodies eager to see the British landscape protected for the benefit of the public and made accessible for them to enjoy. Three things follow from this background: the Act was concerned with the rural environment; it was set in the context of land use planning; and it was primarily about landscape and amenity rather than nature conservation. It is not surprising, therefore, that marine conservation did not get a look in.

It is not necessarily the case that nature conservation was considered less important than landscape protection. The committees set up to explore the case for national parks recognised the need for consideration of measures for nature conservation and soon established specialist committees to undertake this work. These were the Wild Life Conservation (England and Wales) Special Committee under the chairmanship of Julian Huxley (see Cmd 7122, 1947) and its equivalent in Scotland under the chairmanship of James Ritchie. Although both nature conservation and landscape protection are about the maintenance of 'natural beauty', thinking at the time focused on the differences between the two concepts rather than their similarities. Nature conservation was regarded as a scientific activity with a scientific purpose. It was, therefore, left to the scientists to deal with. The administrative framework set up by the 1949 Act for the management of National Parks centred on the local authority model supported by a central National Parks Commission. The Nature Conservancy was established in 1949 by Royal Charter in response to the Huxley Committee's report. There was no need, therefore, to provide an administrative structure for conservation in the 1949 Act.

There was, however, some provision in the Act for the creation of protected areas for nature conservation purposes. Part III of the Act provides for the declaration of nature reserves by the Nature Conservancy and includes powers for the making of byelaws for their management. The Act also introduced the concept of Sites of Special Scientific Interest (SSSIs), designed to give effect to the recommendations of the Huxley Committee that small areas of conservation interest should be identified so that their scientific interest could be taken into account when changes in land use were proposed. The 1949 SSSI is thus a label, with the sole purpose of drawing attention to the planning authorities. The close relationship between nature conservation and planning established by the Act is a clear reflection of the perception of nature conservation at that time. Sir Dudley Stamp who, as Vice-Chairman of the influential Scott Committee on Land Utilisation in Rural Areas (Cmd 6378), was instrumental in drawing attention to the need for conservation, described conservation as 'an aspect of planned land use' (Stamp, 1969).

There is nothing in the Act to prevent nature reserves or SSSIs from being designated at sea but this is, in practice, rendered impossible by the way in which the Act is implemented. Section 23 required the Nature Conservancy to notify the local planning authority of the existence of an SSSI. It is accepted that the jurisdiction of local authorities generally extends to low water mark only. In England and Wales, this is taken to be mean low water mark of ordinary tides; in Scotland it is low water of ordinary spring tides. It follows, then, that there would be no authority to notify in respect of a marine SSSI and, therefore, no possibility of making the designation. Because of the policy of designating nature reserves as SSSIs, there was no real prospect of using the legislation to create nature reserves at sea either.

Does this mean that the post war society was indifferent to the needs of marine conservation? Probably not. In hindsight, it is difficult to understand why the legislators failed to appreciate the potential impact of modern agricultural practice on British wildlife. It was taken for granted that farmers created the countryside and there was no controversy over the SSSI measures. If terrestrial conservation was regarded as adequately provided for without stronger legal measures, it is not surprising that marine conservation was not seen to be an issue at all. It is important to judge the approach to conservation in the context of the time. Nature conservation was the remit of the scientist and science was about discovery and research rather than protection. Difficulties of marine exploration meant that we knew very little about marine wildlife beyond the intertidal zone.

1949–1981: INCREASING AWARENESS

The *Torrey Canyon* oil tanker spill in 1967 did much to bring marine wildlife to the attention of the public. It was the first of the big oil spills, when a tanker carrying 117,000 tonnes of Kuwait crude was wrecked off Land's End, leaving some 40,000 tonnes on the beaches of Cornwall and Brittany. This incident also motivated the scientific community to give consideration to the subject of marine conservation. In 1969, the Nature Conservancy put forward a paper on conservation policy in shallow seas, for consideration by the Natural Environment Research Council. Unfortunately, the NERC decided not to pursue the possibility of extending conservation measures below low water mark because it was felt that there was insufficient evidence of any real need. By July of 1969, interest in marine conservation was being voiced in Parliament. In response to a question by Lord Wakefield on marine nature reserves, Lord Chalfont confirmed that no action was being taken ([303] HL Debs, c 555, 2 July 1969). He referred to the complexities of sublittoral conservation, including scientific, legal and practical considerations. In view of the increased interest in the subject, however, the NERC set up a working party under the chairmanship of Professor Bob Clark. Their report, (NERC, 1973) drew attention to the lack of scientific data that would be needed for making an accurate assessment of the need for marine conservation but also concluded that 'there was insufficient evidence of habitats becoming endangered to justify the creation of sublittoral NNRs'.

Ten years later, in 1979, the Nature Conservancy Council and NERC published a joint report on marine conservation which was produced in direct response to the recommendations of Clark's committee. The report covered both scientific and legal aspects of marine conservation and commented on the differences between the terrestrial and the marine environments. Unlike its predecessor, the joint working group responsible for the report was convinced that there was sufficient justification for marine site protection. It fell short of making any firm recommendations for specific legislation for marine conservation, however, largely because of the perceived legal difficulties. Instead, it recommended 'that the NCC should seek clarification of the legal situation and consider obtaining legislation to permit the establishment and management of conservation areas below the present low water limit of its powers' (NCC/NERC, 1979).

Within a year, non-governmental organisations such as the Marine Conservation Society and the World Wildlife Fund were spearheading an intensive lobbying campaign to get marine nature reserves included in the Wildlife & Countryside Act 1981. The Government was reluctant to do this, allegedly because insufficient thought had been given to the type of legislation needed. In his winding up speech to conclude the second reading debate on the Bill, Lord Avon said 'that following the publication [in 1979] of the Nature Conservancy Council's and the Natural Environment Research Council's joint report . . . discussions have taken place on their suggestion of establishing statutorily-protected marine nature reserves. The issues are, however, much more complex than they appeared at first sight, and the Government are hoping to issue a consultation paper in the very near future' ([415] HL Debs, c 1094, 16 December 1980). Ministers were prepared to consult on the matter but, unfortunately, the deadline for responses to their consultation paper was after the end of the parliamentary session and, therefore, too late for the exercise to have an impact on the content of the Act. Promises to legislate at a future date did not placate the Opposition, which is not surprising, given the previous pattern of one piece of environmental legislation every ten years or thereabout. Instead, the NGOs intensified their efforts to such an extent that the Government eventually had to concede and measures for the creation of marine nature reserves were included in the Act (Warren, 1989). At the time, this was regarded as a victory for the conservation movement and a step forward for marine conservation, but subsequent experience with the implementation of this legislation has highlighted the inadequacies of the measures.

Prior to the issuing of the public consultation paper on marine conservation, a governmental Interdepartmental Working Group had met to discuss the possibility of legislation for marine nature reserves. The failure of this group to reach agreement probably had much to do with the absence of a marine nature reserve clause in the original Wildlife and Countryside Bill when it came before Parliament in 1980. Conservationists interpreted these events as just one more example of the Conservative Government's antipathy towards conservation and failed to consider whether there were particular difficulties with the marine situation that made the typical protected area mechanism inappropriate. While it is no doubt true that the difficulties with the implementation of the marine nature reserve provisions in the 1981 Act are due largely to the less than enthusiastic attitude of successive governments, I think this reason masks a more fundamental difficulty with the concept of marine nature reserves - one which had been recognised by the Interdepartmental Working Group on marine nature reserves. This difficulty relates to the legal and administrative arrangements for marine affairs and not the science of marine conservation. Whatever differences there may be between the sea (and seabed) and the dry land as a provider of habitats for wildlife, the conservation objectives are broadly similar. Lack of scientific knowledge confuses the issue by making it more difficult to define the management needs for marine wildlife or to assess the effectiveness of legal protection, but this is only a difference in degree. The crucial difference between the two environments lies in the legal regime that has been formulated to regulate the way in which we use land and sea.

On land, individual property rights are of paramount importance. The SSSI notification, as modified by the 1981 Act, is essentially designed to make minor adjustments to the way owners and occupiers of land can use their property. The National Nature Reserve is possible only where the statutory nature conservation body can exercise effective control over the rights of the owner of the land. Other developments in environmental law, notably the use of tortious claims in trespass, nuisance or negligence, have been limited by the underlying principle that the purpose of the action is to redress wrongful interference with property or personal rights. Even in the area of judicial review, which provides for public actions to be challenged, the need to show personal interest has restricted the development of the law as a measure for championing environmental protection.

At sea, private property rights are largely irrelevant. The seabed is part of the Crown Estate and the water column is owned by no one. The legal regime for the sea is based on the public rights of fishing and navigation coupled with an assumed right of access by the public at large.

THE WILDLIFE AND COUNTRYSIDE ACT 1981

Legislation for marine nature reserves (MNRs) is contained in sections 36 and 37 and schedule 12 of the Wildlife and Countryside Act 1981. For the first time in Great Britain it became possible to designate a protected area at sea. The legislation was based on the provisions for nature reserves in sections 19 and 20 of the 1949 Act, but with some crucial differences designed to reflect the more complex pattern of interests in the marine environment. Experience within the Interdepartmental Working Group, which comprised representatives of most, if not all, government departments, gave an indication of the difficulties involved in trying to get agreement across a wide range of different interests. For terrestrial reserves, designation could be declared by the Nature Conservancy Council provided that management could be secured in the long term by acquiring ownership or entering into a management agreement with a suitable owner. Because ownership of the seabed attracts far fewer rights and responsibilities, similar arrangements could not be used to deliver conservation objectives. Instead, it was necessary to control the activities of a whole range of different actors, all working independently of each other. As some of these actors were government departments or public bodies, it was not considered appropriate for the nature conservation body to make the designation. Section 36(1), therefore, provides for the Secretary of State to declare an MNR following a submission by the nature conservation body.

It is logical to expect that a dedicated nature conservation body might be more readily prepared to make a designation than a government minister with a range of other, competing, and possibly conflicting, issues to take into account. The reluctance to act has, in practice, reached unacceptable extremes largely because of an earlier ministerial commitment not to make an MNR designation unless there is consensus support amongst all interested parties. Although the Act provides for the possibility of a public inquiry to air the differences of opinion over a designation, this route has never been taken. Instead, the Government has relied on the nature conservation bodies to negotiate with those who oppose designation.

The practical implementation of the MNR provisions provides a classic example of the dangers inherent in trying to impose voluntary commitment from above. Time after time, local interest groups have been united in their opposition to interference from outside bodies telling them how to run their lives.

Even when an MNR is finally declared, designation carries with it little in the way of legal protection. Byelaw-making powers comparable to those applicable to NNRs are contained in section 37 but these are limited in their effect by the inclusion of a number of actual and *de facto* exceptions. In the latest case, the proposed MNR for the Menai Strait, the Countryside Council for Wales has decided that a proposed byelaw regulating interference with wildlife in the reserve would achieve nothing except ill will and have withdrawn it.

Leaving aside these practical difficulties, it is worth summarising what could, in theory, be achieved under this legislation, before going on to consider subsequent measures.

THE MARINE NATURE RESERVE

Under the Wildlife and Countryside Act 1981, MNRs can be established out to three miles from the territorial sea baseline and inland to the extent of tidal waters. The Territorial Sea Act 1987 makes it possible for the outer limit to be extended to twelve nautical miles by Order in Council: the territorial sea baseline is defined as generally the low water mark except where straight baselines have been drawn. There is no upper or lower limitation on horizontal extent. It would be possible, therefore, to use the MNR regime to establish large Marine Parks with smaller, highly protected reserve areas within them, thereby creating a buffer zone around the most sensitive areas.

The statutory purpose of the MNR (section 36 (1)) is to conserve wildlife or physical features of special interest or to provide opportunities for research and education. In order to achieve this purpose, it is possible to restrict access into the reserve by all users except for boats other than pleasure boats. Features of interest in the reserve can be protected by byelaws making it an offence to kill, take, destroy, molest or disturb animals or plants or to do anything to interfere with the sea bed or damage any object in the reserve. The legislation applies to all wildlife while it is in the reserve including, for example, birds, feeding on the water. There is only limited power to make byelaws in relation to fish, however. In England, for example, fishing is regulated by sea fisheries committees. Because section 36(6) prevents the MNR legislation from interfering with the functions of any relevant authorities, amongst which the sea fisheries committees are included, MNR byelaws cannot be used to regulate fishing, even for nature conservation purposes. There is only limited power to control pollution and activities undertaken outside the reserve boundaries that might have an adverse impact inside the reserve cannot be controlled.

Interest in marine conservation in the 1980s focused on the lack of progress with the MNR designations (Gibson and Warren, 1995). Despite plans to declare seven sites in the first round of designations, there are still only two MNRs in Great Britain nearly thirty years after the Wildlife and Countryside Act came into force. Further progress with the MNR designation seems unlikely, not least because it has got left behind in the Government's efforts to implement the EC Habitats Directive.

MARINE CONSERVATION SINCE 1992

The United Nations Conference on Environment and Development (UNCED), held in Rio in the summer of 1992, heralded a new era in environmental policy making and legislation. One of the most significant outcomes of the conference was the signing of the Convention on Biological

Diversity. For the first time ever, conservation appeared on the global political agenda alongside other pressing environmental issues such as climate change. The key to this greater prominence was the realisation that action had to be taken to halt the worldwide loss of plant and animal species. It was an approach that had been championed in the *World Conservation Strategy* published in 1980 by a consortium of IUCN, UNEP and WWF. The importance of conservation as a means of maintaining and enhancing exploitable resources was recognised at last.

The Convention defines biodiversity as 'the variability among living organisms from all sources including, *inter alia*, terrestrial, marine and other aquatic ecosystems and the ecological complexes of which they are part; this includes diversity within species, between species and of ecosystems'.

In 1994, the Government published *Biodiversity: the UK Action Plan* (Cm 2438), a national strategy for the conservation of biodiversity and the sustainable use of biological resources. Marine conservation is covered as a specific topic. The authors observe that 'progress with improving our information base [on marine ecosystems] is currently disappointingly slow' and conclude that 'marine conservation is at a point similar to that for terrestrial ecology in the 1950s'. This was despite the output of a major research programme, the Marine Nature Conservation Review (MNCR), coordinated by the Joint Nature Conservation Committee, the objectives of which were, *inter alia*, to extend our knowledge of British marine ecosystems and assess their nature conservation importance. The Government went on to commit itself to the following planned action on the marine area:

- Complete the MNCR
- Continue to devise arrangements to prevent uncontrolled introductions of non-native marine species
- Promote active management of bay marine wildlife areas including management plans to secure the integrated management of vulnerable areas
- Review the intertidal SSSI network to ensure it covers the important marine wildlife habitats and species
- Utilise voluntary and statutory marine reserves and other relevant initiatives as mechanisms to involve individuals and communities in practical marine conservation work
- Designate sufficient marine SACs and SPAs and ensure that mechanisms are in place for their effective conservation under the Habitats and Birds Directives.

In practice, greatest commitment seems to have been given to marine conservation under the EC Habitats Directive which was adopted in the same year as the Rio conference. The Directive aims to protect biodiversity through the establishment of a network of protected areas known as Natura 2000. Member States are responsible for proposing sites for designation as Special Areas of Conservation (SAC) and are required to take appropriate steps to avoid deterioration of these sites. In particular, there is a requirement to assess the implications of any proposed plans or projects that are likely to have a significant effect on the integrity of an SAC. If an adverse impact is predicted then the proposal can only be taken forward under exceptional circumstances. Member States are also obliged to undertake positive management for designated sites, including, if necessary, the formulation of appropriate management plans.

The Directive is implemented in Great Britain by the Conservation (Natural Habitats, etc.) Regulations 1994 (SI 1994/2716). There are special provisions for European Marine Sites which are designed to take account of the fact that a wide variety of activities undertaken at sea come under the control of public bodies. The Government had earlier issued a consultation paper entitled *Implementation in Great Britain of the Council Directive on the Conservation of Natural Habitats and of Wild Fauna and Flora (92/43/EEC), 'The Habitats Directive'* (issued jointly by the Department of the Environment and the Welsh Office in October 1993). This set out its ideas for implementation, proposing that conservation of marine habitats under the Directive should be achieved without unnecessary interference with the activities of legitimate users of the sea. Activities were to be controlled only in so far as they posed a threat to marine wildlife. The MNR legal regime was considered inappropriate for the implementation of the Directive and the Government concluded that it would not be feasible to legislate for offshore SSSIs. Instead, the Regulations introduce a new type of protection which attempts to promote integrated management of European marine sites so as to protect their conservation interest while, at the same time, allowing activities to continue as far as possible. They provide for relevant authorities to devise a management scheme for the site under which their functions are to be exercised so as to secure compliance with the Directive. Relevant authorities are defined in Regulation 5 and include, *inter alia*, nature conservation agencies, local authorities, the Environment Agency, the Scottish Environmental Protection Agency, harbour authorities, sea fisheries committees and navigation authorities. Only one scheme is to be put in place for any one site and any of the relevant authorities can take the lead in preparing it.

The management scheme cannot regulate activities that do not come under the control of the relevant authorities. It does not, therefore, have any impact on most recreational users. These can, however, be controlled by byelaws made by the nature conservation agency using the MNR powers under section

37 of the Wildlife and Countryside Act. The constraints applying to MNR byelaws also apply to byelaws made to protect European Marine Sites. In addition, any competent authority with functions relevant to marine conservation must exercise those functions so as to secure compliance with the Directive. Competent authorities include ministers, government departments and other public bodies.

The selection of marine sites to be submitted to the European Commission as potential SACs has not been easy. Annex III of the Directive sets out criteria to be used in site selection. These are based on the representivity of the specified habitat type on the site; the area of the site covered by that habitat type in relation to its total area in the Member State's national territory; the present state of the site and its potential for restoration; and a global assessment of the value of the site for conservation of the specified habitat. There are obvious difficulties in applying these criteria to marine sites, especially given the list of marine habitats specified in Annex I. These include estuaries, mudflats, shallow immersed sandbanks, large shallow bays and inlets, lagoons and reefs. Despite years of marine survey work, we still do not have sufficient knowledge of the subtidal environment of the British Isles to be able to judge sites against these criteria. The problem is exacerbated in relation to potential SACs to be identified because of particular species, rather than habitats. A number of native marine species are included in Annex II, including two species of cetaceans and two seals. The criteria for the selection of sites for species include the size and density of the population of the species present on the site in relation to the total population present within the national territory. The Directive acknowledges the difficulties that might be encountered in applying this criterion and adds the following proviso (Article 4(1): 'For aquatic species which range over wide areas, sites will be proposed only where there is a clearly identifiable area representing the physical and biological factors essential to their life and reproduction.'

The Directive applied to the European territory of a Member State. There was some uncertainty as to whether this means that marine sites were restricted to territorial waters, i.e. out to twelve nautical miles, or whether they could extend to the limits of the 200 mile exclusive economic zone. Under the Conservation (Natural Habitats, etc.) Regulations 1994, European marine sites are confined to territorial waters. However, a recent case in the High Court (*R v Secretary of State for Trade and Industry ex parte Greenpeace Ltd.*, CO/1336/1999, 5 Nov. 1999) decided that the Directive applies to the full extent of the continental shelf and, therefore, extends to at least 200 miles offshore. It will be difficult to give effect to this decision, not least because of the lack of scientific knowledge about diversity in offshore waters. Furthermore, there are doubts as to whether the nature conservation agencies have the legal competence to give advice in respect of offshore waters. In the meantime, the nature conservation agencies have concentrated on identifying sites within territorial waters. Following a moderation exercise carried out by the European Commission in 1999, the Government has been instructed to increase both the number and size of sites put forward as proposed SACs. As a result of this moderation exercise a considerable proportion of the British coastline and nearshore waters is likely to come under protective designation.

It is too soon to assess the value of SACs in practice. No SACs have, as yet, been designated so it is too soon to assess the effectiveness of the Natura 2000 scheme for marine conservation. In theory, however, a marine SAC will enjoy absolute protection. It will be managed to provide for the ecological needs of its specific habitats and species and the Government will be under a duty to prevent its deterioration. All proposals for activities on the site that might have a significant adverse effect will have to be assessed and, if it is concluded that damage is likely to result, they will only be allowed to proceed if there are imperative reasons of overriding public interest.

It would seem then, that for the immediate future at least, the protected area designation will be the main mechanism for marine conservation. It does not follow that it is the best method or even that will be effective at all. The existing Marine Nature Reserves are on such a small scale that it is impossible to extrapolate from them. It may be the case that a system of marine management, covering all waters might be more effective. Various suggestions for coastal and marine management planning have been put forward over the last twenty years but have come to nothing. It is possible, however, that the Government's working group on the protection of marine sites and species, which was set up in 1999 following the publication of its consultation paper on SSSIs, may come up with some original proposals. It is noteworthy, however, that the latest piece of environmental legislation, the Countryside and Rights of Way Act 2000, mirrors its predecessor of 1949, and makes no reference to marine sites.

REFERENCES

Gibson, J. and Warren, L.M. (1995). 'Legislative requirements', in Gubbay, S. (ed.), *Marine Protected Areas: Principles and Techniques for Management,* 32–60.

NCC/NERC, (1979). *Nature Conservation in the Marine Environment,* Nature Conservancy Council and Natural Environment Research Council, HMSO.

NERC, (1973). *Marine Wildlife Conservation,* Natural Environment Research Council, HMSO.

Stamp, L.D. (1969). *Nature Conservation in Britain,* Collins, London.

Warren, L. (1989). *Statutory Marine Nature Reserves in Great Britain. A Progress Report.* World Wide Fund for Nature.

11

The Challenge of Change:
Demands and Expectations for Farmed Land

Janet Dwyer and Ian Hodge

I. THE CHANGING CONTEXT

JUST OVER FIFTY years ago, the basis for post-war agricultural policy was established in the 1947 Agriculture Act. The central objective of this Act was to establish a stable and efficient agriculture sector that was capable of producing such part of the nation's food that it was desirable to produce in the United Kingdom at minimum prices. This was to be pursued consistently with proper remuneration and living conditions for farmers and workers in agriculture, and an adequate return on capital.

Despite changes to the mechanisms of agricultural support, particularly the switch from deficiency payments to the maintenance of market prices, the general philosophy of rural policy was maintained following the UK's entry into the European Community in 1973 and survived into the early 1980s. Thus two roles placed agriculture at the centre of rural policy: to secure food supplies from efficient agricultural production; and to support the rural population, rural services and the rural economy through a prosperous agricultural sector. In this perspective, the maintenance of rural landscapes and amenity was seen as a natural by-product of farming activity.

However, the influences of technological change and agricultural policy on the landscape since the Second World War have increasingly, and fundamentally, challenged this perspective. These changes, and their structural and environmental effects, have been widely documented and discussed.

The changes in incentives arising from policy, in combination with the enhanced capacity of technology to respond to these incentives, have had severe consequences for the environment. With mechanisation and increases in land and labour productivity, farms became larger and concentrated on fewer enterprises. The eastern counties increasingly specialised in arable cropping in general, and in cereals in particular. The west of the country specialised in grazing livestock. Many enterprises, particularly pig and poultry production which were once common on practically all farms, became concentrated in specialist production units. New technology increasingly encouraged a larger scale of operation, with larger farms and larger field sizes.

Developments in agricultural technology also profoundly altered rural landscapes and biodiversity. Particularly in those areas where production was traditionally limited by natural constraints, these changes facilitated the drainage of wetlands, the improvement of upland pastures and the ploughing up of permanent grassland, moor and heath. The statistics of habitat loss have become familiar. In the forty years following the Second World War, about 95% of lowland meadow was lost, 80% of chalk downland; 60% of lowland bogs, 50% of lowland marsh, and 40% of lowland heath (Nature Conservancy Council, 1984). Even in the already productive countryside, landscapes changed profoundly as a result of farm structural change and the increased use of chemical fertilisers and pesticides. For example, the length of hedgerows declined from 495,000 miles in 1947 to 386,000 miles in 1985 (Countryside Commission 1986), and evidence suggests that the decline has continued since then, although at a slower rate than in previous periods (Countryside Commission 1998). There has also been continuing concern at the loss of wildlife, recent studies emphasising both direct and indirect consequences of pesticide use, associated with the lack of food sources for birds and mammals, in intensively farmed areas (Campbell *et al.* 1997). An overview of the environmental impacts of agriculture has been provided by Skinner *et al.* (1997).

Perhaps less discussed have been the institutional changes that could be seen as a third set of factors influencing the relationship between agriculture and the environment since 1947. The post-war drive to increase food production from farmed land was institutionalised through policy support, and through the establishment of public-funded, sectorally focused, extension and marketing bodies. These policies and organisations promoted the role of farmer as food producer above all else, and favoured the emergence of a more 'efficient' farm structure. The policy tools for promoting such a straightforward objective could be relatively simple: investing in the modernisation of farm holdings, and providing incentives to individual farmers to produce more through guaranteed output prices.

These policies and institutions thus encouraged a 'horizontal individualisation' in land management, where each farmer responded to the signals of a centralised and standardised policy regime, and in which prices affected whole sector markets across the UK, rather than particular regions or localities. In this way, each farm became increasingly independent of neighbouring and local land uses and other economic activity. The approach promoted the characterisation of farming as an industry (as opposed to 'a way of life'), in which the countryside was its 'factory floor'. This vision was strengthened over successive decades by increasing vertical integration of farmers into the wider food industry, as suppliers of raw materials to the growing ranks of large-scale food processors and retailers.

At the same time as these sectoral policies and institutions were encouraging a single-purpose view of agriculture, fundamental change was occurring in the socio-economic composition of rural areas. This change was broadly associated with the process of counter-urbanisation, which was first identified and described in Britain from the results of 1981 census, but which more recent analysis has suggested is a continuing, although easing, trend (Champion, 1994). A number of processes have been involved, including the relocation of employment to more rural areas, increasing retirement migration and the growth of weekend/holiday homes and other tourism-related residency, and perhaps most widespread, increased commuting from a rural hinterland to larger towns and cities. Each of these processes is affected by different factors, so the phenomenon is both complex and spatially variable: the changes in South Devon and Cumbria have been quite different to those in the Berkshire and Sussex Downs, for example.

At a national level, counter-urbanisation has tended to cause population decline in the larger conurbations and the growth of smaller settlements in rural areas. However, there is commonly a continuing decline of population within the smallest villages (Weekley, 1988). At the same time many of the local, collectively-used services in rural areas have continued to decline, especially public transport, and shops, Post Offices and schools in the smaller villages, as demand has been affected by improved private transport and economies of size in the provision of retail services.

Within the last three decades, these changes have formed the subject of an increasing body of rural sociological research, which has traced the increasing diversity of rural communities across Britain and highlighted the ways in which farmers have ceased to play a 'natural focal role' in many communities. Indeed, in some areas, farmers have become relatively isolated and criticised by their immediate neighbours. Such criticism is most often related to perceptions fuelled by growing public awareness of the negative environmental and structural impacts of modern agriculture, as encouraged by post-war policy. The majority of rural residents now have no connection with the agricultural economy, and their concern relates almost exclusively to the quality of the physical environment produced by farmers, in which they live and spend their leisure. Thus rural areas have increasingly become zones of consumption rather than production (Marsden and Murdoch, 1994). More broadly, the consumption of food has become increasingly distanced from the initial production process. For many people, urban and rural alike, little connection is now drawn between activities on the land and the products on display in the supermarket (ERM, 1998).

2. PRESSURES FOR CHANGE

Today, there are many pressures for substantial change in the way in which we manage our farmland. These have arisen at different levels, and they have profoundly different implications for the future. For the purposes of this paper, we somewhat crudely characterise these forces as acting in two opposing directions, but of course the reality is more complex than this.

Firstly, there are widespread concerns which can be broadly related to the concept of *sustainability and sustainable development*, embracing environmental, social and economic dimensions. Without seeking to offer a precise definition (see DETR, 1999 for a recent government statement), the aim of environmental sustainability is broadly to reduce the short-term exploitation of the natural environment, to enhance the production of countryside goods and to adopt a precautionary approach towards technology and environmental risk. In social terms too, the concept has relevance to society's expectations from farmed land and its management. Social sustainability encapsulates a 'bottom up' locally-focused, partnership approach to decisions about resource use, in stark contrast to the 'individualist operator responding to top-down policy' that has characterised so much land management change in recent decades, as described above.

These aims are associated with a more general philosophy, as espoused by many environmental politicians and economists, that has expressed scepticism about the outcome of unfettered market forces and increasingly questioned whether the pursuit of individual interests through market mechanisms is consistent with the attainment of wider, social goals. This philosophical perspective identifies an important role for collective decision-making, as represented by public policies at all levels of governance, in limiting the pursuit of self interest through various forms of intervention.

Secondly, an entirely contrasting pressure for change arises from the increasing global discourse about economic development, the pursuit of *competitiveness and the need for freer trading markets and level playing fields*. The free trade rhetoric believes in promoting improved wealth and welfare through increased market activity. It tends to view interventionist policies as interfering with, and hindering, the capacity of the individual innovation and spirit which would otherwise take forward economic and social development, through this process.

This view is not necessarily anti-environmental. A variety of voices in the 'liberalising' camp would claim that it offers the best chance for environmental conservation. In theory, liberalisation can promote free market environment-alism (Anderson and Leal, 1991), as well as reducing environmentally damaging government subsidies (e.g. Myers, 1997) which could bring some environmental benefit by reducing the current incentives to maximise farm output. Following the logic of the 'environmental Kuznets curve' (e.g. World Bank, 1992), the view is also advanced that once we are richer as a result of increased trade, we are better able to afford and more likely to demand a higher quality environment.

These contrasting pressures for change are expressed in different ways at different scales (as illustrated in Table 1).

Table 1. Contrasting Pressures for Change

	The 'sustainability' agenda (collective, social environmental choice)	The 'free trade' agenda (individual, private environmental choice)
International	International conventions: • Agenda 21 • Biodiversity • Climate change (Kyoto)	• International trade agreements and processes – GATT/ WTO: new round begins 1999
European	• European environmental legislation (eg Birds, Habitats, Nitrates, Water Framework, Environmental Impact Assessment) • Sustainable rural/regional development policies (ERDF, Rural Development under CAP)	• Single European market • Harmonisation of environmental and health regulations
Domestic	• Demands for 'public goods' – environmental conservation, wildlife and landscape, access • Social and demographic change – changing preferences of rural communities • Leisure industry growth – demands for beautiful yet multi-purpose land use • Growing appreciation of cultural diversity, threatened by homogenising trends in rural areas • Resurgence of interest in quality products, regional specialities and 'ethical consumption'	• Demand for greater access to markets, level playing fields (EU and beyond) • Exchequer pressure to reduce agriculture/EU budgets • Continuing consumer demand for cheap(er) food, year-round product choice • Demand for lower land prices (allowing purchase for non-farm uses – e.g. leisure/nature)

At the global level, government has signed up to international conventions that pledge certain actions domestically, which may be more or less binding

upon their subsequent policy decisions. Examples include both sustainability and trade obligations. At the European level, the UK works with
other Member States to influence the future direction and implementation
of European legislation, which includes the Common Agricultural Policy – a
common sectoral policy operating within a single market – as well as a
significant suite of policies promoting regional development, and a growing
number of environmental Directives. And domestically, there remain many
decisions to be made about how this mix of international goals and
European policies should be refined and delivered alongside national and
regional policy objectives, in a way which promotes desirable changes on
farmed land. The devolution of decision-making to new assemblies in
Scotland and Wales, and the establishment of the Regional Development
Agencies in England suggests that, in future, we will see greater variation at
sub-national level, although the precise scope for this has yet to be
determined.

At the centre of these pressures sits Europe's Common Agricultural Policy,
which is undoubtedly the single greatest policy influence upon rural land
management in the UK. The agreed need for its reform was affirmed by Heads
of State in their Agenda 2000 agreement in March 1999. However, as Table 1
illustrates, agreement that the policy needs reform can obscure fundamental
disagreements about why and in what direction reform should be taken
forward. This is further complicated by a variety of more specific contexts and
concerns within different EU Member States.

In general, a few countries support the argument for liberalisation, for
reducing the burden on taxpayers and consumers, limiting the interference
of the state in markets, and enhancing the opportunities available to farmers
as a result. However, it is probably fair to say that the majority of Member
States only accept this argument to a limited extent and not least as a result
of international trading pressure and broader fears about future EU finan-
cing. At the same time, there are strong arguments across Europe that are
built upon a perceived need to transform the role of the CAP from
production support towards support for rural society and the provision
of environmental and social 'countryside goods', that markets alone may
under-provide. It is perhaps this argument that has most common currency
among the Member States.

For the time being, the European Commission has used arguments from
both these sides, in pressing the case for reform. Its views are described in the
context of a proposed 'European Model of Agriculture'. In policy terms, it
advocates relative trade liberalisation to allow farmers to compete in freer
markets, alongside the maintenance of a significant support policy for rural
areas, in which resources shift away from agricultural production towards

broader environmental and social support, including support for sustainable rural development.

Of course, the Agenda 2000 reforms, as with so many previous attempts at reform, have not moved as far in this direction as the Commission had hoped. For some years beyond 2000, the bulk of CAP expenditure will remain targeted towards support linked to agricultural production – the direct aids to producers which compensate them for price cuts. However, most commentators now accept that the longer-term trajectory of change will be towards a more significant dismantling of production supports and their replacement by payments for social and environmental purposes. And Agenda 2000 does offer new opportunities to develop such new policies within the reformed CAP, through environmental cross-compliance and the new rural development regulation (to which we return later), and through the scope for Member States to switch resources at national level from production to rural development, through applying 'modulation'.

3: ROLES – ON BEING A FARMER; BECOMING A LAND MANAGER

The main message to farmers as a result of these current pressures is a profound one. It signals that policies will move away from emphasising the farmer's role as food producer towards encouragement for the multi-purpose management of land and natural resources.

- The 'collective sustainability' goal of policy reform emphasises environmental and social values, thus increasing the pressure for all land management to be 'environmentally responsible' and encouraging farmers to aim to produce a variety of countryside goods rather than simply to pursue increased agricultural output. These trends should generally be beneficial for nature conservation and rural communities.
- The 'free market' goal of reform encourages farmers to pursue greater competitiveness through an increased quality and diversity of production, encouraging the market to help define the value and range of alternative outputs that farmers, as land managers, choose to produce. However, the social and environmental implications of increased competition and reduced production support are less clear.

So, how will farmers react to these pressures for change? There are different views about how increased market liberalisation may impact upon rural areas. These views arise from differing perspectives on the fundamental relationship between agriculture and the environment.

THE 'INPUT MODEL' OF ENVIRONMENTAL IMPACT

The approach often favoured by North American and Australian commentators models the impact of agriculture on the environment as an external cost associated with input use (e.g. Anderson, 1992; Dunn and Shortle, 1992, Just and Antle, 1990; Zilberman, *et al.* 1997). The paradigmatic example is of water pollution: fertiliser and chemicals applied by farmers run off or are leached from farm land into aquifers and watercourses, imposing external costs on water users and damaging ecosystems. Reductions in output prices lower the returns to the inputs used, lowering optimal levels and hence lessening environmental damage. This approach implies an inevitable relationship between output prices and environmental quality; a reduction in the level of price support inevitably leads to a reduced intensity of production and thus to an improvement in environmental quality (Hodge, 2000).

THE 'OUTPUT MODEL' OF ENVIRONMENTAL IMPACT

A different model is often adopted by European commentators. This views marketed food and environmental quality as separate *products* of the land (e.g. Buckwell, 1989, Russell, 1993, Traill, 1988). These are portrayed as joint products that can be produced in varying combinations. In this case, the environmental focus for the model concentrates on the need for active land management to generate environmental benefits (e.g. landscape diversity and semi-natural habitats).

In this model, there are still levels at which environment and agricultural production are competitive – for example in very high intensity agricultural systems. A reduction in agricultural production in these cases would generally increase environmental quality. However, for some, usually less intensive production systems, agricultural and environmental outputs can be complementary, such that a reduction in agricultural prices can *reduce* environmental quality. For example, as the price paid for livestock products falls, grazing in marginal areas may become sufficiently extensive for undesirable scrub species to invade pastures that would otherwise support wildflowers. Similarly, if such farms enlarge and shed more labour in response to falling prices, their field boundaries will become increasingly redundant and fall into decline, as stock are left more to their own devices. This suggests that price reductions will not be unambiguously beneficial. There is likely to be less chemical pollution but also potentially fewer countryside services, particularly in economically marginal areas or in relation to less productive areas and features on farms.

The relationship between production and the environment may be mirrored by relationships between production and social variables. Traditional agricultural systems have also co-evolved with particular local communities and cultures. Thus the preservation of certain cultural and community values – such as their defining skills, knowledge and customs – may also depend upon the protection of the agricultural systems which have engendered them. Perhaps the most obvious example of this in Britain is crofting.

Viewed from this 'output' perspective, we should anticipate both positive and negative environmental impacts, as farmers adjust to more liberalised agricultural markets. Some recent research (e.g. Doyle, *et al.* 1997; Potter, *et al.* 1999) has indeed suggested that the changes could be significant and damaging to landscapes and biodiversity in both marginal and mixed farming areas.

Equally, there remain uncertainties about how farmers will react to a more comprehensive shift of support towards explicit rural environmental and social goals. In the UK at least, we have nearly twenty years of experience with schemes promoting environmental goals. Our voluntary agri-environment schemes started with the Broads Grazing Marshes Experiment in the early 1980s. To date, the experience of these schemes has demonstrated several interesting points:

- Farmers are increasingly willing to accept the notion of being paid to deliver countryside goods such as wildlife habitats, well-maintained hedgerows and other landscape features on farms. The number and variety of farms enrolling in the schemes continues to grow year by year and indeed, several of the current schemes are heavily over-subscribed with applicants.
- Nevertheless, the compatibility of these schemes with commercial farming activity has limits. These limits may be in relation to the scale of scheme impact, such that agreements or activities may be confined only to small parts of the farm such as field margins and less productive areas. Alternatively, they may relate to the degree of change which can be negotiated by an agreement – for example securing some restraint of grazing densities on upland or semi-natural pastures, but failing to encourage farmers to agree to more radical stocking reductions where these could bring increased benefits (e.g. ADAS, 1998). It is not yet clear to what extent these limits arise mainly because the balance of policy support still encourages high-output farming, or whether they would persist even if this support were removed.
- Finally, these voluntary schemes take time and effort to apply for and they generally expect farmers to invest in a proportion of the work agreed to – particularly in relation to 'capital works' such as hedge and

tree planting. Studies of entrants and non-entrants suggest that schemes therefore tend to miss a potentially large proportion of the farm sector which remains unwilling or unable to invest the time and money required, such as smaller farms (particularly dairy), farmers nearing retirement or landowners whose interests – financial and other – are elsewhere.

So, it may be important to think about the extent to which the priorities for landscapes, species and habitat protection will coincide with the likely 'policy reach' of voluntary agri-environmental schemes, as they expand; and whether schemes could be amended locally to make them more accessible to particular types of farmer, where necessary.

But agri-environment schemes are only one part of the future environmental and social policy measures that will apply in rural Europe. Increasingly, land managers will have access to a wider range of aid for 'Integrated Rural Development' (IRD), including for environmental and other training, diversification, farm forestry and marketing and processing. The scale of such aid is likely to remain limited in the first few years beyond 2000, but is expected to eventually become a significant 'pillar' of policy support. So far, Britain has had much more limited experience of aid of this kind. The first IRD experiments date back to the same period as the first agri-environmental schemes, in the early 1980s (e.g. Parker, 1984). However it has only been with the significant increase in European Regional Development aid for the UK since 1994 that many rural areas have had access to such funds, through the Objectives 5b, 1 and 2 programmes.

Broadly speaking, the ongoing evaluation of these programmes appears to suggest that the farming sector may have been relatively slow to engage in the process of rural development planning (Ward, *pers comm*), and many programmes have been designed in ways which have made farmer participation particularly difficult because of the small scale of most farm businesses, and their particular need for management flexibility. Nevertheless, there have been some imaginative and promising projects in some regions. Initiatives such as the North York Moors' Moorland Regeneration Programme, Cumbria Farm Link, and integrated farming and regional marketing schemes in many areas including the Marches, Southwest England and East Anglia have begun to demonstrate ways in which farmers can be encouraged to develop new and successful commercial activities which also bring environmental benefits.

But these projects are mostly still in their infancy. Among the farming sector in general, despite a growing proportion of holdings with non-agricultural incomes (NFU, 1999) there remains much scepticism about farmers' ability to 'change track'. It is commonly claimed that diversification is only an option for the favoured few, that markets for regional products, organic foods or farm tourism are fragile and could be easily saturated. Whatever the true situation, it seems clear that the coming decade will be a very challenging time for farmers in Britain and that there will no doubt be a certain amount of 'fall out' from the industry, as it tries to adjust to the new agenda.

4. REDEFINING PROPERTY RIGHTS

The previous discussion focused upon the demands placed on rural land managers, and farmers in particular, describing how changes in support are encouraging farmers to think about pursuing a broader set of goals than before. This is not only associated with the way in which the land should be used, but also to the duties attached to land ownership. Important developments are underway which affect the formal rules governing the use of land and the informal pressures exerted over landowners. These help to determine the nature of property itself, the values that are enjoyed by the owners of property rights over land.

Changing social values and attitudes lead to changing perceptions and rules of land ownership. As has been emphasised by the current administration, rights go together with responsibilities. The rights of landowners are defined in many ways, such as through environmental regulations, the operation of the planning system, decisions in the courts, definitions of rights of way and so on. The regulatory framework sets the context within which countryside management takes place, and thus defines the nature of property itself.

One major area in which land owners' rights are defined is through the planning system (Hodge, 1999). Until recently, agricultural and forestry activities have been largely excluded from the sphere of planning control. The 1947 Town and Country Planning Act provided the means for urban containment; to keep the countryside free for the production of food. The use of land for farming and forestry was expressly excluded from the definition of development under the Act. Even today, under the 1990 Town and Country Planning Act, s.55 provides that 'the use of any land for the purpose of agriculture or forestry (including afforestation) and the use for any of those purposes of any building occupied together with land so used' does not constitute 'development' and thus is excluded from the operation of the planning system.

Back in 1947, government did not perceive the extent to which changes in land use and management over the next fifty years would bring farming and forestry into conflict with other interests and values in rural land. In that sense therefore, the legacy of the 1947 Act has been more a history of responsibilities overlooked than of unconstrained rights affirmed.

Within the last 20 years, there have been growing calls to bring agriculture more comprehensively into the planning framework. Shoard (1980) advocated the extension of planning controls to cover the changes taking place in the countryside. Cox, Lowe and Winter (1988) rejected a comprehensive extension of controls, arguing that the negative controls available would be insufficiently sensitive to deal with the dynamics of organic change. However, they regarded the blanket exemption of agriculture through the General Development Order as an 'indefensible anomaly', and proposed an extension of a general order-making power to prevent the removal or alteration of specified landscape features or the undertaking of a notifiable operation that might damage the conservation interest of a site.

Since then, some changes have been made. The General Development Order was amended in 1988 to introduce restrictions on the building of intensive livestock units (Marsden, *et al.* 1993). In changes introduced in 1992, development is, in certain cases, subject to a requirement to give prior notification to the local planning authority, to enable them to determine whether their prior approval should be required with respect to the siting, design and external appearance of the building or other development. This applies for instance to new farm buildings, significant extensions and alterations (to all extensions and alterations in National Parks) and to farm roads. Further controls introduced in 1997 require the removal of buildings erected under agricultural permitted development rights, where buildings cease to be used for agricultural purposes within ten years of their substantial completion, and where planning permission has not been granted for re-use for non-agricultural purposes (DoE 1997).

The UK Round Table on Sustainable Development (1998) has commented that:

> the lack of clarity of current planning controls over agricultural buildings and over the carrying out of excavations or engineering operations for the purposes of agriculture, and the general inconsistency of approach in comparison with the requirements which apply to other industries, is unjustifiable. It is important that controls do not stifle legitimate diversification of the economy in rural areas. But all development should be subject to proper control.

They recommend that:

> government should introduce requirements for full development control on all agricultural buildings and on the carrying out of excavations or engineering operations for the purposes of agriculture. (p.19)

The issue of the exemptions of planning controls over agricultural development has also recently been raised in Scotland by the Land Reform Policy
Group (1998).

We can also observe evidence of a shift in social expectations for farmed
land in other ways. The strengthening in the Countryside and Rights of Way
Act (HMG 2000) of the protection and management of SSSIs also
represents a shift in the balance of rights and responsibilities of land
management. These empower, in England and Wales, conservation agencies
to refuse permission to landowners to undertake potentially damaging
operations and remove the presumption of compensation for net profits
foregone. Conservation agencies have also been given powers to enforce
positive conservation management orders, similar to the powers already
available in relation to the built heritage.

Another development has been the introduction of legislation for the
protection of hedges in England and Wales from deliberate removal, which
was finally included in the 1995 Environment Act after several previous
attempts. Although concerns remain among environmental groups that the
regulations are far too narrow and that local authorities lack the manpower
and resources to enforce them adequately, these effectively extend a form of
planning control over features on farm land (DETR, 1998b). Furthermore, in
the near future the UK must implement European legislation which requires
Environmental Impact Assessments, with a public power of veto, for any
significant projects which involve agricultural intensification on uncultivated
and semi-natural land (CPRE leaflet, 1999).

New environmental and amenity regulations also affect the balance of
rights and responsibilities in land use and management. The implementation
of EU Directives in relation to Nitrates and Water, the future need to limit
greenhouse gas production from agriculture in order to meet international
climate change obligations, and changing policies as a result of domestic
demand, such as access to open countryside in England and Wales, will all
have their impacts.

The introduction of environmental cross-compliance as part of the Agenda
2000 CAP reforms signals another shift. This is the first explicit statement that
the continuing receipt of agricultural support payments should in future be
dependent upon achieving some degree of environmentally-responsible farming across Europe. While there may be considerable practical difficulties in
identifying, agreeing and implementing such a policy effectively, the fact that
it was retained in the reform package indicates that notions about basic
environmental responsibilities in relation to land use and ownership are now
widely accepted. Such notions are also evident in the proposal by the UK
Round Table on Sustainable Development (1998) for a 'duty of care' for

landowners and land managers that would provide a uniform and basic level of legal obligation.

5. POINTERS FOR THE FUTURE

We have attempted to sketch out some key challenges and expectations for farmed land over the coming decade or so, highlighting their variety in scale and likely impact, and showing how they are reflected in a combination of shifting purposes in support for agriculture, and shifting definitions of the rights and responsibilities of landholding. At both national and European level, these challenges are now perceived as requiring a re-definition of the basic relationship between farming and society. Here in Britain, this has been evident in the rhetoric of Rural White Papers published in England, Wales and Scotland and it has been a common thread in many commentaries on the CAP reform process (e.g. Country Agencies, 1998; Wildlife and Countryside Link, 1998; MAFF, 1999).

At European level, the same perspective is emphasised in the Commission's future vision of 'the European model of agriculture'. Fischler (1998) has defined the vision as meaning that agriculture:

> must be able to perform all functions on a sustainable basis across the whole Community. European farming must perform its market function, providing consumers and the processing industry with healthy, high quality food and renewable raw materials. At the same time it must also carry out its environmental functions, ensuring the sustainable use of natural resources, safeguarding the wide variety of ecosystems and protecting the diversity of Europe's farmlands. European agriculture must also provide a wide range of services, performing new functions that are in increasing public demand such as tourism or in the social sector. Finally, it has a major role to play in providing employment in rural areas.

In the short term, this revised 'contract' between agriculture and society is to be pursued within the currently limited new elements of the CAP – environmental cross compliance and new regional or national programmes for Rural Development, which incorporate a mix of agri-environmental and other aids. In the longer term, it is widely anticipated that these elements will become a more substantial feature of the policy.

Elsewhere in Europe, we can already find some possible pointers to the future. In Switzerland (Curry and Stuki, 1997), in response to consumer pressure and the growing international trend towards liberalisation, the government introduced radical reform of its agricultural policy some years ago, in which support was fully decoupled from agricultural production and instead, devoted to the promotion of environmental benefits through a suite of voluntary schemes. The basic tier scheme required farmers to adopt 'integrated farming systems', a generalised approach which involves reduced use of pesticides and fertilisers and increased use of alternative husbandry techniques, including nutrient budgeting systems and biological pest control. Higher tier schemes included organic farming, and the protection and restoration of natural and semi-natural habitats and features.

Because Swiss agricultural production had traditionally been very heavily supported, the response of farmers to this sudden shift was swift and positive – within a couple of years, over 90% of farms had enrolled in one or more of the environmental schemes, probably mainly in order to protect their incomes. In this context, therefore, the policy has achieved a widespread adoption and appreciation by farmers of new techniques of more environmentally-sensitive land management. Furthermore, in a recent review of the policy, the Swiss government has discussed the possibility that the 'basic tier' of integrated farming should no longer attract specific payments, but should simply become a basic standard underpinning all other support for agriculture.

The Swiss approach, of making a radical shift away from production support and into a 'broad but shallow' agri-environmental policy, contrasts with the British experience to date of fairly carefully targeted schemes which must compete against mainstream CAP payments. If there is a more radical reform of CAP within the next five to ten years, as many commentators predict (e.g. *Agra Europe*, 1999), it is possible to envisage the need for similar broad and shallow schemes here, to maintain the basic fabric of our countryside.

Within the EU, some countries and regions have much longer experience of integrated rural development than we have here in the UK. In many cases, their experiences suggest that the current difficulties of our programmes can be overcome, given time and increased sensitivity to local circumstances. A variety of recent reports (eg Ambroise, 1998, Dwyer, 1998, Parker, 1997, Mitchell, 1999) relate the benefits generated by communities in Austria, France, Germany, Spain, Greece and Portugal as a result of innovative projects involving farmers working in partnership with other local interests to promote new commercial and environmentally-sensitive economic development.

Among these examples there are common factors:

(i) successful policies combining rural development and land management demonstrate a much greater degree of local influence in their design and implementation than has traditionally been the case in Britain;

(ii) partnerships between farmers, environmental and public authorities, and non-farm commercial expertise appear to offer the best scope for developing projects which generate economic and environmental benefits – these can take time and effort to establish;

(iii) developing a strong local profile as a marketing tool, both for local consumers and for tourists, is beneficial. It can also help to foster collective action between different local groups;

(iv) the generation of multi-purpose outputs from farming is promoted by multipurpose policy instruments – public funds for environmental, social and economic objectives are combined at grassroots level into single, simple packages.

If we are to develop a new 'social contract' for farming, how might it differ from the past? The various elements in this paper would suggest the following:

(i) it will be more dependent upon location and upon the rest of the rural population and (rural) economy than it has been for the past 50 years;

(ii) it will present a much greater variety of future options for individual farm businesses but there may be also increased private risk as markets are no longer guaranteed;

(iii) it will require more involvement by the farming sector in collective decision-making, as more integrated and locally devolved policies are developed to meet the new multifunctional agenda;

(iv) it will need to improve the connections between agricultural production activities and consumption of food, in order to promote better understanding of food products, production techniques and associated risks to consumers.

These elements also need to be complemented by action at the global level. In particular, we foresee an increasing need to challenge the methodological assumptions in the 'free trade' agenda of the WTO, because of its inability to deal with society's desire to protect the institutional and social capital of rural areas, and adequately to address concerns about the risks of new technologies. The future World Trade rhetoric may need to be tempered by a greater acceptance of the concepts and policy mechanisms of the 'sustainability agenda', in order to accommodate these needs.

REFERENCES

Abler, D.G. and J.S. Shortle, (1992). Potential for environmental and agricultural policy linkages and reforms in the EC. *American Journal of Agricultural Economics,* 74, (3) 775–781.

ADAS (1997). *Environmental Monitoring in the Lake District Environmentally Sensitive Area, 1993–1996.* ADAS report to the Ministry of Agriculture, Fisheries and Food. MAFF, London.

Agra Europe (1999). Analysis section, various editions April – June 1999.

Ambroise, R., Barnaud, M., Manchon, O. and Vedel, G. (1998) 'Bilan et experience des plans de developpement durable du point de vue de la relation agriculture-environnement', *Le Courrier de l'Environnement de l'INRA*, 34 (juillet 1998), *5–20.*

Anderson, K. (1992). 'Agricultural trade liberalisation and the environment: A global perspective'. *The World Economy*, 15, (1) 153–171.

Anderson, T.L. and Leal, D.R. (1991). *Free Market Environmentalism.* Westview Press, Boulder. 1991

Buckwell, A. (1989). 'Economic signals, farmers' response and environmental change'. *Journal of Rural Studies*, 5, (2) 149–160.

Campbell, L.H, Avery, M., Donald, P. Evans, A.D., Green, R.E. and Wilson, J.D. (1997). *A Review of the Indirect Effects of Pesticides on Birds.* JNCC Report 227, JNCC, Peterborough.

Champion, A. (1994). Population change and migration in Britain since 1981: evidence for continuing deconcentration. *Environment and Planning A* 26, 1501–1520.

Countryside Agencies (1998*). Agenda 2000 – CAP Draft Regulations 1998: working papers from the countryside agencies of Great Britain.* Countryside Council for Wales (with Countryside Commission, Scottish Natural Heritage, English Nature), Bangor.

Countryside Commission (1986). What is Really Happening to the Landscape? *Countryside Commission News* 23, 4–5.

Countryside Commission (1998). *Agricultural Landscapes: A Third Look.* CCP521, Countryside Commission, Cheltenham.

Cox, G., Lowe, P. and Winter, M. (1988). Private rights and public responsibilities: the prospects for agricultural and environmental controls. *Journal of Rural Studies* 4: 323–337.

CPRE (1999). Leaflet highlighting *the UK's obligations to implement the EU Directive on Environmental Impact Assessment in respect of agricultural operations on semi-natural and uncultivated land.* Council for the Protection of Rural England, London.

Curry, N. and Stuki, E. (1997). Swiss agricultural policy and the environment: An example for the rest of Europe to follow? *Journal of Environmental Planning and Management*, 40 (4) 465–482.

DETR (1998a). *Access to the Open Countryside in England and Wales. A consultation paper.* Department of Environment, Transport and the Regions, London.

DETR (1998b). *Review of the Hedgerows Regulations 1997.* DETR, London.

DETR (1999). *A Better Quality of Life: A strategy for sustainable development for the United Kingdom.* DETR, London.

DoE (1997). *The Countryside: Environmental quality and economic and social development.* Planning Policy Guidance 7, HMSO, London.

Doyle, C., Ashworth, S. and McCracken, D. (1997). *Agricultural trade liberalisation and its environmental effects.* Report to the Land Use Policy Group of the GB Countryside Agencies. Scottish Agricultural College, Edinburgh.

Dwyer, J.C. (1998). *European experience of promoting countryside products.* Unpublished paper to Countryside Commission workshop, London, October 1998. Institute for European Environmental Policy, London.

Ecotec (1999). Evaluation of Structural Fund programmes in the UK. Ecotec, Birmingham.

ERM (1998). *Countryside Products.* Unpublished report for the Countryside Commission. Environmental Resources Management, London.

Fischler, F. (1998). A strong agriculture in a strong Europe: the European model. Speech to European Agriculture Congress, Ljubljana, 1 October 1998.

HMG (2000). *Countryside and Rights of Way Act 2000.* The Stationery Office, London.

Hodge, Ian (1999). Countryside planning: From urban containment to sustainable development, pp. 91–104, Chapter 7 in J.B. Cullingworth (ed.) *British Planning Policy: 50 Years of Urban and Regional Change.* The Athlone Press, London.

Hodge, Ian (2000). Agri-environmental relationships and the choice of policy mechanism. *The World Economy* (forthcoming).

Just, R.E. and J.M. Antle (1990). 'Interaction between agricultural and environmental policies: A conceptual framework'. *American Economic Review* 80, (2) 197–202.

Land Reform Policy Group (1998). *Identifying the Problems.* The Scottish Office, Edinburgh.

MAFF (1999). *Europe's Agriculture: The case for change.* Ministry of Agriculture, Fisheries and Food, London.

Marsden, T. *et al.* (1993). *Constructing the Countryside.* Restructuring Rural Areas 1, UCL Press, London.

Marsden, T. and Murdoch, J. (1994). *Reconstituting rurality: Class community and power in the development process.* UCL Press, London.

Mitchell, K. (ed.) (1999). *EU Structural Funds 2000–2006: Conserving Nature, Creating Jobs.* Information dossiers for all EU member states. Institute for European Environmental Policy, London.

Myers, N. (1998). *Perverse Subsidies: Tax dollars undercutting our economies and environments alike.* International Institute for Sustainable Development, Winnipeg.

Nature Conservancy Council (1984). *Nature Conservation in Great Britain.* Nature Conservancy Council, Shrewsbury.

NFU (1999). Unpublished *results of a survey of non-agricultural incomes conducted through the UK Farm Business Survey, 1998.* National Farmers Union, London.

Parker, K. (1984). *A Tale of Two Villages.* Peak Park Planning Board, Bakewell.

Parker, K. (1998). *Pride in Place: Report on a 1995 Churchill Fellowship Study of countryside conservation linked to rural economic development in Austria and France.* Peak National Park Authority, Bakewell.

Potter, C., Lobley, M. and Bull, R. (1999). *Agricultural liberalisation and its environmental effects.* Report to the Land Use Policy Group of the GB Countryside Agencies, Wye College, University of London.

Russell, N. (1993). 'Efficiency of rural conservation and supply control policies'. *European Review of Agricultural Economics,* 20, (3) 315–326.

Shoard, M. (1980). *The Theft of the Countryside.* Maurice Temple Smith, London.

Skinner, J.A., Lewis, K.A., Bardon, K.S., Tucker, P., Catt, J.A. and Chambers, B.J. (1997). An Overview of The Environmental Impact of Agriculture in the UK. *Journal of Environmental Management* 50, (2) 111–128.

Traill, B. (1988). The rural environment: what role for Europe? pp. 78–86 in M. Whitby and J. Ollerenshaw (eds.) *Land Use and the European Environment.* Belhaven Press, London.

UK Round Table on Sustainable Development (1998). *Aspects of Sustainable agriculture and rural policy.* UK Round Table on Sustainable Development, London.

Weekley, I. (1988). Rural depopulation and counterurbanization: a paradox. *Area* 20, 127–134.

Wildlife and Countryside Link (1998). *Building the pyramid: report of a one-day seminar on the future vision for rural support policy.* Wildlife and Countryside Link, London.

World Bank (1992). *World Development Report 1992: Development and the Environment.* Oxford University Press, New York.

Zilberman, D., M. Khanna, and L. Lipper (1997). Economics of new technologies for sustainable agriculture. *The Australian Journal of Agricultural and Resource Economics,* 41, (1) 63–80.

12

Beyond NIMBYism: The Evolution of Social Attitudes to Biotechnology

Joyce Tait

THE NIMBY CONCEPT AND ITS LIMITATIONS

THE TERM NIMBY ('not in *my* back yard') has been used since the mid-1980s to describe negative public responses to new developments and proposals for change (Gervers, 1987). It is generally used in a pejorative manner by those whose proposals are being obstructed, to imply that the objections are based on narrow self-interest with no consideration of the wider public good.

However, the NIMBY description does not do justice to the range and subtlety of human motivations for opposing any issue or development or to the variety of social and economic networks within which we all operate. It arose from a regulatory culture which does not recognise the validity, legal or intellectual, of any objections which are not based on 'rational self-interest' supported by strong scientific evidence. People whose objections are based on ethical and value-based concerns, or on an alternative conception of what is 'in the public interest', have had no way of being heard other than to dress up their concerns in a fake guise of rationality. However, a wrong or simplistic identification of the human motivations underlying any conflict makes it very difficult for government and policy-makers to engage in a meaningful dialogue about the issue and will probably exacerbate conflicts.

The alternative term NIABY ('not in *anybody's* backyard') was coined to make a much needed distinction between genuinely interest-based (NIMBY) motivations and those based on fundamental values or ethical judgements (Tait, 1988). Table 1 shows how relatively easy it is to deal with interest-based conflicts, compared to those based on values and ethics, and suggests some of the difficulties that can arise when there is a wrong diagnosis of the nature of the conflict.

This table describes the most extreme positions in what will usually be a mixture of motivations. In any community of individuals, in a few cases the basis of their concerns will be purely NIMBY or NIABY, but for most it will be a mixture of the two. There will be a continuum of shades of attitude to a

Table 1. Environmental and risk-based conflicts and their resolution

NIMBY conflicts	NIABY conflicts
Based on self interest of protagonists	Based on ethics or values of protagonists
Likely to be restricted to specific developments	Likely to spread across all related developments
Likely to be location-specific, locally organised	Likely to be organised on a national or international basis
Can usually be resolved by the provision of: – information; – compensation; or – negotiation	Very difficult to resolve: – information is viewed as propaganda; – compensation is viewed as bribery; – negotiation is viewed as betrayal

single issue among and within individuals. Also, our attitude systems are complex. We are all capable of holding a number of contradictory attitudes and opinions simultaneously and, for those interested in risk analysis and communication, the interesting questions are: which attitudes will remain dormant and which will be expressed in some form of overt disruptive or supportive behaviour; to what extent is a response to an issue based on interests and to what extent on values; when will personal or group interests over-ride values or vice versa; how and when might an individual or group response change from one form to another. A flip from NIMBY to NIABY can be achieved fairly rapidly, for example, by an incident which leads to loss of public trust in regulators, but a change in the reverse direction is a difficult and slow process.

As our more subtle understanding of the nature of public responses to contentious issues was developing in the 1980s, an alternative, more pre-cautionary approach to risk regulation was also evolving in Europe, beginning in Germany as the *Vorsorgeprinzip* in 1976 (von Moltke, 1987) and then spreading more widely (Royal Commission on Environmental Pollution (RCEP), 1988). One of the best examples of the impact of this shift can be seen in the regulatory systems that evolved in the 1960s and 70s to control the production and use of pesticides, and those which evolved in the 1980s and 1990s to control the emerging biotechnology industry, particularly the introduction of genetically modified (GM) crops.

The link between these issues and nature conservation may not be immediately obvious but they are in fact of supreme importance. The resolution of the current debate about the introduction of GM crops will determine the types of farming system we have in Europe in the next century, the nature of rural landscapes over large areas of the continent, the number of wildlife species which are able to co-exist with our farming systems and the nature and viability of rural societies.

REACTIVE/PREVENTIVE RISK REGULATION

Risk regulation of the agrochemical industry has always been reactive rather than precautionary in nature, in theory responding to scientifically rational interpretation of factual information. No attempts have been made to predict previously unforeseen hazards before a product was placed on the market. Only after a hazard had been identified did the regulatory system *react* to *prevent* future generations of products from giving rise to similar problems.

In the case of the organochlorine insecticides, for example, a very convincing standard of scientific proof of environmental damage was demanded before any action was taken to limit their use (Moore, 1987). However, once the risks had been officially accepted, any chemical which showed undue persistence in the environment, or a tendency to accumulate in food chains, was eliminated from the R&D pipelines of the agrochemical companies at a very early stage. Persistence in the environment changed from being an attractive attribute in a pesticide (because of the long term protection provided to the farmer's crops by a single application) to being an absolute prohibition to its further development.

Negative environmental impacts of subsequent generations of pesticides were, if considered sufficiently serious, incorporated into the regulatory system after their existence had been proved scientifically. One such example was the use of the insecticide carbophenothion as a seed dressing to replace dieldrin. This was found to be selectively toxic to geese (Jennings *et al.*, 1975) and its use in the UK was prohibited in areas where large numbers of geese over-winter, such as the Humber estuary.

There was a different official response to the finding that the fungicides benomyl and thiophanate methyl were lethal to earthworms (Stringer and Lyons, 1974). In this case the benefits of using the fungicides were seen as outweighing the agricultural value of earthworms and the use of these pesticides was not restricted.

These examples serve to illustrate the main characteristics of a reactive/preventive system of risk regulation (Tait and Levidow, 1992):

- the industry concerned and/or its products are controlled by a system set up *in response to* scientifically proven adverse impacts that have arisen in previous generations of products;
- new products and processes are screened to make sure that they do not give rise to any similar hazards;
- the regulatory system is built up slowly in a piecemeal fashion as new generations of product or process exhibit different hazards;

- decisions about the need for regulation and the level of regulation required are based on an analysis of relevant costs and benefits.

Even although the pesticide regulatory system incorporates elements of predictive toxicology, it is still essentially reactive in nature – it does not attempt to envisage *types* of hazard in new products that have not been scientifically proved to arise from similar products in the past.

Those who advocate a risk-based or science-based approach to potential hazards would claim that the type of system described above has a role to play in safeguarding the environment and at the same time avoiding unnecessary conflict by setting clear parameters for decision making. However, in the case of the organochlorine insecticides, such a convincing standard of proof of damage was demanded that many species suffered local extinction in regions of the UK before any action was taken. The agrochemical industry's reluctance to accept the possibility of environmental damage in this case undermined public trust and this has tended to push all subsequent conflicts involving the industry, including those over GM crops, into the NIABY rather than the NIMBY category.

Pesticides in general have also been blamed for the serious declines in numbers of some farm birds, although the intensive farming systems made possible by the use of pesticides are probably the major culprit, rather than pesticides *per se*. It has not proved easy to develop an effective *scientific* basis for analysing the complexity of modern farming systems, where many farmers apply numerous pesticides with widely varying toxicity profiles and environmental impacts, often in repeat doses.

Such problems have placed major strains on our science-based systems of pesticide regulation. Jasanoff (1990, pp123–151) has described how this advisory process, instead of facilitating consensus in the USA, created an adversarial environment because there were no mechanisms for reconciling conflicting constructions of science which emerged in hearings conducted behind closed doors. The end result was ' to create incentives for interested parties to remove the risk debate to the media and the corridors of politics, where it can be conducted under different and more flexible ground rules from those acceptable to science.' The science-based approach to pesticide regulation has not in practice been able to forestall conflicts, whether based on interests or values, over pesticide use

PRECAUTIONARY RISK REGULATION

Because of the actual environmental and health risks and also the public relations difficulties experienced in implementing the reactive/preventive approach to pesticide regulation, when research and development work began on GM crops those involved were more prepared than before to consider new ideas. Scientists, industry and regulators co-operated in applying the precautionary principle (PP) which was increasingly being advocated by European regulators for a range of potentially hazardous activities.

The RCEP (1989) report on 'The Release of Genetically Engineered Organisms to the Environment' described the potential role of the PP as follows: 'The opportunity exists to learn from the experiences and predictions of the past in order to build environmental foresight into any necessary regulation of these new products.' The precautionary approach as applied to the biotechnology industry was described as follows (Tait and Levidow, 1992):

- the industry concerned, and its products, are controlled by a system set up to avoid potential hazards;
- these hazards are predicted in advance of the development and/or marketing of products and before there is any empirical evidence for their existence; and
- safety issues and the formation of the regulatory system become an integral part of the development of the industry itself as well as its products.

The precautionary principle advocates restraints on development on reasonable suspicion of possible environmental damage without waiting for scientific proof and therefore, inevitably, without considering the costs and benefits of such actions. Such an approach could easily paralyse all future development, so some limitations on its scope are needed. A clear statement of the circumstances where it is justified is given in the Scottish Natural Heritage (1993) report on sustainable development:

- where the impacts envisaged are significant and/or potentially irreversible;
- where there are major gaps in our knowledge of the relevant systems and hence uncertainty over the nature and extent of possible impacts; and/or
- where the complexity of the system interactions is so great that it would be impossible to predict or identify the impact of a single development or activity.

The nascent biotechnology industry has been regulated in a precautionary manner, particularly in Europe, since the earliest stages of research and development. This has been justified mainly on grounds of uncertainty about the possible environmental impacts of GM crops. The novelty of the genetic combinations and the fact that many could not arise by natural means was presumed to give rise to unpredictable hazards.

IMPLEMENTING THE PRECAUTIONARY PRINCIPLE
FOR GM CROPS – WHAT WENT WRONG?

As noted above, there was a long standing lack of public trust in the agrochemical industry and both industry and regulators accepted the PP at least partly on the assumption that it would help to allay public fears about the new technology and smooth the path of new products through to the market place (Levidow, 1994, p 130–131). This is clearly not happening in Europe where the PP has been incorporated more consistently into the regulatory process than elsewhere in the world. The press, pressure group and public response to the introduction of new products, in the UK and several other European countries, is extremely hostile. It would appear that the strategy adopted in Europe has gone badly wrong, both in terms of protecting the environment and of allaying public fears. We need to have a better understanding of the nature and antecedents of the current conflict before we can begin to resolve it.

Figure 1 shows the range of human motivations on the NIMBY and NIABY dimensions and how different groups have located themselves on these dimensions in response to the introduction of GM crops. Research done in 1990 (Martin and Tait, 1992) showed that most members of the public were fairly neutral in their attitudes to biotechnology (point O). Not many of them knew what biotechnology was, they did not think that it was likely to affect their interests directly, and it did not seem relevant to any of their strongly-held values. The same survey interviewed members of environmental pressure groups and research scientists working on biotechnology in a university. The environmental pressure group members were located well into the top right hand corner at point D (biotechnology was perceived to be inimical to their fundamental values which were opposed to intensive farming and also against their interests as they believed it would have adverse effects on the development of organic agriculture). Scientists were mostly in the bottom left hand corner at point A (it was in their interests for their research to lead to marketable products at the end of the day and they also had strongly pro-GM values, seeing the crops as an unmitigated benefit to humanity with less risk attached to them than current chemical-based technology).

Public statements from organic farmers would locate them at point D, along with the environmental pressure groups who support them. Informal discussions with intensive arable farmers (as part of the SNH TIBRE initiative (Tait and Pitkin, 1995)) placed them at point C – they felt that GM crops were essentially a good thing (positive on the value dimension) but they were concerned about the impact on their business as a result of negative public opinion if they adopted the technology. Research on companies (Chataway and Tait, 1993) showed that multinational companies (MNCs) were located at point 'A' with GM crops contributing positively on interest and value dimensions, while small and medium-sized enterprises (SMEs) developing biotechnology products for agriculture had attitudes similar to intensive farmers, leading many of them to avoid investing in products that involved genetic modification.

Figure 1. Public Motivations in Responding to Biotechnology Issues

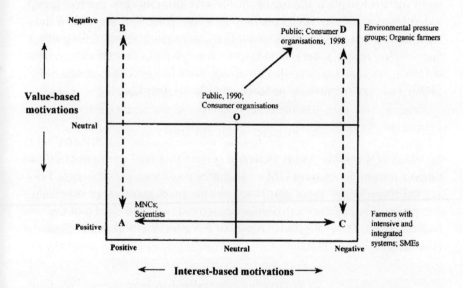

The strength and ratio of the two dimensions, interests and values, in dictating overall attitudes and motivations on any issue will be subject to change over time. When a shift takes place upwards out of either of the two boxes below the neutral line in Figure 1, the tendency will be to gravitate towards point D and once such a change has occurred it is very difficult to reverse. There are generally no 'half measures' in negative value-based motivations and they tend to over-ride interest-based motivations and to be more stable for the reasons described in Table 1.

Shifts in interest-based motivations, in either direction along the trajectory A C in Figure 1 will happen fairly readily as part of the normal processes of interaction between neighbours, business partners or competitors. If the business environment should change, non-organic farmers and SMEs would readily move back from point C to A. The most interesting part of Figure 1 from the point of view of this paper is the major shift in public opinion and the views of consumer organisations from the neutral point O in 1990–92 to point D in 1998. The triggers that drove their motivations into the top right corner of this diagram, rather than the bottom left included a series of events, related and unrelated, and some unfortunate coincidences.

1. INFLUENCES ON PUBLIC OPINION

The Martin and Tait (1992) survey and several others conducted since then asked which sources of information people would trust if they wanted to find out more about biotechnology. At the top of the list were environmental pressure groups and consumer organisations. Low down the list, along with the tabloid press, were industry and government sources. Thus, although members of the public at that time had generally not yet made up their minds about biotechnology, if they did want more information, they would be more likely to trust sources which already had very negative, value-based attitudes to the technology.

2. PUBLIC REQUIREMENTS

Members of the public had indicated in surveys that they were more likely to support the development of GM crops if they could see a public benefit (such as a reduction in the use of pesticides) in addition to commercial benefits for companies. They also indicated that they wanted to be reassured that the new technology was being effectively regulated but were doubtful that it would be (Martin and Tait, 1992).

3. INDUSTRY PERSPECTIVES

Encouraged by the support for deregulation by right-wing governments in Europe and the USA in the early 1990s, industry was pressing strongly for abandonment of the precautionary approach to biotechnology regulation, at least in the case of GM crops. Following several years of trials, these were seen to pose no hazards over and above those of traditionally bred crop varieties.

These pressures succeeded in the USA but were less successful in the EU. Industry set up a high-profile lobby group in Brussels, the Senior Advisory Group for Biotechnology (SAGB), to campaign for the relaxation of the precautionary approach to risk regulation in Europe. An influential report of the House of Lords Select Committee on Science and Technology (1993) also recommended relaxation of the PP on the grounds that it was unnecessarily inhibiting the competitiveness of European companies.

The agrochemical industry in the early 1990s was already experiencing the commercial pressures that are leading to today's spate of mergers and acquisitions and European companies did feel selectively disadvantaged compared to their American counterparts. They had invested heavily in biotechnology and the pay-off period was looking increasingly uncertain. The extent to which the technology has already been adopted in the USA demonstrates that this assessment was correct, although the more precautionary European approach may still prove to have been justified.

The multinational agrochemical companies were also inhibited from promoting GM crops on the sort of basis that the public would like to hear – reduction in the levels of use of pesticides. While it would probably have been in their interests to do this, any suggestion that it was 'a good thing' to promote lower levels of pesticide use would have seriously conflicted with companies' value systems and also with their commercial interests. Monsanto was the only MNC which was not inhibited in this way – its only major pesticide product was a herbicide, glyphosate, and development of herbicide resistant crops would promote rather than inhibit its use.

4. ENVIRONMENTAL PRESSURE GROUP RESPONSES

Up till the early 1990s, Greenpeace had been opposed to biotechnology developments for agriculture but had not adopted an overt campaigning stance. Co-incidentally with publication of the results of surveys showing that they were likely to be an important source of public influence and also with the setting up of SAGB, Greenpeace advertised for its first staff member to lead a campaign against biotechnology.

The campaign stance of environmental pressure groups reflected a value-driven opposition to biotechnology. They argued, for example, that it would result in further intensification of farming systems and even greater reliance on the use of pesticides and fertilisers. Biotechnology also facilitates the control of world food production systems in the hands of multinational companies and this effect is strengthened by vertical integration of production from development and distribution of seeds, through growing of the crops, to their processing and distribution.

Invoking the PP, pressure groups also predicted that GM crops could have a range of damaging effects on beneficial organisms and wildlife both on the farm where they were grown and beyond.

Pressure group campaigns were initially low-key. However, the widely publicised news that bovine spongiform encephalopathy (BSE or 'mad cow disease') could potentially infect humans was used as a powerful and apparently very effective argument in their campaign (Grove White *et al,*

1997). The value-based line of argument was that BSE was the result of careless over-intensification of farming systems; GM crops would result in yet further intensification; and therefore there would be new examples of unpredicted and uncontrollable impacts like BSE arising from GM developments. The fact that Government regulators had claimed for some time that BSE posed no risk to humans undermined public trust in official statements that GM crops were safe and seems to have been at least partly responsible for the shift in public opinion from 'O' to 'D' in Figure 1.

5. THE ROLE OF CONSUMER ORGANISATIONS

For a long time consumer organisations took a much more neutral, interest-based stance on GM crops than the environmental pressure groups. They could envisage potential risks but were happy with the precautionary approach that was being applied in Europe and they could also envisage consumer benefits. The turning point came in March 1998 with a publication from the National Consumer Council (1998) announcing that they were now opposed to GM crops *in principle*, i.e. they had also moved to point 'D' on Figure 1, invoking a similar argument about BSE to that used by environmental groups.

In this case they were following rather than leading public opinion. However, their change of stance seems to have had an important influence in encouraging the environmental groups to raise the profile of their campaigns and may also have encouraged the press to take a stronger interest in the issue.

Once GM crops began to be imported into Europe from the USA the views of consumer organisations became highly influential in the debate over the issue of labeling foods containing GM ingredients. This point could be presented as an interest-based argument but the issues raised during the debate (democratic freedom to avoid food derived from production systems of which consumers disapproved, rather than actual expected risks from its consumption) placed it more strongly in the value-based category.

Even this extensive list of influences on the conflict over the introduction of GM crops in Europe does not do justice to the full complexity of the situation. However it does cover some of its most important features and illustrates some of the most salient interactions.

One important factor has been the formal incorporation of the PP into EU legislation in the context of biotechnology. For many of the regulators involved and for industry managers, this was seen as justified in the early stages of development of the technology on grounds of public reassurance rather than environmental protection. Unfortunately for the trajectory of this conflict, the commercial inconvenience of the PP for industry became unsupportable before its role in public reassurance became obvious. The existence of the PP also enabled pressure groups to bring into the debate about GM crops issues such as the role of intensive farming systems in food production which would not have been legitimate in a strictly risk-based regulatory system. This contributed to shifting the negative public reaction, when it came, onto a value-based rather than a risk-based dimension, making it more difficult to resolve.

As the influence of environmental pressure groups on the press and the public has become stronger and their value-based arguments have been more widely accepted, statements from some groups have become gradually more extreme, less based on conceivable potential risks and taking less account of the risks and benefits of GM crops and of alternative technologies. This is fueling unnecessary public alarm and undermining intelligent debate about important public issues.

The links made between transmission of BSE to humans and the risks of GM crops, which had such an important role in the conflict trajectory, could have been rendered less convincing if not altogether avoidable. BSE arose in a sector of the agriculture industry that was poorly regulated and poorly supervised whereas GM crops had been developed under a highly precautionary regime by an industry that was well accustomed to high levels of regulation. However, by arguing so strongly against the PP in the early 1990s, industry had lost this potential argument from its armoury. Some industry managers will now admit that they left the public relations arena wide open to occupation by environmental pressure groups, allowing the majority of the public to move to a value-based opposition to GM crops. As Table 1 shows, once this situation has been reached, it takes more than an expensive advertising campaign to reverse it.

NEW MODES OF REGULATION

Although not superficially linked to nature conservation, the issues discussed here are very relevant to important decisions at a European and world level which will have a bearing on the part played by nature conservation in all our lives. We are developing new modes of interaction between nature, landscapes and people which owe a major debt to the thinking of those involved with the 1949 Act, and subsequently extended and shaped by many other important actors (some of whom are taking part in this conference). They placed nature conservation firmly on the agenda of a wide range of organisations, particularly those concerned with industry and agriculture.

The challenge today is to find mechanisms to enable us to continue to have a concern for nature conservation, even beyond our national boundaries, in the face of strong economic and industrial pressures against any action which appears to hinder free trade and the processes of globalisation.

There are pressures from some quarters, particularly the USA, for the EU to abandon the PP because it is not based on scientifically demonstrable risks and because it is being used by EU countries to inhibit free trade in GM crops. As indicated above, many of the value-based arguments put forward by pressure groups invoke the PP and refer to the impacts of GM crops in the further intensification of European farming systems and in undermining traditional farming systems in developing countries. These are issues which the PP has allowed to enter into the debate and for which there is currently no alternative forum.

Neither the science-based approach to risk regulation (as exemplified by the case of pesticides) nor the PP (as applied to GM crops) is able to forestall conflict over major technological changes which affect our natural environment and our food production systems. We should expect to engage in a wide ranging public debate about such issues. But the debate will be more constructive and more likely to lead to helpful outcomes if issues are discussed in a more appropriate context.

For example, rapid globalisation of our food production and distribution systems is likely to continue whether or not we allow the development of GM crops. We may see major increases in the extent of organic farming but it is unlikely ever to become economically competitive in the context of globalisation. GM crops may permit globalisation to take place while allowing us to give greater protection to the natural environment and to set aside large areas of countryside to provide wildlife refuges. Pursuit of globalisation without the use of GM crops and other modern technological innovations may result in agricultural systems that are more environmentally damaging than those we have today.

BALANCED PRECAUTION

There is no evidence that abandoning the PP is the answer to developing more constructive public or institutional debate about contentious issues such as the introduction of GM crops. Indeed, we are likely to need to invoke the PP increasingly often, as human impacts on the environment become more complex and more long term, and as the forces of globalisation become stronger and better organised. However, it is clear that we need to learn to use it more effectively than we have done to date.

For example, precautionary regulatory systems do not currently recognise that some predicted outcomes may be more scientifically plausible than others or that some types of scientist may be better placed than others to make specific types of prediction. In the early stages of GM crop development, predictions from ecologists that GM organisms could survive and establish themselves in the wild or could disperse their novel genetic material more widely in the natural environment (Tiedje, 1989) were largely discounted in favour of the views of laboratory based scientists who were much more sanguine about the risks (Kornberg, 1988). However, many of the ecologists' predictions are now being borne out by scientific research. It should be possible to develop guidelines on making a precautionary judgement between different sets of scientific expertise based on the relevance of the expertise to the issue.

We need to become more consistently sceptical in our judgement of human nature. At the moment we are too prone to reject arguments put forward by industry (for example that GM crops will be needed to provide food for a hungry world) and too prone to accept uncritically arguments put forward by environmental pressure groups (for example that GM crops will lead to dramatic reductions in biodiversity on farmed land). We should recognise that each group has its own reasons for exaggerating particular points and attempt to judge the information accordingly. Part of this process will be to discriminate between arguments which are evidence-based and those which are not (including in the latter case those based on the PP): and in both cases to develop methods to assess the extent to which arguments derive from the interests and/or values of protagonists. Such assessments should be more openly taken into account in regulatory and policy decision-making.

We should also indicate clearly where we expect the limits of precaution to be located. For example for GM crops, should we be precautionary only at the early stages of research and development or should we maintain precaution through to the stage of farm level commercial crop production? What constitutes 'precaution' will be different at each stage – how would this be implemented? What would be our criteria for deciding when we can relinquish the PP and will we need to maintain a readiness to re-instate it if any unforeseen events should occur? If the answer to the last question is 'yes', what plans might we have in place? With hindsight, these are the decisions we should have made in the early stages of implementing a precautionary approach to the development of GM crops. We should certainly have them in mind the next time such a need arises.

The above issues could all be subsumed under what I call *balanced precaution* – we need to ensure that all issues about which one ought to be precautionary are considered and treated in a balanced way (Tait, in press). For example in the case of GM crops, why do we accept unconditionally the need to be precautionary about their environmental impacts but reject the need to be precautionary about protecting our food supplies?

SELECTING THE APPROPRIATE LEVEL FOR DEBATE

The most difficult conflict situations often arise where an issue happens to be selected as a proxy for public concerns which have no other forum for discussion. As noted above, the context of GM crops is being used to provoke debate on a set of wider issues to do with the future nature of European farming systems, the role of organic production, and control of world food production and distribution systems, to which the GM issue is related, but not central.

If we want to have a debate about the role of organic food production systems let us investigate in an open-minded way where organic systems could co-exist with farming systems based on GM crops in the same way that they have been co-existing for years with farming systems based on pesticides.

If we want to have a debate about the protection of wildlife within intensive farming systems, let us take an open-minded look at where GM crops would support this overall aim, where they might be incompatible with it, and where they might be neutral.

The World Trade Organisation will soon be opening up a new round of negotiations on the General Agreement on Tariffs and Trade (GATT) in which GM crops are likely to feature prominently. Expected to be on the agenda is the extent to which European nations can protect their distinctive, non-intensive farming systems which preserve particular landscapes and wildlife habitats, and how this can be achieved within a world-wide free-market trading system.

Less attention is being given at the moment to the impact of free market trading conditions on fully competitive, intensive farming systems, how this will affect the crop management decisions of farmers as Common Agricultural Policy supports are gradually withdrawn in Europe, what the resulting landscapes will be and what will be the role of wildlife in such systems. These issues need to be discussed in their own right and in their full complexity, not as an adjunct to pressure group and industry agendas on GM crops. There is an urgent need to foster intelligent public debate about these higher-level issues.

REFERENCES

Chataway, J. and J. Tait (1993). Management of agriculture-related biotechnology: constraints on innovation. *Technology Analysis and Strategic Management 5(4)*: 345–367.

Gervers, J. H. (1987). The NIMBY Syndrome: is it Inevitable? *Environment 29(8)*: 18–20.

Grove-White, R., P. Macnaughten, S. Mayer, B. Wynne (1997). *Uncertain World: Genetically Modified Organisms, Food and Public Attitudes in Britain*. Lancaster University, March 1997.

House of Lords Select Committee on Science and Technology (1993). *Regulation of the United Kingdom Biotechnology Industry and Global Competitiveness*, 7th Report, Session 1992/93. London: HMSO HL Paper 80–I

Jasanoff, S. (1990). *The Fifth Branch: Science Advisers as Policy Makers*. Cambridge, Massachusetts, Harvard University Press.

Jennings, D. M. *et. al.* (1975). Organophosphorus poisoning: a comparative study of the toxicity of carbophenothion to the Canada goose, the pigeon and the Japanese quail. *Pesticide Science 6*: 245–257.

Kornberg, Sir Hans (1988). Opening Remarks. *The Release of Genetically Engineered Microorganisms*. M. Sussman, C.H. Collins, F.A. Skinner and D.E. Stewart-Tull(eds.), pp 1–5).

Levidow, L. (1994). *Contested Rationality: Early Regulation of GMO Releases in Britain*. Ph.D. Thesis, Centre for Technology Strategy. Milton Keynes, Open University.

Martin, S. and J. Tait (1992). Attitudes of selected public groups in the UK to biotechnology. *Biotechnology in Public: a review of recent research*. J. Durrant. London, Science Museum for the European Federation of Biotechnology: 28–41.

Moore, N. W. (1987). *The Bird of Time: the Science and Politics of Nature Conservation*. Cambridge, Cambridge University Press.

National Consumer Council (1998). *Farm Policies and our Food: the Need for Change*. London, National Consumer Council, March 1998, PD11/B2/98.

RCEP (1988). *Best Practicable Environmental Option*. London, HMSO.

RCEP (1989). *Thirteenth Report: the Release of Genetically Engineered Organisms to the Environment*. London, HMSO.

Scottish Natural Heritage (1993). *Sustainable Development and the Natural Heritage: the SNH Approach*. Perth, Scottish Natural Heritage.

Stringer, A. and C. H. Lyons (1974). The effect of benomyl and thiophanate methyl on earthworm populations in apple orchards. *Pesticide Science 5*: 189–196.

Tait, J. (1988). NIMBY and NIABY: Public perception of biotechnology. *International Industrial Biotechnology 8(6)*: 5–9.

Tait, J. and L. Levidow (1992). Proactive and reactive approaches to risk regulation: the case of biotechnology. *Futures (April 1992)*: 219–231.

Tait, J. and P. Pitkin (1995). The role of new technology in promoting sustainable agricultural development. *Integrated crop protection: towards sustainability*. R. G. McKinlay and D. Atkinson, British Crop Protection Council. Symposium Proceedings no 63: 339–346.

Tait, J. (in press, 2001). More Faust than Frankenstein: the European debate about risk regulation for genetically modified crops. *Journal of Risk Research*.

Tiedje, R.K. *et al.* (1989). The planned introduction of genetically engineered organisms: ecological considerations and recommendations. *Ecology, 70(2)*, 298–315.

von Moltke, K. (1987). *The Vorsorgeprinzip in West German Environmental Policy*. London, Institute for European Environmental Policy.

13

Can Ecologists Recreate Habitats and Restore Absent Species?

J. A. Thomas

INTRODUCTION

THE AIM OF this paper is to consider the opportunities that may exist, as ecological knowledge increases, to restore declining species to new sites in the UK, to re-establish extinct species, and to recreate on degraded land, ecosystems that achieve functional parity with the most valued examples of their kind elsewhere in Britain.

CHANGING ATTITUDES TO HABITAT AND SPECIES RESTORATION

The high importance placed on habitat and species restoration in the current strategies of both government and non-statutory UK agencies (and those of many other countries) marks a fundamental shift in philosophy following the Rio summit of 1992. This change is still resented by some individual conservationists who consider that it interferes with the 'naturalness' of nature. Yet in reality, it represents little more than the culmination of a trend in the acceptability of human interference from the predominantly non-interventionist policies that dominated the early years of nature conservation.

The greatest achievement of the founding fathers of modern conservation – led by Charles Rothschild, the Society for the Promotion of Nature Reserves, the National Trust and the Royal Society for the Protection of Birds – was to establish the concept that the finest representative sites of every type of 'natural community' in the British Isles should be preserved as nature reserves for future generations to enjoy (Rothschild & Marren, 1997). They began putting this idea into practice from the late nineteenth century onwards, until the untimely death of Rothschild in 1923 created a hiatus that was to last for a quarter of a century. To these early conservationists, human interference on the land was seen almost entirely as a detrimental activity. Tellingly, their newly established reserves were often referred to as 'preserves', and on most sites a strict policy of non-intervention was established to allow nature to flourish in a natural way. The results were sometimes disastrous. Many valued species and communities were quickly lost from the early reserves, the scrubbing over of Wood Walton Fen being one of the more dramatic examples.

Rothschild's vision of establishing a network of representative nature reserves was eventually implemented on a national scale following the foundation in 1949 of the Nature Conservancy (NC). By then, the new discipline of Ecology had become established within Biology, and Tansley's concepts of succession and semi-natural communities were increasingly accepted. Such ideas, together with the loss of species from early nature reserves, led the more perceptive officers in the NC to realise that many ecosystems were dynamic and that active management by man would be required to maintain the valued communities of wildlife for which each reserve had been established. These fledgling ideas caused Max Nicholson, with considerable foresight, to establish within his Nature Conservancy a research arm manned by ecologists whose remit was to provide a scientific basis for the conservation of British wildlife. By the late 1960s, these scientists outnumbered the executive staff in the Nature Conservancy, and the (generally harmonious) cross-fertilisation of ideas and their application between scientist and practitioner was both effective and much admired and imitated by conservation bodies throughout the world. Indeed, in my view, the most serious weakening of the conservation movement in the UK during the second half of the twentieth century came not from the division of NCC into agencies but from the loss of NC's research branch in 1972. This divorce between scientists and practitioners resulted, on the one hand, in a gradual reduction of exposure of NCC officers to new (or indeed established) ideas in ecology while, on the other hand, the programmes of UK ecologists often became more theoretical, less focussed on answering the problems faced by conservationists, and their hypotheses were seldom subjected to large-scale long-term testing in the field as had occurred when applied to conservation projects.

It is beyond the scope of this paper to explore the concept of 'naturalness' in UK ecosystems, except to report that a recurring conclusion from the two decades of the research by NC ecologists (and others such as Oliver Rackham in Cambridge and many abroad) was that most terrestrial ecosystems throughout the British Isles have been shaped by man's activities to a degree that would have surprised even Tansley and his fellow ecologists. A similar situation is now recognised throughout most sub-boreal and sub-montane regions of the Palaearctic. For example, we now accept that several grassland SSSI's existed as arable land during the Napoleonic wars; that the Norfolk Broads are artefacts created by the flooding of ancient peat diggings; and that lowland heathland, as now classified, was created through Roman and prehistoric woodland clearings.

More recently, Warren (1993) demonstrated that 42% of the current prime calcareous sites for butterflies consist of artefacts such as embankments and abandoned quarries, and that 86% of the key sites for fritillaries and other woodland species were not ancient broad-leaved woodland but modern conifer plantations, admittedly often planted on ancient woodland sites; the few populations inhabiting broadleaved woods had generally persisted only where traditional management practices, such as annual coppicing, had been maintained. Similarly, I demonstrated that one sixth of the UK butterfly species appear to have been wholly dependent on man-managed sites since records began, about 200 years ago (Thomas, 1993). I suggested that these and other ground-dwelling invertebrates may have been living 'artificially' for the past few thousand years (= generations) several hundred kilometres further north than their 'natural' climatic range-limits, due to the unnatural abundance of very warm, early successional micro-habitats that was created on most downs, heaths and in woods by traditional forms of agriculture and woodmanship. Furthermore, I suggested that many terrestrial insects (and perhaps other taxa) have become adapted to the spatial and temporal dynamics of antique anthropomorphic habitats, following exposure (and often restriction) to them for perhaps a few thousand generations. This would explain why a high proportion of the UK insects studied to date are much more sedentary than ecological theory predicts, spreading, in the case of the slowest butterflies, by no more than 1 km a decade (= 100 metres per generation) when introduced to unoccupied landscapes containing an abundance of their optimum habitat. In particular, the dispersal behaviour of those butterfly species that traditionally bred in the ground layer of coppice woodland may have become adapted to a situation whereby their short-lived habitat patches were, for over a thousand generations, annually recreated in adjoining blocks within every woodland, requiring the adults seldom to fly more than a few metres in order to track the creation of new patches of habitat. In ecological terms, UK (and Palaearctic) conservationists may have to cope with the problem of conserving, in modern landscapes, populations of extreme *r*-selected species (see Gimingham and Usher, this volume) whose life-history traits are adapted to exploiting ephemeral habitat patches, yet which have evolved in their sedentariness one attribute that is characteristic of an extreme *K*-selected species (Thomas, 1991).

I conclude that many assemblages, communities, and even species, have been shaped by human practices through prehistory and history. I therefore have few philosophical problems with the policies of interference that are implicit in both the UK national and local Biodiversity Action Plans (BAPs). It is worth noting, however, how ambitious are the goals set in BAPs and how radical a shift they represent in recent attitudes. For example, in my early career in the 1970s, most colleagues were content to dig ponds and plant trees – and accepted RSPB constructions to attract avocets to Mimsmere – yet rejected most other forms of habitat creation as artificial tampering or gardening, dismissing the results, if wild flower seed were sown, as the creation of no more than an empty floral facsimile of a real ecosystem. Today the current BAP to which Government is committed (Anon, 1994) instructs UK agencies to restore many declining species to former sites and, for example, to implement such ambitious goals for ecosystems as:

- *Reed beds*:   'Create 1200 ha of new reed bed on land of low [current] nature conservation value by 2010'
- *Saline lagoons* 'Create, by the year 2010, sufficient lagoon habitat to offset losses over the last 50 years'.
- *Fen*   'Initiate rehabilitation at priority fen sites by the year 2005 . . . ensure appropriate water quality and water quantity for the continued existence of all SSSI/ASSI fens'
- *Heathland*   'Encourage re-establishment of a further 6000 ha of heathland'

My prime concern is not whether these are appropriate goals but whether they are tractable given current ecological knowledge. Is it really possible to create, say on arable land, fully functional ecosystems of a defined and valued type? Under what circumstances can one expect to succeed in restoring absent species to sites from which they have disappeared?

THE RE-ESTABLISHMENT OF EXTINCT SPECIES

In practical terms, it is useful to distinguish between three types of reintroduction: viz. those involving species for which there is still an abundance of habitat in the countryside, but which declined as a result of pesticides or pollution; those for which there also remains an abundance of habitat, but which were over-hunted to extinction as sport or were specifically persecuted as pests because they were thought to compete with sporting or other interests; and those involving species that were lost primarily because their habitats deteriorated or disappeared.

The recovery of the sparrowhawk, the peregrine falcon and other species in the first group has been one of the success stories of twentieth-century conservation. It is described in this volume by Norman Moore, the leader of this science-based project. By and large, affected species were sufficiently mobile and fecund to reoccupy vacant habitats within two decades after the pollutants causing their decline had been identified and withdrawn. In only a few species, such as the otter, have a combination of low initial densities, a low intrinsic rate of increase, social traits and more fragmented habitat made it desirable to introduce groups artificially to former localities.

The second group of species is small but includes most of the large spectacular vertebrates that became extinct in historical times, notably wild boar, beaver, wolf, bear, lynx and certain large birds of prey. Both ecological research and practice suggest that there is considerable scope to re-establish most or all of these species in the British Isles, merely by releasing into vacant habitats groups of individuals that are large enough to establish socially coherent populations. Considerable political and ecological skills may be required to achieve the initial establishment, but after perhaps for a year or two supplementary feeding, all that may be needed thereafter is limited protection from persecution. The accidental establishment of at least two wild boar population in English woods (albeit slightly diluted by breeding with domestic pigs), and the successful re-establishment of sea-eagles to Scotland, of goshawks and of red kites to three English regions, one population of which reared more than 290 chicks in 1998–99 (Anon, 1999), are testimony to the large areas of vacant habitat that exist for extinct vertebrates in the British countryside. In central Europe, even lynx and wolf populations have been successfully restored to the Alps (Bretenmoser, 1998). Lynx, in particular, have capitalised on the large increase in deer populations that resulted in these wooded landscapes from the abandonment of much upland pasture and hay meadow, and their subsequent succession to scrublands. Farmers require compensation for the loss of livestock, but these secretive predators have caused few other problems, apart from their need for protection from human hunters. A sea-change is required before public perceptions in the UK match those of the rest of Europe, enabling either lynx or wolf to be restored to the British mainland. However, their habitats appear to be present and, if established, might benefit forestry by reducing the current high populations of small deer species, particularly munjack and sika. These may be pipe dreams. Nevertheless, I strongly advocate the restoration of wild boar and beaver populations to Britain, not just as attractive animals in their own sakes but because both are keystone species (Simberloff, 1998) whose activities impact significantly on their environment. Their return would restore fascinating communities to certain biotopes that have been missing from Britain since medieval times.

Unfortunately, the great majority of declining or extinct species listed in UK BAPs are believed to have declined because of habitat loss. For these species, the track record of reintroduction is poor (Hodder & Bullock, 1997). For example, Oates and Warren (1990) showed that 26% of butterfly introductions failed within three years, and that only 6% persisted for more than ten years. Moreover, with this and other taxa, many of the original losses occurred from Nature Reserves and SSSIs, usually for unknown reasons. In an early analysis (Thomas, 1991), I cited the recent local extinction of eleven scarce or rare species of butterfly that had been breeding in the 157 ha broad-leaved woodland of Monks Wood when it was established as a NNR. Similar examples are to be found for most ecosystems. It is hardly surprising that reintroductions of species have generally failed, when the causes of the original decline were so little understood that it proved impossible to maintain existing populations on nature reserves. Yet this is not an intractable problem. Clearly, current funding (and the supply of competent ecologists) is inadequate for every species listed in BAPs to be intensively studied for the two-five years usually needed before the cause of a decline is identified. Instead, I believe that an increase in targeted research would lead to the establishment of more general rules to solve the problem. The success, to date, of the reintroduction of the large blue butterfly illustrates some of the reasons for my optimism.

The large blue is famed for its beauty, rarity, and for a highly specialised life-style that involves feeding briefly as a larva on the flowers of wild thyme before living underground for ten months as a social parasite inside the nests of red (*Myrmica*) ants. Although formerly known from about a hundred British sites, the butterfly had been in almost continuous decline since records began. Each of a wide variety of conservation measures taken since the 1920s failed to save it, even though the dependency on red ants was known. The enigma (as with many insects) was that even the strongest populations of large blue would inexplicably go extinct when no change was apparent in either its metapo-pulation structure or, within sites, in the general habitat or in the abundance of thyme and *Myrmica*. As a last resort, intensive ecological research was initiated in the 1970s on the final small population. This revealed (as with many insects) that the requirements of the larvae were more specialised than had been realised (Thomas, 1994). Larvae were adapted to survive with only one of the four similar-looking species of *Myrmica* that commonly foraged beneath thyme on large blue sites, and this ant, *Myrmica sabuleti*, had virtually disappeared from UK sites. The cause had been a reduction in the traditional heavy grazing of these sites after this form of agriculture became uneconomic, exacerbated by the loss of rabbits through myxomatosis. *M.sabuleti* requires warmer soil during spring and autumn than other species of *Myrmica*, and under British climates suitable conditions exist only when the sward is short enough for the sun's rays to penetrate to the ground.

It took five years of intensive research to elicit these simple facts, and a further five years before altered management plans delivered large populations of *Myrmica sabuleti*. Unfortunately, by then the last population of the butterfly was extinct. A re-establishment programme was soon devised, and by 1983 the large blue had been introduced from Sweden and was again flying on a British site. After sixteen generations, this population still thrives. Since then, the project has expanded and currently involves thirteen organisations and more than 70 individuals. By 1999 the butterfly had been introduced, or had spread, to a further eight sites, where informed management had again resulted in high densities of *M. sabuleti*. To date, two of these introductions have failed to establish, but others formed large populations that have persisted at high densities for up to seven years.

Considering the time and effort required to re-establish the large blue, what hope is there for the hundreds of other unstudied species listed in UK BAPs? There are two grounds for optimism. First, the technical lessons and insights from this and other projects means that autecological research can be more selective than hitherto, and hence quicker, cheaper and more effective. Secondly, the most important lesson from the large blue is that its conservation resulted in the restoration of a particular type of habitat – unusually warm, but not xerophyllic, grassland on certain well-drained acidic and calcareous soils – that had always been rare in UK and north European biotopes, and which had almost disappeared in the twentieth century. Not surprisingly, the restoration of this warm-soiled grassland benefited a wide variety of other thermophilous species, several of which are listed on BAPs. For example, on the more acidic sites, the rare pale heath violet, *Viola lactea* has increased by about one hundred-fold in the areas managed for the large blue, as have other violet species. As a result, four scarce and listed species of fritillary butterfly which feed on violets have either colonised or increased in density by seven to ten-fold on these sites; elsewhere during the same period up to 50% of their populations became extinct and those that survived typically declined to 5–50% of former densities. Similar increases on large blue sites occurred in the grayling butterfly, a tiger beetle, and a rare cockroach and bee-fly, and one site was colonised by the wood lark, an endangered bird with a similar habitat to the large blue. Recent research suggests that the restoration of 'large blue habitat' on the Atlantic coast of Cornwall may also enable the chough to be re-introduced there; and so on. In short, ecological theory and experience suggest that the restoration of conditions for one declining species will almost inevitably benefit associated species of a similar functional type, which had been declining for the same general reason. This gives hope that obtaining the knowledge needed to re-establish all the species listed on UK BAPs will be less onerous than these lengthy lists suggest.

THE RESTORATION OF ECOSYSTEMS

It is not such a large step, from restoring the habitat of a single endangered species and finding one has created conditions for a wide variety of associated wildlife, to aiming to restore a listed ecosystem from the outset. Recent attempts to create wetlands, heathland and mesotrophic and calcareous grassland suggest that it is indeed becoming possible, given sufficient resources and time, to achieve fully-functioning replicas of certain semi-natural eco-systems on former sites that had been fundamentally changed, for example on intensively farmed arable land (Urbanska & Grodzińska, 1995, Urbanska *et al*, 1997). No-one, however, is yet claiming the ability to restore ancient woodland, with its saproxylic (rotting wood) communities, at least within a time-scale of decades rather than centuries.

This potential is illustrated by the restoration of species-rich chalk grassland to Twyford Down following the construction of the M3 motorway (Snazell, 1998). Contrary to popular belief, Twyford Down was predominantly an arable field, that had been ploughed and fertilised for decades before the motorway was constructed. Early surveys confirmed that these arable fields were typically bereft of wildlife, although about 0.15 ha of species-rich calcareous grassland lay elsewhere along the proposed route. With the construction of the M3 (and in response to environmental protesters), an opportunity arose to attempt to restore downland of similar quality to that on the neighbouring St Catherine's Hill SSSI, both to the arable land that was not consumed by the motorway cutting and along 3km of the redundant route of the former Winchester by-pass.

Fuller details of this project are given by Morris *et al* (1994), Snazell (1998) and Thomas *et al* (2000). Three restoration sites were designed, totalling nine ha. The former cutting of the Winchester bypass was filled with more than a million tons of chalk rubble, shaped to match its original contours and coated with a thin layer of unfertilised top-soil. In contrast, the arable land was stripped of most of its enriched top-soil, and in places the remainder was harrowed into the bedrock. From the outset, considerable heterogeneity of microhabitats within the proposed grassland was planned, involving a variety of soil depths, ranging from thin to skeletal, distributed over a range of aspects and micro-topographical features. Since the preservation of the chalkhill blue and other butterflies of St Catherine's Hill had been the focus of much environmental protest, we sought especially to create new areas of habitat not only for every species of butterfly currently found on that SSSI but also for some rarer species that had disappeared from it earlier this century. The calcareous grassland on the motorway route was retrieved using a tractor-mounted turf cutter, designed to extract large (2.4 x 1.2 m) turves, cut to the depth of the bedrock. These were relocated, in a variety of formations, on appropriate aspects on one restoration site. These, however, occupied a small area, and 96% of land, including the whole of two restoration sites, was seeded with mixtures of calcareous plant seed, designed to match the communities on

St Catherine's SSSI. Much seed was collected from that SSSI, the rest being of local provenance. The precise mixture varied locally within each restoration site, according to the variety of microhabitat planned for each spot. Six characteristic species of plant that were known to be difficult to establish from seed were also introduced as rooted plantlets, again of local provenance.

Five to seven years after the initial construction, the restorations appear to have succeeded. All but one species of calcareous plant found on the neighbouring SSSI appears to be established on the former arable land and along the route of the by-pass, including several species that were not in the seed mix. These include an abundance of orchids (another focus of the anti-road protest): although, to date, only pyramidal and spotted orchid have spread through the seeded areas, the appearance of several frog orchid in the translocated turf – a species not previously recorded in it before translocation – was another welcome addition to the plant list of Twyford Down. More importantly, after an initial period when a few plants dominated, the relative abundance of different species' populations soon resembled that of ancient calcareous grassland.

Despite its attractiveness, the real test of this restoration is whether it supports characteristic communities of invertebrates and other wildlife that were not introduced, except possibly within the turf to a small part of one site. Fortunately, this project is unusual in that its budget allowed for most taxa to be monitored, including the butterflies, beetles, bugs, grasshoppers, ants and other hymenoptera, spiders and molluscs. These groups show the same pattern of success as the plants, including on the sites that received no turf. Not only has every species of butterfly that inhabits St Catherines' SSSI established separate (additional) populations on one or more of the restoration areas, but two species that had disappeared from the SSSI have also colonised the new habitats. Thus, not only are the two celebrated populations of chalkhill blue within the SSSI undiminished since the M3 was opened, they are now supplemented by two additional populations on the restoration sites, and between 1% and 5% of adults disperse between the four colonies each year, theoretically adding stability to the metapopulation of this species in the region. More generally, we can apply to these restoration sites the current scoring system, devised by the NCC, to provide an objective assessment of whether a site is of adequate quality to be classed as a SSSI (Anon, 1989). This gives 100 points for a Red Data Book species, 50 for a Nationally Notable species, and so on, with a total of 200 points being the threshold for consideration as a SSSI. To date the restoration areas on Twyford Down exceed this threshold score by an order of magnitude, with the invertebrates alone totalling 3350 points. It is recognised that these areas are situated near strong source populations for many invertebrates; also, that intensive sampling of the finest UK sites generally produces scores of this magnitude, or greater, for invertebrates. Nevertheless, these results suggest that the restored grasslands on Twyford Down are far from being an attractive floral facsimile, but within five years of establishment support a diversity of characteristic wildlife that matches those of ancient semi-natural ecosystems of the same type.

CONCLUSION

Species and habitat restoration is a rapidly developing branch of conservation throughout the developed world. Enough successful examples exist, encompassing a variety of species and ecosystems, to suggest that this approach will play a major role in future conservation strategies (Urbanska *et al*, 1997). Although priority should still be given to conserving existing ecosystems and species' populations, restoration schemes can complement them. At present most restoration projects are expensive and time-consuming, but costs are rapidly being reduced as techniques improve and can be applied on greater scales, and as experience and ecological knowledge increases. Having witnessed a large variety of restoration schemes over the past decade, I conclude with four observations: i) With increased knowledge and resources, I believe that valuable examples of most, but not necessarily all, types of ecosystem and species' populations can be restored to degraded land. In many cases this is already possible. ii) Certain gaps in ecological knowledge make several goals in current UK BAPs untenable pending further research. iii) Despite genuine gaps in knowledge, I am disappointed that so many restoration schemes are being started with little or no ecological input in the plan or design. Much current knowledge is being ignored to the great detriment of projects. iv) Ecologists, too, would greatly benefit from involvement in restoration schemes, which offer unparalleled opportunities to test new ideas on scales that would otherwise be impossible.

REFERENCES

Anon. (1989). *Guidelines for selection of biological SSSIs.* Nature Conservancy Council, Peterborough.
Anon. (1994). *Biodiversity: the UK Action Plan.* HMSO, London.
Anon. (1999). Kites move north. *English Nature magazine* **45**: 10–11.
Breitenmoser, U. (1998). Large predators in the alps: the fall and rise of man's competitors. *Biological Conservation* **83**: 279–290.
Hodder, K.H. & Bullock, J.M. (1997). Translocations of native species in the UK: implications for biodiversity. *Journal of Applied Ecology* **34**: 547–565.
Oates, M.R. & Warren, M.S. (1990). *A review of butterfly introductions in Britain.* WWF, Godalming.
Rothschild, M. & Marren, P. (1997). *Rothschild's reserves.* Harley Books, Colchester.

Simberloff, D. (1998). Flagships, umbrellas, and keystone species: is single-species management passé in the landscape era? *Biological Conservation* **83**: 247–258.

Thomas, J.A. (1991). Rare species conservation: case studies of European butterflies. In *The scientific management of temperate communities for conservation*. Eds. Spellerberg, I., Goldsmith, B. & Morris, M.G. *BES Symposium* **29**: 149–197. Blackwells, Oxford.

Thomas, J.A. (1993). Holocene climate change and warm man-made refugia may explain why a sixth of British butterflies inhabit unnatural early-successional habitats. *Ecography* **16**: 278–284.

Thomas, J.A. (1994). The ecology and conservation of *Maculinea arion* and other European species of large blue. In *Ecology and conservation of butterflies* Ed. Pullin, A., Chapman & Hall, London: Chapter **13**: 180–196.

Thomas, J.A., Snazell, R.S. & Ward, L.K. (2001). Are roads harmful or potentially beneficial to butterflies and other insects? In *The impact of roads on wildlife*. Ed. by J.A. Burton. *Symposium of the Linnean Society.*

Urbanska, K.M. & Grodzińska, K. (1995). *Restoration ecology in Europe.* Geobotanisal Institute SFIT, Zürich.

Urbanska, K.M., Webb, N.R. & Edwards, P.J. (1997). *Restorable ecology and sustainable devlopment.* Cambridge University press, Cambridge.

Warren, M.S. (1993). A review of butterfly conservation in central southern Britain II: site management and habitat selection of key species. *Biological Conservation* **64**: 37–50.

14

Recreation and Conservation in the Countryside: Policy Challenges

Nigel Curry

CHANGING POLICY PREOCCUPATIONS FOR RECREATION AND CONSERVATION SINCE THE 1949 ACT

NOTIONS OF CONSERVATION in the 1949 Act were fairly clear cut. Nature conservation was the province of specialists. These elements of the Bill were passed through Parliament unscathed since few felt that they had the received knowledge to dispute them. The proposed agency infrastructure was to be discrete, staffed by scientists and was concerned with designating and managing defined areas considered to be of important scientific value. Amenity (as it was termed at the time) on the other hand, was a concept about which everyone had, or felt that they ought to have, a view. The actual location of designated areas here, National Parks and AONBs, was hotly debated (Blunden and Curry, 1990).

Elements of this distinction have endured to the present day. Scientific conservation has developed against internationally measurable benchmarks that have allowed global protocols (for example the World Conservation Strategy) and European Directives to be produced at regular intervals defining, in policy terms, a comprehensive value system for the custodianship of nature. Amenity, perhaps more recently tagged 'landscape conservation', has remained apart from this. For these aesthetic conservation values, supranational Directives have remained notably absent. In part this is because value systems are much more subjective in this area, but essentially such values have much to do with local distinctiveness: they provide the antitheses in value terms of internationally measurable benchmarks. The fact that everyone had a view about them has perhaps also inhibited a common consensus value. As a result of the precise nature of scientific conservation and the amorphous nature of landscape conservation, the former has fully occupied centre stage in respect of policy priorities.

Three key elements of these post-war conceptions of conservation, however, have shifted radically in policy rhetoric since that time. Firstly, the notion that conservation should be the province, in policy terms, of designated areas only, has been dismantled. The implication that those areas not so designated were of no value at all, had to be overcome. Conceptions of a more pervasive conservation ethos now prevail. Designated areas have given way to notions of conservation of all parts of the wider countryside as a more integrated system (Selman and Wragg, 1999).

Secondly, hand in hand with a shift in the designation/non-designation distinction, the dividing line between amenity and scientific conservation also is being blurred. Disciplines such as landscape ecology have grown to develop thinking in this area (Forman, 1995) but in policy terms the substitution of this old language with the rhetoric of sustainable development has allowed conservation to be embraced more holistically in a wider set of guiding principles for sensitive development and custodianship (Adams, 1996). 'Conservation' is being displaced by 'environment', which itself is only part of sustainability.

The third element of change in the conservation ethos, which is considered more fully later in this chapter, has been an attempt in many ways to 'demystify' the province of conservation and to allow a greater public or 'lay' voice in the influence of policy. In setting down principles for sustainable development the Bruntland Report (WECD, 1987) in particular extolled the virtues of the devolution of responsibility to the wider community. The subsequent Earth Summit in Rio formalised this exhortation into a commitment to the development of Local Agenda 21 programmes where local populations were given the opportunity (and the responsibility) to be more deterministic in the shaping of their local environmental destiny (UNCED, 1992).

Conceptions of recreation have oscillated quite starkly in terms of policy concern since the 1949 Act. This Act was preoccupied with *access*. In introducing the Statutory Rights of Way system and Definitive Maps, it fundamentally shifted the rights of citizens to access over private land, without compensation. This was a concern, therefore, to alter legal rights structures. *Recreation* in the Act, which is the consideration of public enjoyment, was more blandly extolled as an opportunity, for those who wanted it, dominantly in the new National Parks (even AONBs, let alone the wider countryside, specifically excluded recreation objectives in their remit).

Whilst the Rights of Way system has developed falteringly ever since the Act, the perceived growth in the consumption of rural leisure during the 1950s and 1960s brought policies for recreation to the fore. The 1968 Countryside Act introduced a comprehensive national network of managed recreation sites, country parks and picnic sites, to allow public enjoyment, but in a controlled way. Lip service to access was manifest only in the requirement to signpost and waymark rights of way in recognition that much of the general public did not actually know where they were.

Consumer surveys during the 1970s and 1980s, however, showed clearly that these managed recreation areas were not what people wanted. From the late 1980s it was recognised that access to the wider unmanaged countryside could only really be met by the now creaking Rights of Way system. This has become the clear policy preoccupation since that time, crowned, in terms of this concern for access rights generally, with the proposed introduction of the rights of access to open country in England and Wales. Recreation as public enjoyment has been subsumed under different policy imperatives: as a vehicle for exploiting community involvement (Millennium Greens), for integration with environmental objectives (Greenways) or as a component part of rural tourism, which has moved up the policy agenda because of its potential for employment creation and income generation as well as for enjoyment.

Despite all of these changing policy interpretations of the notions of conservation and recreation since 1949, there has been a structural inertia in the organisation of governance. The integration of English Nature (nature conservation) and the Countryside Commission (amenity conservation) was successfully resisted in England (though not in Scotland and Wales) during the early 1990s. The changing portfolios of government Ministries (for example the emergence of MAFF as a player in the environmental and recreation area from the late 1980s) have not led to a reconceptualisation of how such responsibilities should be organised. Perhaps the only accession in this area has been in the merging of the Countryside Commission (responsible for recreation and access) and the Rural Development Commission (responsible for rural tourism). Here, for the first time, the access and recreation functions have been administratively separated with the formation of two branches, for access on the one hand and recreation and tourism on the other, in the new Countryside Agency.

CHANGES IN GOVERNANCE:
THE GROWTH IN COMMUNITY PARTICIPATION

These maturations of the interpretation of the meanings of conservation and recreation in public policy since 1949 have taken place in tandem with much broader shifts in the very nature of government itself. These shifts have had a significant impact in the way in which conservation and recreation polices have been developed and implemented. As Lowe *et al* (1995) have noted, from the early 1980s, but particularly during the 1990s, the post-war notions of the welfare state, equity, industrial efficiency and international security have given way to new sets of political concerns to do with citizenship, competitiveness and globalisation. This may be in part an inevitable consequence of a mature democracy placing more rights and responsibilities on its citizens and less on the state (Etzioni, 1995). Certainly, though, it is common to view government as shifting from an 'executive' to an 'enabling' role (LGMB, 1991): from government to governance (Burns *et al* 1994).

As a trigger to this new policy style, members of the 'global' society have become more individualistic, but rather than creating a self-centred culture, this has led to a desire on the part of the population at large to find new expressions of social cohesion and social involvement (Giddens, 1998). Globalisation, too, has loosened associations with the nation state and has led individuals to identify, in part, with supra-national organisations such as the European Union, in order to be globally visible. Dominantly, however, a desire to associate with the more local and to appreciate and celebrate local distinctiveness has become a central part of this global culture (Adams, 1996). Governments have responded to these natural consequences of globalisation – new forms of social commitment and at a devolved and more local level – by acknowledging and even institutionalising the potential of communities themselves, with the state acting as an enabler, to become actively involved in decision-making and implementation in rural areas.

Earlier moves in this direction had been crystallised by the mid -1990s in the 1995 Rural White Paper for England (Department of the Environment, 1995). Introduced under a Conservative administration, this championed the cause of community participation approaches generally for rural areas. The White Paper stressed the traditional strengths of rural communities in respect of independence and self-help (Lowe, 1996). It was clearly asserted that rural decision-making would be more responsive to local circumstances than to uniform plans and that quality of life started with local people and local initiative (Hodge, 1996).

The focus for local decision-making was not now to be local government but rather, rural communities themselves. The role of central government was characterised as working in partnership with local people, developing resource effective and 'enabling' policies rather than imposing 'top down' solutions. The state was to help communities to help themselves through the diffusion of best practice. As Murdoch (1997) notes, this was a clear statement of government moving away from its managerialist or 'executive' role. That such a change in governance is an all-party phenomenon is borne out by the Labour Government's deliberations over a second Rural White Paper for England. In its recent discussion document *Rural England* (MAFF, DETR, 1999), the consultative phase of the new Rural White Paper, the principles of partnership working are commended. It clearly acknowledges that decisions on rural issues are best taken at the local level.

Such community involvement has now become more than exhortation in policy. National Planning Policy Guidance for Scotland, for example (NPPG

15, Rural Development, Scottish Office, 1999), now *requires* that development plans for countryside areas have to be reconciled with strategies developed by local communities. Planning authorities must work with local communities to outline ways that land should be used in general terms to promote economic, environmental and social well-being. The community planning approach is to ensure that rural development strategies take full account of community aspirations. Community participation is not now merely encouraged by government, but would appear to be a mandatory element in the development of rural policies and plans.

The formalisation, or indeed post-rationalisation of this new style of governance, embraced in the broader notion of 'Third Way' politics (Giddens, 1998), is a much more recent phenomenon than the growth of acts of 'Community Participation' (CP), in conservation, the environment and recreation. Their genesis, according to Gittins (1993) predates the current policy concern and even contemporary notions of citizenship and social cohesion induced by globalisation. They were rather, part of a deeply held and very British idea of 'getting involved' in voluntary work. He cites the British Trust for Conservation Volunteers (BTCV – formed as the Conservation Corps in 1959) as a foundation stone in this post-war movement, formed as a voluntary organisation for practical conservation work in National Nature Reserves and Sites of Special Scientific Interest (designated under the 1949 Act), but broadening its base to include education and practical tasks for the wider countryside in 1964.

The Council for Europe's European Conservation year in 1970 induced further conservation action through CP and by this time had embraced the commercial sector in such development. Shell UK (with grass roots action from the Women's Institute) funded a scheme to encourage school children to participate in active projects to improve the environment. Other long-standing organisations, too, (for example County Wildlife Trusts, the Ramblers' Association, the National Trust and the Inland Waterways Recovery Group) were exploiting voluntary action systematically by this time and the Rural Community Councils, through their annual 'Best Kept Village' competition, were leading a range of parish-based initiatives.

During the 1980s, these community aspirations became more widely endorsed by the commercial sector, still in the absence of any coherent policy framework from Government. The Shell Better Britain Campaign (driven by BTCV and the Civic Trust, although with endorsement from the then Nature Conservancy Council) supported local practical action by volunteers, to improve the environment. This induced, among others, Sainsbury's, Marks and Spencer, British Gas, Esso and ICI into funding local communities for direct action projects for environmental and social purposes.

Formal governmental action in this area was as much responsive as ideologically based. Indeed, early involvement was experimental. Some 17 projects were set up by the (then) Countryside Commission running from 1985 to 1989 under the programme Community Action for the Rural Environment (CARE). These were formalised by the (then) Department of the Environment into the programme Rural Action for the Environment in September 1992, where three rural agencies, the Countryside Commission, the Rural Development Commission and English Nature, committed an annual budget of £400,000 each to a programme of action 'to help people living in the English countryside care for their own local environment' (Bovaird *et al*, 1994). This formalisation of CP in rural policy in England was taking place in tandem with similar international initiatives such as Local Agenda 21 programmes (UNCED, 1992) and a range of commensurate European projects such as the LEADER programmes (Chanan, 1992).

Specifically for conservation and the environment this voluntarism was manifest in the wider countryside by the continued success and growth of the Farming and Wildlife Advisory Group (Cox *et al*, 1990, Winter 1996a, 1996b). Formed in 1970, FWAG was initially a national forum for the exchange of views between farmers and conservationists. The development of a county organisational structure and an advisory capacity followed, so that by the early 1990s nearly all counties in England and Scotland, but not Wales, had one or more FWAG advisers available to guide farmers on all aspects of conservation. FWAG is a blend of public and private initiative with leading figures in the farming community heavily involved. It is thus 'acceptable' to many farmers in a way that official conservation agencies might not be. It is based firmly on the principles of voluntarism and compromise. Farmers are encouraged to seek its advice and much emphasis is placed on the agricultural knowledge and sympathies of those giving advice.

FWAG's reliance on effective voluntary local organisation and, indeed, a continuing element of local funding, provides for both its strength and its Achilles heel. At best, county FWAGs have brought leading farming figures into the conservation arena and facilitated the provision of good technical advice for a significant proportion of farmers. At worst, county FWAGs are resource-starved, appearing somewhat amateurish, with too little impact in the farming community. It is fair to say, at the close of the 1990s, that a positive image of FWAG prevails in most counties. FWAG is a good example of how a public-private initiative can demonstrate a high degree of flexibility, adapting to changing circumstances and opportunities with greater facility than might be the case within mainstream government departments. Thus, FWAG is no longer merely concerned with cosmetic conservation around the margins of the farmed landscape, for now it adopts a whole farm approach. It adapted to the arrival of agri-environment schemes by reorienting its efforts territorially where the arrival of new project officers, as in the English ESAs, warranted this or, alternatively, acting as in a crucial catalytic manner in recruiting farmers to other schemes such as the Countryside Stewardship Scheme. More recently, its ability to adapt to new demands has found it involved in experimenting with Farm Biodiversity Action Plans in partnership with one of the main food retailers promoting quality assurance in food.

In other respects, too, the world of conservation has dramatically shifted during the 1990s with attention shifting away from the old concern with designation to new forms of dealing with conservation policy, particularly in the wider countryside. The first innovation was the assumption of new responsibilities by MAFF. The Ministry was given a responsibility to promote conservation under the terms of the Agriculture Act 1986 and ESAs became the first of a raft of agri-environmental policies developed in the late 1980s and 1990s. Later schemes included the Countryside Stewardship Scheme, the Habitats Scheme and the Moorland Scheme. Although these policies are top-down in the sense that they are mostly initiated and led by MAFF, they are novel in their focus on the wider countryside and enlisting farmers, albeit through financial inducements, into conservation management. They have changed the face of conservation policy in Britain.

A change of a very different type, but of equal significance, has come about through the emergence of biodiversity action planning. Whereas the agri-environmental scheme has brought a single new central government player into the conservation policy arena, BAP has brought many new partners into conservation policy at the local (usually county) level. Commitments made by the UK under the terms of the *Fifth Environmental Action Programme* of the EU (1992–2000) and the UN Rio *Convention on Biological Diversity* of 1992 prompted the UK's *Action Plan on Biodiversity* (Cmnd 2428) launched in 1994. The targets set by the plan were primarily directed towards the continuation of well established procedures, the improvement of monitoring and the honouring of commitments. For example, the Government committed itself to compliance with the timetable for the designation of SACs under the Habitats Directive by the year 2004.

As Wragg and Selman (1998) explain:

> The UK Biodiversity Action Plan has been cascaded down to county level through a process initially entailing the production of 'Biodiversity Challenge' documents which outline the locally important habitats and species towards which conservation priority should be directed.' Subsequent local 'Biodiversity Action Plans' (BAPs) then convert county

'challenges' into specific objectives and methods for each prioritised species and habitat. Crucially, these action plans are to be prepared, publicised and implemented on as consensual a basis as possible, through a local network of public, private and voluntary sector organisations, and expert and lay individuals.

The local BAPs are charged to:

- translate national biodiversity targets to a local level;
- identify targets for species and habitats in the local area;
- develop partnerships;
- raise awareness;
- consider all opportunities for conservation of the whole biodiversity resource;
- provide a basis for monitoring progress in conserving biodiversity.

(Local Government Management Board 1997)

This is major policy innovation, in that a partnership approach is adopted which gives considerable responsibility to local actors in partnership with national government and agencies. In most counties where the preparation of BAPs is well advanced, local authorities and county wildlife trusts have taken the lead acting in tandem with the local offices of English Nature and other bodies. This process has led to a clear identification of weaknesses within current designation and protection policies and incentive schemes. In some instances this has resulted in innovative local projects which have had a serious positive impact on local conservation management. For example, in Devon the failure to achieve ESA status for a large tract of north and west Devon led to a highly successful campaign of advice for farmers to safeguard Culm grasslands, led by the Devon Wildlife Trust (Winter and Winter, 1999).

In its evolutionary context, CP in countryside recreation had a number of discrete origins. Its genesis probably lies in the integrated land management experiments of the early 1970s, developed to 'exploit a growing community interest in becoming involved in practical management tasks' (Centre for Leisure Research, 1986, p 34). They were to consider the relationships between agriculture, conservation and recreation in tandem, but for recreation in particular they had a valuable role in assisting authorities to meet urban space standards and in providing new uses for derelict land (Curry, 1994).

In urban areas too, threats of development as a result of the freeing up of the planning system in the early 1980s had led to much building on urban vacant land. At the same time, selling off school playing fields was encouraged and local authorities had been relieved of their obligation to maintain open space standards (NCVO and OSS, 1991). Community responses became visible from the mid-1980s under formal sanction of the Department of the Environment (1986) considering them at the time to be cost effective.

The success of these initiatives into the 1990s, has led to a broadening of the base of open space provision from parks and allotments to newer forms such as community gardens, urban forestry projects, arts initiatives and city farms (OSS, 1992). The official merit of such developments in the 1990s is now not seen as cost effectiveness, or even notions of a reduction in vandalism through a sense of ownership (Department of the Environment, 1996). Rather, CP in urban open space provision is now championed by government because, it is claimed, it provides a means of allowing parks to play a much more central role in urban life.

In the forestry sector, the need to develop recreation for reasons of economic viability led, by the 1980s, to the development of the National Forest and Community Forests, many of which are being actively developed and managed by parish councils and other community groups. More singularly, by 1993, the Forestry Commission had introduced grant aid, through the Community Woodland Supplement (as part of the Woodland Grant Scheme) for providing recreation though consultation with, and the active involvement of, the local community. By the start of 1998, in excess of 1,300 individual Community Woodland schemes had been approved (Forestry Commission *et al*, 1997).

European structural funding also has nurtured this CP movement, this time specifically in the development of community tourism initiatives. Objective 5b funding in particular has allowed rural community groups, through full consultation, to develop their own tourism and marketing strategies (Harper, 1997). Funding also has allowed the development of tourism infrastructure very much at the behest of local people (Tregear *et al*, 1997).

Centrally in the new governance style, however, principal recent CP outdoor recreation initiatives have been used to assist in the improvement of the statutory rights of way system. Originating at the level of the highways authority, a range of Community Path initiatives and Adopt a Path schemes were developed in the early 1990s to encourage parish councils and other groups to take an active part in path maintenance and publicity (PACEC, 1995). These initiatives were mimicked in the national context with the introduction of the Parish Paths Partnership by the Countryside Commission in 1992 and almost 1,000 parishes had joined the scheme in its first three years of operation (Parker, 1996). Such was the scheme's considered success and national visibility, that it was cited in the 1995 Rural White Paper as an exemplar of good CP practice. The development of Greenways, too, with the purpose of blending nature conservation and access, has more recently been proposed as a means of increasing recreation provision through community effort (Land Use Consultants, 1997).

Perhaps the 'flagship' of CP in outdoor recreation, certainly in terms of a national Government policy initiative, has been the development of Millennium Greens (MG). These are areas of open space to be enjoyed and held in trust by the local community in perpetuity, normally through the purchase or donation of the freehold of the land. They are to be developed, implemented and managed into the longer term by communities themselves after full local consultation to ensure public support. MGs may be on the edge of any settlement, from city to hamlet and may be of any size up to around 15 hectares. They should be within easy walking distance of a residential community and be accessible safely. The central tenets of the scheme are therefore both to create new public open space and to generate high levels of community commitment (Curry and Selman, 1999).

Participatory action, community involvement, devolved power and local autonomy have therefore all impacted on the development of conservation and recreation during the 1990s as part of a longer term shift in government style.

<h3 style="text-align:center">RETAINING THE OLD ORDER:
NEW POLICIES IN THE OLD STYLE AND SOME POLICY INACTION</h3>

Despite these pervasive shifts, some areas of conservation and recreation policy tenaciously hold on to the old style top-down imposed policies.

This is particularly the case with regard to the system of designated sites, especially SSSIs. Here the Wildlife and Countryside Act 1981 might appropriately be considered to be old style policy. The Act sought to strengthen site protection through comprehensive re-notification and an elaborate system of management agreements based on compensatory payments. The SSSI remains a cornerstone of site protection policy and, in the 1990s, has become central to the UK's claims that it meets its obligations under *European Directives on the Conservation of Wild Birds* (1979) and *the Conservation of Natural Habitats and of Wild Fauna and Flora* (1992).

For all the appearance of dirigiste policy, the SSSI system is crucially flawed in two very different respects. First, it is dependent, in part, on the operation of the land use planning system which, by its very nature, is open to contestation and can offer no ultimate watertight safeguards for particular sites, whether of international importance or not. Secondly, despite the strengthening of protection under the 1981 Act, agriculture remains outside the planning mechanism and the means to protect SSSIs from the consequence of changes in agricultural management on or adjacent to sites are in some respects severely limited. These criticisms were apparent even before the ink was dry on the paper of the 1981 Act and have sharpened in the 1990s but there has been a slowness on the part of governments to legislate, at least before the year 2000. Alternative routes have been attempted, some emanating from government, some from the statutory agencies charged with managing the SSSI resource.

Government, for example, has continued to provide a steer through planning circulars. For example, PPG9 in October 1994 affirms that developments affecting SSSIs will be 'subject to special scrutiny'. English Nature for its part, came to recognise that the complexities of site by site negotiations made the SSSI management agreement both cumbersome and costly. The cost of agreements rose from £0.3 million in 1983/84 to £7 million in 1993/94 (constant 1992/93 prices: NAO, 1994). In 1992 it introduced the *Wildlife Enhancement Scheme* (WES) in three pilot areas to introduce a set of standardised and simplified payments to encourage positive management on SSSIs. Administration costs for WES agreements amount to 10% of total cost compared to 24% in standard SSSI management agreements (NAO, 1994). In addition to the simplified payment formula, the scheme differs from the standard SSSI management agreement in so much as English Nature informs all land occupiers and invites them to participate, in stark contrast to the situation in other SSSIs where the occupier has to threaten to perform a damaging operation in order to trigger the offer of a management agreement.

An opportunity to remedy some of the perceived weaknesses of the 1981 Act was provided by the Environmental Protection Act 1990, although many suggestions made by the (then) Nature Conservancy Council and others were rejected (Ball, 1991). One innovation was a clause allowing management agreements to be negotiated with owners and occupiers of land adjacent to SSSIs, a development that could help where existing SSSIs are adversely affected by activities, such as drainage, on near-by land. But an amendment to extend this to the wider countryside was rejected 'on the grounds that the Council's money was better targeted on the protection of key sites' (Ball, 1991: 82). However there has long been scientific recognition that it is inappropriate to consider isolated sites without reference to conditions in the remainder of the countryside (Diamond 1975) and there is growing pressure to recognise that 'the survival of the wildlife interest of the SSSIs themselves depends to an extent on the nature of the landscape of the wider countryside' (Adams *et al*, 1992). In Scotland, a new Natural Heritage Area designation was introduced (but has hitherto not been used) under the terms of the Natural Heritage (Scotland) Act 1991, in an attempt to broaden the base of valued environments.

Despite all these efforts, there is evidence of continuing damage to SSSIs.

English Nature figures show that between 1990 and 1997, one in five SSSIs in England was damaged. In Dorset, 33% of the county's sites were damaged and in Norfolk 25%. In 1998, the Government issued a consultation paper on SSSIs which included proposals that legislation should be amended to clarify the status of SSSIs with regard to national and international importance, that stronger powers should be introduced to require restoration of a site after deliberate damage, stronger penalties for deliberate damage to SSSIs, and better targeting of incentive payments to reward positive management for wildlife. This forms the basis for legislation coming before Parliament in 2000.

For recreation, a commitment on the part of the Labour Government to introduce legislation for access to open country (DETR and Welsh Office, 1999) is quintessentially of the 'old order'. The debates over the imposition of such public rights over private land have been fully aired in the consultation phase of this proposal (DETR and Welsh Office, 1998) and are not considered further here. Such a policy, however, does seem to run against more recent styles of negotiation and consensus building in conflict resolution in the countryside (Selman and Wragg, 1999) which themselves have been very much developed at the behest of Government.

The proposed legislation too, seems to negate the ethos of the Rural White papers, both extant and proposed, of the devolution of such kinds of developments to the local community. Certainly some would argue (Shoard, 1999) that such access for recreation purposes is the right of the nation as a whole based on the historic freedoms that have been eroded through land acquisition (legitimate or otherwise) initially triggered by the Agricultural Revolution. But such access was never available to the nation as a whole (it was essentially customary use by local populations and was not, in its historical context, deployed for recreation purposes – it was simply for a right of passage) (Curry, 1997). If historical precedent is to be used in shaping this policy, therefore, *local* negotiation of access rights for recreation purposes might seem more appropriate.

Such an approach also would be more consistent with the new community-based recreation policy approaches of Millennium Greens, Greenways and the Parish Paths Partnership. Indeed, local level agreement over local access use has been one of the success stories of the 1990s, through the creation and development of access liaison groups (Parker, 1996). These have brought all stakeholders together, usually at the county level, to thrash out and commonly resolve, differences of opinion about the use of land for access purposes: the contemporary consensual approach that the old style enforced legislation for access to open country runs a danger of impairing.

This imposition of such a stark change in access rights over open country does seem to have its impetus in a deeper history. This is not so much a history of the struggle for access *per se,* but rather a history of the political affiliations associated with this struggle. Many members of the Labour Government that introduced the 1949 Act (which despite provisions in the Bill that preceded it, failed to introduce access to open country) were active in pursuing the access cause through their membership of pressure groups. Indeed, Lewis Silkin, the Minister of Planning who introduced the Act had been a member of the Ramblers' Association. Others, such as Barbara Castle had remained active in championing such wider access from the time of the Act well into the 1990s (Blunden and Curry, 1990). And John Smith too, leader of the Labour Party until his untimely death in the mid-1990s, held the broadening of such rights high on his personal agenda.

The proposed legislation in some ways then, can be construed as a tribute to Old Labour rather than an innovative dynamic in New Labour thinking. Perhaps, too, it has limitations in serving the public well. As is suggested in the next section of this paper, new access to vast tracts of open country simply may not be needed in terms of recreation and access demands.

POLICY INERTIA

In other areas of conservation, but particularly recreation, neither the new style of governance nor the old order appear to have had much impact during the 1990s.

This is manifest in recreation and access terms in the enduring problems relating to the Statutory Rights of Way system. This was firmly established in the 1949 Act as the principal means by which public access over private land was to be secured. Definitive Maps were to be produced by county highways authorities within five years of the Act, to identify beyond question where legal rights of way were located. They were to be those linear routes that had been used for twenty years or more without interruption. Constant inadequacy of resources and the unforeseen magnitude of legal disputes over where such routes were, meant that by the late 1980s, no county councils had their rights of way legally defined, properly maintained or appropriately publicised as the Act had directed. Rather than pushing government for more resources in this area, the Countryside Commission, in the early 1990s introduced a business planning approach for making progress with rights of way, known as the Milestones Statement.

Whilst this assisted with progress in some authorities, it certainly identified the magnitude of the problem more clearly than had been done before. Some authorities would not complete the Definitive Map until well beyond 2010 and some even felt that they never would (Ravenscroft *et al,* 1996). The problem was resources. The national system was at least £150 million deficient in respect of meeting Milestones targets, but no further funding was forthcoming by government despite considerable expenditure on new means of access, which are considered further in the next section, developed through the 1990s. Application for additional funding (together with proposals for a simplification of the processes surrounding the development of Statutory Rights of Way) has indeed now gone to government, however, (Countryside Commission, 1998) but is in danger of being occluded by a preoccupation with the access-to-open-country issue.

SUPPLY-BASED POLICIES:
PURSUING POLICY-MAKER RATHER THAN PUBLIC GOALS

The policy bases considered in the previous two sections have perhaps inevitably been concerned with controlling and developing the resources concerned with conservation and recreation, rather than their use. Policy-makers have been preoccupied with supply-based policies. Traditionally this has been considered legitimate for conservation goods since there are no comprehensive markets, or other appropriate mechanisms, through which either citizens or consumers can express their preferences. The state intervenes to ensure an 'appropriate' supply (in terms of both quality and quantity) of conservation in the absence of comprehensive data on the preferences of the nation. Levels of provision are based, rather, on notions of the environmental health of the nation, both now and for future generations.

But the situation for recreation is somewhat different since this is directly consumed either through the assertion of rights, participation through the market place or recreation through state support, for example in the agri-environment schemes. Here, the revealed preferences of consumers can be made known and there is an opportunity for policy to respond to such preferences directly. The remainder of this section is concerned to outline some of the shortcomings of supply-based policies for recreation that do not make appropriate acknowledgement of consumer behaviour. Combining supply driven policies with notions of demand management and manipulation through public policy is likely to lead to a more efficient and equitable allocation of recreation resources nationally.

Research conducted for the Country Landowners' Association (1998) has attempted to provide estimates of the *net* change in the publicly available recreation resource (both for area and linear access) between 1990 and 1997. Whilst this invariably is not exhaustive (changes in water company and Ministry of Defence provision for example, could not be procured) it is comprehensive of all of the agri-environment scheme access provision, local authority and other access agreements, permissive access on farmland without any formal agreement at all and Millennium Greens. The estimates of the net new growth in access supply are presented in figure 1 below. In statistical terms the figures for access through 'other written agreements' and 'access with not formal agreement' are accurate with 95% confidence and a sampling error of + or - 4%. All other data are from official government sources.

Figure 1.   Estimates of net new growth in access supply, 1990 – 1997 in England and Wales as a whole

Type of Access	Area Access (ha)	Linear Access (km)
Countryside Stewardship Scheme	10,282	518
Tir Cymen	25,935	41
Environmentally Sensitive Area Access	41	N/A
Countryside Access Scheme	1,143	N/A
Woodland Grant Scheme/ Farm Woodland Premium Supplement	24,202	N/A
Other Written Agreements	82,932	1,978
Access with no Formal Agreement	314,853	17,492
Total	*459,388*	*20,072*

Source: Country Landowners' Association, 1998

From this figure, there has been a *net* growth in access opportunities as a whole in England and Wales since 1990 in excess of 450,000 hectares of land and some 20,000 kilometres of linear access. Of these, approximately 13.4% of area access has been provided through some form of state support, the other 86.6% having been provided by increases in informal access opportunities (68.5%) and through bi-lateral agreements with user groups (18.1%). For linear access, only 2.8% has been provided by the state, with the remainder being increases in informal access (87%) or through bilateral agreement (10.2%). Overall, it was estimated that access opportunities in England and Wales may have grown somewhere in the region of 20% between 1990 and 1997.

But is this increase in provision a response to a growth in consumption? There actually is no consistent time series data that allows changes in overall countryside recreation consumption to be charted with any accuracy during the 1990s. Some time series data are available for the 1980s drawn from the National Surveys of Countryside Recreation conducted by the Countryside Commission, but which ceased in 1990. Data from these surveys indicate a slight decline in the proportion of the population making countryside trips between 1984 and 1989 and also a decline in the number of trips made by recreation active households (Curry, 1994). The total number of trips to the countryside made by the population as a whole during this period is shown in figure 2 below.

Figure 2. Total Number of trips to the countryside made by the population as a whole, England and Wales, 1984 – 1989 (base year 1984 = 100)

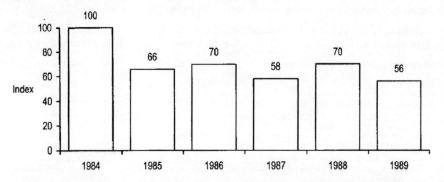

Source: derived from the National Surveys of Countryside Recreation (Curry, 1994)

This figure does suggest a slight structural decline in participation nationally during this period. This is certainly the view offered by Roberts (1979) who suggests that national countryside recreation participation peaked in about 1977 and, according to Patmore (1989) and Curry (1997) has exhibited a structural decline ever since. This, they contend, is not due to any inherent declining interest in the countryside, but rather, a shift in leisure lifestyles towards more home-centred leisure activity. This has been triggered by increasing home ownership (and an increase in DIY) and the increasing popularity of home-centred consumer goods such as CDs, video and computers.

In the absence of any reliable data for the 1990s (the UK Leisure Day Visits Survey which has covered countryside recreation issues since 1990 has not used consistent questions or sample bases), the Countryside Commission's official position is that year on year, the consumption of countryside recreation is in aggregate terms for England and Wales, at best, static (Countryside Commission, 1998, personal communication). The House of Commons Committee on the Environment (1995), too, concluded that a growth in overall countryside recreation is a thing of the past. Certainly there is no evidence at all to suggest any aggregate growth in countryside recreation consumption during the 1990s.

Clearly, a preoccupation with recreation supply in public policy must raise issues about the effectiveness of public expenditure in this area in the face of the widening gap between production and consumption. Is financial support of the agri-environment schemes for access really more to do with direct income support for farmers than enhancing recreation opportunities? Is the estimated £100 million in tax revenues forgone since 1975 through Heritage Tax exemptions for access land, a wise use of public money, when it is difficult to find where these areas are because tax matters are confidential? Is it effective to develop a whole new financial and bureaucratic infrastructure for access to open country when the Rights of Way system remains cash starved?

Closer consideration of consumption characteristics lends further weight to a reconsideration of the allocation of public resources for recreation. All consumer surveys since the 1960s have shown that those who undertake trips to the countryside in their leisure time are dominantly amongst the upper social, income and occupational groups. Public expenditure in this area thus tends to benefit the already privileged and active relative to the less well off. In short, it is socially regressive.

Recreation and access policy therefore needs to become more integrated (the Countryside Agency, MAFF, the Forestry Commission and the Environment Agency, for example, might consider the aggregate effects of their individual supply-based polices more closely) and more fine grained in responding to consumer preferences. Further public expenditure on net new provision might be questioned in the context of consumer needs. Public rights through the rights of way system should be vigorously defended (and fully resourced) as a system instituted in 1949 that has never been properly set up. Surveys show that this is the system that people understand and like to use: linear access is favoured by consumers (over area access), it is comprehensively signposted and waymarked and it is on the Ordinance Survey map.

Beyond this, public policy might usefully shift more towards its new-found enabling role. Certainly, by far the largest area of net new growth in recreation opportunities since 1990 (figure 1) has been through informal permissive mechanisms based on locally determined arrangements. Such a development is an exemplar in the new style of governance.

Closer consideration also might be given to enabling the development of markets, since recreation is clearly a consumer good. Certainly, markets would avoid the inefficiencies of public expenditure brought about by new provision for which there is no concomitant increase in aggregate demand. Markets also would avoid the problem of regressive public expenditure. Those who have an effective demand can pay and taxpayers who do not have an effective demand will not have to subsidise provision. This is the market operating efficiently and equitably. If there is a demand, providers can exploit it fully. If there is not, there can be little justification for state support in this area.

REFERENCES

Adams, W. (1996). *Future Nature.* Earthscan Publications, London.

Adams, W.M., Bourn, N.A.D. and Hodge, I. (1992). Conservation in the wider countryside: SSSIs and wildlife habitat in eastern England. *Land Use Policy,* 9 (4), 235–248.

Ball, S. (1991). Law and the countryside: the Environmental Protection Act 1990 and nature conservation. *Land Management and Environmental Law Report,* 3 (3), 81–84.

BDOR (1992). *Countryside Community Action – an Appraisal.* BDOR, Bristol, the Countryside Commission, Cheltenham.

Blunden and Curry (eds.) (1990). *A People's Charter?* HMSO, London.

Bovaird, T., Dando, M., Green, J., Martin, S., McVeigh, T., Millward, A. and Tricker, M. (1994). *An Evaluation of Rural Action for the Environment.* Aston Business School, Public Sector Management Research Centre, University of Aston, November.

Burns, D. Hambleton, R. and Hoggart, P. (1994). *The Politics of Decentralisation: Revitalising Local Democracy.* Macmillan, London.

Centre for Leisure Research (1986). *Access to the Countryside for Recreation and Sport.* CCP 217, Countryside Commission and the Sports Council, Cheltenham and London

Chanan, G. (1992). *Out of the Shadows: Local Community Action and the European Community.* Office for Official Publications of the European Community, Brussels.

Country Landowners' Association (1998). *Access to the Countryside.* The CLA's Response to the Government's Consultation Paper, Volume 2, June.

Countryside Commission (1998). *Rights of Way in the 21st Century.* CCP543, the Commission, Cheltenham.

Curry, N.R. (1994). *Countryside Recreation, Access and Land Use Planning.* E and FN Spon, London

Curry, N.R. (1997). Enhancing Countryside Recreation Benefits Through the Rights of Way System in England and Wales. *Town Planning Review,* 68 (4), 449–463.

Curry, N.R. and Selman, P. (1999). *Feedback Concerning the Process of Applying for A Millennium Greens Grant.* Final report to the Countryside Agency, Countryside and Community Research Unit, Cheltenham, May.

Department of the Environment (1986). *Evaluation of Environmental Projects Funded Under the Urban Programme.* HMSO, London.

Department of the Environment (1995). *Rural England.* HMSO, London.

Department of the Environment (1996). *People, Parks and Cities, a Guide to Good Practice in Urban Parks.* HMSO, London, March.

Department of the Environment, Transport and the Regions and the Welsh Office (1998). *Access to Open Countryside in England and Wales, a Consultation Paper.* February, DETR/WO, London and Cardiff.

Department of the Environment, Transport and the Regions and the Welsh Office (1999). *Access to the Countryside in England and Wales: the Government's Framework for Action.* March, DETR/WO, London and Cardiff.

Diamond, J.M. (1975). The island dilemma: lessons of modern biogeographic studies for the design of natural reserves. *Biological Conservation,* 7, 129–145.

Etzioni, A. (1995). *The Spirit of Community: Rights, Responsibilities and the Communitarian Agenda.* Fontana, London.

Forestry Commission, Ministry of Agriculture, Fisheries and Food, Welsh Office Agriculture Department and the Scottish Office (1997). *A Guide to the Woodland Grant Scheme.* Forestry Commission, Edinburgh.

Forman, R.T.T.(1995). Some General Principles of Landscape and Regional Ecology. *Landscape Ecology* 10 (3), 133–142.

Giddens, A. (1998). *The Third Way: the Renewal of Social Democracy.* Polity Press, Cambridge.

Gittins, J. (1993). Community Involvement in Environment and Recreation, Chapter 15 in

Glyptis, S. (ed.) *Leisure and the Environment: Essays in Honour of Professor A. J. Patmore.* Belhaven Press, London and New York, 193–194.

Harper, P. (1997). The Importance of Community Involvement in Sustainable Tourism Development, in M. Stabler, (ed.) *Tourism and Sustainability, Principles and Practice.* CAB International, Wallingford, 129–142.

Hodge, I. (1996). On Penguins and Icebergs: the Rural White Paper and the Assumptions of Rural Policy. *Journal of Rural Studies,* 12(4), 331–337.

House of Commons Environment Committee (1995). *The Impact of Leisure Activities on the Environment.* HC 246–1, HMSO, London.

Land Use Consultants (1997). *Greenways: Consensus Building and Conflict Resolution.* Countryside Commission, Cheltenham, April.

Local Government Management Board (1997). *Guidance for Local Biodiversity Action Plans, Note 1.* LGMB, Norwich.

Local Government Management Board (1991). *Reinventing Government.* LGMB, London

Lowe, P. (1996). The British Rural White Papers. Centre for Rural Economy, University of Newcastle upon Tyne, Working paper 21, December.

Lowe, P., Ward, N., Ward, S. and Murdoch, J. (1995). *Countryside Prospectus, 1995–2010: Some Future Trends.* Centre for Rural Economy Research Report, Newcastle University.

Ministry of Agriculture, Fisheries and Food and the Department of the Environment, Transport and the Regions (1999). Rural England: A Discussion Document. MAFF, DETR, London.

Murdoch, J. (1997). The Shifting Territory of Government: Some Insights from the Rural White Paper. *Area,* 29(2), 109–118.

NAO (1994). *Protecting and Managing Sites of Special Scientific Interest in England.* Report by the Comptroller and Auditor General of the National Audit Office, London: HMSO.

National Council for Voluntary Organisations and the Open Spaces Society (1991). *Spaces Between: Community Action for Urban Open Space.* NCVO, OSS, London and Oxfordshire, January.

Open Spaces Society (1992). *Making Space: Protecting and Creating Open Space for Local Communities.* OSS, Oxfordshire.

PA Cambridge Economic Consultants (1995). *Parish Paths Partnership: Final Report.* Prepared for the Countryside Commission, Cambridge Economic Consultants Limited, Cambridge.

Parker, G. (1996). Citizens' Rights and Private Property Rights in the English Countryside: A Study of Countryside recreational Access Provision. Unpublished PhD thesis, University of Bristol, October.

Patmore, A. (1989). Land and Leisure: a Contemporary Perspective, in A. Patmore (ed.) *Recreation and Conservation, Themes in Applied Geography.* Hull, University of Hull.

Ravenscroft, N., Curry, N.R. and Markwell, S. (1996). *Evaluation of Highways Authorities Milestones Statements for Public Rights of Way.* Final report to the Countryside Commission, Centre for Environment and Land Tenure Studies, University of Reading, May.

Roberts, K. (1979). Countryside Recreation and Social Class. Unpublished report to the Countryside Commission, the Commission, Cheltenham.

Scottish Office (1999). *National Planning Policy Guidance, NPPG 15, Rural Development,* The Scottish Office, Edinburgh.

Selman, P. and Wragg, A. (1999). *Consensus Building for Sustainability in the Wider Countryside.* Final report of the EU framework IV Programme, Countryside and Community Research Unit, Cheltenham and Gloucester College, Cheltenham, February.

Shoard, M. (1999). *The Right to Roam.* Oxford University Press, Oxford.

Tregear, A., McLeay, F. and Moxey, A. (1997). Sustainability and Tourism Marketing: Competitive or Complementary? In M. Stabler (ed.). *Tourism and Sustainability, Principles and Practice.* CAB International, Wallingford, 119–127.

United Nations Conference on Environment and Development (1992). *Agenda 21–Action Plan for the Next Century.* UNCED, Rio de Janeiro.

Winter, M. (1996a). Landwise or land foolish? free conservation advice for farmers in the wider English countryside. *Landscape Research*, 21 (3) 243–263.

Winter, M. (1996b). *Rural Politics: Policies for Agriculture, Forestry and the Environment.* London, Routledge.

Winter, H. and Winter, M. (1999). The Culm Grassland Service, Unpublished Working Paper.

World Commission on Environment and Development (the Bruntland Report) (1987). *Our Common Future.* Oxford University Press, Oxford

Wragg, A. and Selman, P. (1998). Local Biodiversity Action plans: an example of consensus building for sustainable development? Paper presented to Rural Economy & Society Study Group Annual Conference, Aberystwyth.

ACKNOWLEDGEMENT

I acknowledge the assistance of Professor Michael Winter in contributing material on recent developments in nature conservation policy for inclusion in this chapter.

15

Biodiversity into the Twenty-First Century

Derek Langslow

THIS CONTRIBUTION HAS a rather grand title, but it provides an opportunity to present a few observations about the future by examining the past. The 1949 Act makes no reference to 'biodiversity'. It was a word unused at that time and it still fails to merit its own entry in quality dictionaries. But the focus on biodiversity is arguably the key outcome from all the conservation legislation over the fifty years. Many changes and trends in nature conservation and its biodiversity component have occurred over the last fifty years. By using some examples of these changes, I want to discuss what we have learnt from them for the future.

If the last fifty years have taught us one thing, it must be the difficulty of forecasting the changes ahead. While the far sighted legal draughtsmen of fifty years ago, supported by those extraordinary papers produced towards the end of the Second World War, were labouring over the clauses, they could scarcely have envisaged how quickly the face of Britain would change by the Millennium. Unquestionably, the human species has benefited overall, but there have also been significant downsides.

The natural environment has fared far less well. The 1949 Act did not anticipate the forthcoming agricultural revolution. Let the corn bunting serve as an example. Its distribution and abundance across the UK has shrunk greatly. A similar phenomenon has been observed with many farmland birds. Many changes have only been revealed by careful data gathering and seem to have gone unnoticed from anecdotal reports. The complexities of the possible reasons for the decline of the corn bunting also emphasise how many inter-related factors are involved.

I have no intention of making this a doomsday contribution. I believe that we have turned the corner in the last decade on many of the negative aspects of environmental impact. Biodiversity will become a key test of sustainable development and will improve over the next fifty years. The last fifty years has seen an extraordinary growth in interest in wildlife and nature conservation, far beyond that dreamed of by the early ecologists. The enormous societal changes of the last half century have changed the focus, reasoning and ethics of nature conservation beyond recognition from 1949.

So how will we improve our biodiversity in the next half century? The

Convention on Biological Diversity, which emerged from the 1992 Rio conference, provided a major stimulus to work on biodiversity conservation in Britain. The production of national reports on biodiversity was followed by the preparation of species and habitat action plans with their associated targets, the recognition of the need for changes in policy and the need to integrate biodiversity into social and economic issues.

Of course concern for biodiversity is not new. One of the classic examples must surely be Derek Ratcliffe's work on the peregrine. Having entered the Second World War with a population of perhaps 800 pairs, the 1950s saw a catastrophic decline in numbers and breeding success. Patient, determined and thorough scientific work demonstrated the role of organo-chlorine pesticides in the decline. Once their use was banned, recovery has been extraordinary, as the difference in distribution maps between 1968/72 and 1988/91 shows. Indeed there are now far more peregrines about than have ever been known and numbers are still growing. Bird watching thirty years ago in Norfolk, it was a truly extraordinary day if you saw a peregrine in the winter time. Nowadays if you fail to see a couple in a day's birdwatching, you are surprised. The peregrine story continues to provide an important lesson for us all in many different ways.

The Species Action Plans, derived under the UK Biodiversity Action Plan, set a course which has already improved the population of some species and will improve more in the future. As the action planning process proceeds, policy adjustments and renewed efforts will improve progress. Our surveillance systems should now serve as sensitive warning systems which identify new priorities and unexpected changes. However, the story of farmland birds does not necessarily augur well for any area of land used intensively for purposes other than biodiversity conservation.

The 1949 Act introduced SSSIs. They remain a foundation, but *not* the totality, of biodiversity conservation throughout Britain. Long before fifty years from now, I hope we will have achieved that holy grail, 'favourable condition', on all SSSIs. This needs to be secured through positive management agreements since virtually all our habitats are man-modified. But SSSIs will not be enough.

Biodiversity will form a key test of sustainable development. We shall need to make sure that the land and water outside the special sites makes a bigger contribution. Some aspects of 'favourable condition' can be delivered directly by the conservation agencies working with the owners of land. Others require changes in how our society uses freshwater, practises agriculture and delivers planning policies. We have a clear idea of where we want to go on biodiversity targets over the next two decades; our joint objectives will help promote the massive partnership needed to deliver improved biodiversity.

Biodiversity targets are already recognised as a key test of sustainable development. This offers improving prospects, as well as some dangers. Our concerns for biodiversity will be more fully integrated into the overall development of society. Biodiversity indicators need to be geographically and temporally sensitive. They will need reviewing as targets are achieved and other changes occur. These targets will be prominent and accepted in the public and political domains. The new Quality of Life Indicators are a prominent part of the Sustainable Development Strategy. This should ensure that there is an influence on all policies into the future.

One example of how policy change and practical action has improved the population of a declining species concerns the otter in England. Otters suffered in the period following the 1949 Act for a variety of reasons, most notably in relation to water management and quality. Major improvements in water quality, specific help through otter holts and friendlier bankside management and a virtual absence of persecution have produced a remarkable improvement in otter site occupation in England. It also illustrates that we need to be patient. Results do not come overnight. We need determination and consistency over a prolonged period to reap the rewards.

Apart from the Convention on Biological Diversity, there have been a number of other international developments which have affected biodiversity and are likely to be influential in the next century. The most important is the European Union whose influence has grown significantly over the last decade. Everything points to that influence increasing. A balance sheet of the pluses and minuses of the European Union for the environment is quite difficult. There have been a number of Directives beneficial on environmental matters. Almost everyone in this country, but sadly few of our continental partners, recognises the need for a macro change in the Common Agricultural Policy. If the founding fathers of the 1949 Act missed one big issue, it must surely be the post-war agricultural revolution. They recognised fully the potential of built development but overlooked the potential for enormous changes in land use. Surely over the next fifty years we can look forward to a more sustainable agricultural system which provides a better natural environment as well as meeting the needs of society for food. Surely we can create a position of better coexistence of agricultural practices and biodiversity. We have begun to achieve this with forestry in the last decade and the vision of the Forestry Commission in changing to multi-purpose objectives is highly commendable.

If I am still around in 2025, I am confident that our countryside will be richer for wildlife. Lapwings will once again be able to nest in a field of spring cereal and walk their chicks to the nearby water meadow for invertebrates. The lessons we have learnt from our Habitat Restoration Project over the last decade will have been incorporated into planning and agricultural policies. The tide of habitat fragmentation will have turned and key wildlife sites will be bigger, buffered and linked, thereby protecting both habitats and species directly as well as enabling mobile species to move around and take advantage of suitable conditions.

One of the big unknowns for biodiversity in the years ahead is how climate change will influence the populations and distributions of species. Recently, a lot of evidence has been published on changes in butterflies and dragonflies. Are these sensitive indicators of some of the trends to come? A particularly interesting example is the silver-spotted skipper. This species of short turf chalk grassland declined massively from the 1950s, when agricultural improvement and the loss of rabbit grazing combined to reduce the potential habitat area. Where it persisted on south facing slopes, its population was stable for a long period but has shown marked increases in the last decade. All the monitoring sites are managed for conservation and hence improvements partly reflect improved management. Simultaneously, rabbit populations have recovered somewhat but especially the frequency of warm summers has increased notably. This information gives two clear messages. Firstly, that our understanding of the butterfly and its management needs has helped us create the right conditions. Secondly, would the management have worked without the warm summers and the increases in rabbits? Do we need to prepare north-facing slopes? This review for silver-spotted skipper was stimulated by the UK Biodiversity Action Plan. The Action Plan process will help ensure a consistent and regular accumulation of knowledge.

Let me turn to dynamic habitats. We will build on the experience of EU LIFE projects on coasts, wetlands and other landscapes, good examples of future ways of working. The result will be a planning system which is working with nature, rather than against it. The effects of climate change will be recognised and accepted; there will no longer be futile and unsustainable schemes to counter natural coastal processes; flood defence schemes will cater for the natural processes, allowing space for nature.

Then there is the problem of Genetically Modified Organisms. Within the next fifty years, the risks and benefits will, hopefully, have been more clearly identified and demonstrated and action agreed. The current GMO debate will have established the principles in relation to all novel crops – that the precautionary approach must prevail and the implications for any major agents for change in the countryside will first be subject to impartial and intelligent research.

In a further fifty years, the amount of data on biodiversity will be even greater than it is now. However, the National Biodiversity Network will have swept it all into shape, ensuring that biological recording is consistent and to common standards. As well as being greater in quantity, higher in quality, it will be accessible through the wonders of information technology. At the touch of a few buttons, everyone will be able to discover the current status of any of the key species and habitats, both nationally and locally, and to find out their performance against the targets. This information will be available to all, be it at work, at home or at school. Or so we can wish.

This dissemination of data will be the key to public awareness and involvement. Biodiversity will be on every agenda. Businesses will be on board through the championing of particular Biodiversity Action Plan species, and schools will be fully engaged in Local BAP strategies. The benefits of involving youngsters in Local Nature Reserves are evident and represent a long-term future interest, which can be passed down to others. Biodiversity will be a familiar concept in the National Curriculum, and an integral component of higher level courses and professional training.

In order to achieve all this we must help the voluntary conservation organisations to do more. They can be immensely persuasive, snapping around the heels of Government, drawing attention to particular issues. However, a pack of snappy dogs can serve only to confuse the flock of Government. The desired direction must be clear to all, and we must not lose ourselves with internal argument, and being diverted down single interest paths. In this way, biodiversity will be an automatic factor in the consideration of major decisions – as well as local and personal choices.

Some may consider this to be too rosy a view – but I think not. It is, instead, a continuation, a development, of the work of the far-sighted few who laboured so hard to put the 1949 Act into law. It is carrying on the efforts of those who have worked since the 1949 Act and who have achieved so much in the face of apathy, greed and ignorance. By working together we can deliver a natural environment of which we can be proud, and which our children and grandchildren can enjoy and nurture.

16

Beyond 2000: A New People's Charter

Roger Clarke

THE 1949 ACT was described by those promoting it as a 'People's Charter'. It was part of the rebuilding of postwar Britain: creating a society where opportunities would be available to all. It embodied deeply held values about the importance of the countryside to the whole population.

Let us consider what would happen if the 1949 Act were abolished and we made a fresh start on achieving its strategic objectives. What would be the key ingredients? By asking this question I hope to shed light on where we might move forward from the 1949 legacy. My remarks refer to England only. They are personal, and do not necessarily reflect the views of the Countryside Agency.

The 1949 legislation had three broad purposes. It aimed to conserve the beauty and amenity of the countryside, to improve recreational opportunities, and to protect wildlife. It is instructive to note that only twelve sections of the Act dealt with nature conservation, fourteen with National Parks and the National Parks Commission, and 57 sections on the complexities of Rights of Way and access to open countryside.

The focus of my remarks is on those objectives of the 1949 Act which aimed to conserve and enhance the natural beauty of the countryside and to improve opportunities for public recreation. These objectives remain equally valid today. The values on which they are based are still deeply held, especially that the countryside is a national asset for us all to enjoy. But they are not the only objectives of countryside and rural policy, and I shall also explore some of the wider links, though I leave to others, better qualified, the specific issues connected with wildlife conservation.

The approach of the 1949 Act could be described as planning and providing. Much effort was spent on defining the relationship between the new countryside arrangements and the equally newly established town and country planning system. The role of local authorities in planning for development was paramount. A good deal of attention was given to regulatory approaches to rights of way, access and nature conservation.

Now, the role of Government is to set strategy, to establish ground rules and to catalyse and facilitate partnerships in the public, private and voluntary sectors. It is no longer the universal provider. We are concerned today with sustainable development. We want our conservation and recreation objectives to be achieved in parallel with, and as part of, wider efforts for economic prosperity and social justice.

I shall organise my comments about the future in four sections: countryside character and quality; managing local countryside; working with the economic and social grain; and countryside recreation.

COUNTRYSIDE CHARACTER AND QUALITY

One of the cherished concepts in the vocabulary of the old Countryside Commission was the distinction between 'designated areas' and 'the wider countryside'. Such a distinction has no resonance in the popular imagination and relatively little visible impact on the ground. But it was a direct product of the 1949 legislation. That in turn derived from concepts of protected areas based loosely on North American style national parks and the affection in which relatively remote upland areas in England were held by outdoors enthusiasts in the 1930s.

While wilderness and remoteness remain important, would we start with such an approach today? They are not the only things we cherish. Much more relevant to the whole of the countryside is the term 'countryside character'. You will be aware of the efforts of the former Countryside Commission and English Nature to assess the character of each part of the countryside of England, drawing on historical, cultural, habitat and land use data. This produced the 'Countryside Character map' and its sister the 'Natural Areas map'. The maps describe what is present in terms of fields, woodlands, settlement patterns, semi-natural vegetation and intensively managed arable areas. They make no judgement about the quality of the asset.

Closely linked to the character map is the concept of 'environmental capital'. This rather unfriendly term summarises the environmental value of different places. It describes the local, regional and national values or benefits of mountains, moors, heather and lakes. It recognises that the North Norfolk coast has a cluster of 'biodiversity hot-spots' or that Dartmoor is particularly important for archaeological remains. Using Countryside Character and Environmental Capital, it is possible to devise policies to manage the areas or assets identified. Some areas may be relatively degraded and require work to restore water quality, expand heathland or create new native woodland. Other areas may already have a high value and need policies with a greater emphasis on protecting and managing existing assets.

Linked to concepts such as Countryside Character and Environmental Capital we need, in my view, a fresh approach to Town and Country Planning. In spite of lofty ideals, a lot of planning focuses on the identification of sites for different sorts of built development. Indeed, the vocabulary of planning, where land is held in 'reserve' until it is 'released' for development gives a good clue to the orientation of the planning system. 'Captured by development' might be a better phrase since, once built on, it is hard to return land to other uses.

In my view, the planning system should be seen as a tool for achieving long-term sustainability. Two or three facets of this are particularly important. First, the 'development plan' should become a 'sustainability plan', articulating goals for the future of an area and in particular its land use. Second, the plan should be based on the concepts of Countryside Character and Environmental Capital described above. Third, the approach to development should not be as at present 'is the development bad enough to refuse' but 'is it good enough to accept'? Developments should only be permitted where they make a positive net contribution to each of the economic, the social and the environmental well-being of the local area. Where an economic or social development such as a factory or a housing scheme results in environmental damage, the development should only go ahead if there is a realistic means of providing compensating environmental gain.

Armed with these fresh approaches, do we need areas designated for their natural beauty? Clearly some areas enjoy national regard for their high quality, often closely linked to their popularity as recreation destinations. The Lake District and the Cornish coast are good examples. Other areas may be of local importance, but do not enjoy such national recognition.

It appears to me that designation has two main benefits. First it attracts national recognition to a local area, giving it a status in the minds of both local people and the wider community that it would not otherwise enjoy. Designation can bring national leadership to local management through devices such as the appointment of Secretary of State Members to National Park Authorities. The second benefit of designation is that it brings resources to the local area to assist with high quality planning and management: both resources from the Exchequer such as National Park grant and the ability to attract other funds from Europe and the Lottery, often working through local partnerships. The local arrangements thereby developed often strengthen the management infrastructure of otherwise remote and relatively impoverished areas.

What does this imply for designations policy? It points, I think, to the continuing need for national recognition of important areas but not perhaps on the same basis as before. Were we starting today, we might well identify a smaller number of nationally important areas where special management attention was required to preserve high quality. Designation might be based on the national significance and quality of the area, the extent of management pressure, and, in some measure, the local will to take action. We might consider taking a similar approach in areas requiring restoration and regeneration. And we might take a fresh look at management arrangements. It is to this last point that I now turn.

MANAGING LOCAL COUNTRYSIDE

When the National Parks were being created in England and Wales in the 1940s and '50s there was a long-running debate about their degree of independence from local government. Eventually, through changes in 1974 and 1995, National Park Authorities gained greater autonomy from local authorities. However, they remain part of the local government family, with a culture and leadership derived primarily from local government. The control of development has been at the core of their activities and certainly at the core of the expectations of elected members. Many NPAs have adopted imaginative and innovative approaches, for example in preparing management plans, carrying out development control, deploying rangers, and introducing land management schemes. But, as institutions, NPAs have not been at the forefront of pioneering new approaches to local governance. Reflecting the culture of the rural areas in which many of them sit, they have tended instead to be rather conservative bodies, focusing primarily on the local rather than the national dimension of their work.

I believe that if we are to achieve the strategic and catalytic approach I described at the start, we would not today create the kinds of arrangements that we have inherited from the past. Areas requiring special attention such as some of our National Parks would instead have Conservation Boards, responsible for setting a long-term vision for the local area and securing its effective long-term management. Their mandate would be to sustain the quality of the area. Their work would be to conserve the natural and cultural resources of the area and to provide for public recreation through the economic and social development of local communities. Conservation Boards would not primarily be creatures of local government. They would embrace a wide variety of stakeholders including business and NGOs. They would contain a blend of national, regional and local representation. Their accountability would derive in part from direct election and in part from appointment by key stakeholders and other tiers of government. They would work in partnership, catalysing others, seeking new resources and pioneering new approaches. They would be similar in many respects to the Regional Parks in France. They would be required to agree structure and development plans for the local area, with appeal to ministers in the case of serious disagreement. Development control would rest with local authorities. Conservation Boards would have the right to be consulted on cases, and to co-determine those which in the opinion of the conservation board would have a significant and long-term impact on the quality of the area.

Conservation Boards might be appropriate only in a more limited number of areas than the current full suite of AONBs and National Parks in England. But the conservation board model might also be used in areas requiring significant national regeneration effort. Indeed a similar approach is already being used in areas such as the National Forest and the Community Forests and in less formal partnerships throughout the country. Conservation boards would require legislative underpinning and long-term national funding. The life of an individual Board would not be indefinite. Boards might each be given a ten-year mandate with the chance to bid for renewal. Their mandate might be amended or terminated if their job was done or their boundary or constitution required amendment.

WORKING WITH THE ECONOMIC AND SOCIAL GRAIN

As I noted, the legislation of the 1940s was primarily concerned with planning and regulation. These remain important elements. But a fresh approach today would surely place stronger emphasis on working with the economic and the social grain to achieve desired outcomes. We live in a market economy, though markets are shaped by our social and political objectives. To a considerable extent we get the countryside we deserve: our living habits, our travel patterns, our food purchases, shape settlements, transport networks and farming systems. It is not enough to say that 'they' (the housebuilders, the motoring organisations or the supermarkets) have imposed their choices on us.

How shall we harness the power of the market? This is a huge subject. Let me pick out one or two points. Agriculture is clearly unsustainable in its present form. It costs too much. Farm incomes are low, at least in upland areas. Environmental quality has been lost. Numbers employed continue to decline. One of the main shortcomings of the 1949 dispensation was the failure to see agriculture and forestry as key engines of countryside change. Today, we need to chart the way towards more sustainable patterns of agriculture which guarantee a livelihood for farmers running viable businesses (even if these may be part-time), re-integrate farming into the rural community, and make farming, as was envisaged in the 1940s, an ally, not an enemy, of a high quality environment.

We need much closer links between our interest in safe food, whose production contributes to a high quality environment, and our purchasing decisions as consumers. The upsurge of interest in farmers' markets and the

Countryside Agency's preliminary work on 'Countryside Products' show this to be a promising area.

The Rural Development Regulation holds out the promise of being the second pillar of the CAP. At present it is a small stump. We need to built it up. One component might be a new legal 'duty of care' on farmers and foresters to maintain the quality of the countryside, based on a nationally recognised standard of good practice. Another might be universally available land management contracts, to deliver benefits beyond the basic duty of care.

In its Transport White Paper, the Government has signalled a fresh direction for transport policy, relying more on public transport, walking and cycling, and less on the private car as the universal provider. We need to travel wisely, and be prepared to use a wider variety of travel options. This means more projects in rural areas to demonstrate and, later, implement high quality alternatives to private car use. There is an important 'hearts and minds' issue here, as well as practical measures.

Those hostile to countryside conservation often say contemptuously 'you cannot eat the view'. In the Lake District, the West Country and many other rural areas, rural economic development depends very substantially on eating the view. In such areas, the income generated by visitors and tourism for local businesses, far exceeds that generated by what is often a highly subsidised agriculture. This is not to deny that there can be disbenefits to the local community and to the environment from some aspects of tourism. We need to find better ways of harnessing the economic resource that visitors and tourism represents. As tourists, we need to recognise more clearly that our presence brings costs to the local community and the local environment, and be prepared to think of new means of meeting these costs at point of use, for example through car parking charges or visitor taxes.

COUNTRYSIDE RECREATION

The fact that over two-thirds of the 1949 Act focused on recreation provision demonstrates both the importance and the complexity of the subject. In the 1950s, local authorities were required to prepare 'definitive maps' of rights of way. In the 1960s, the Ordnance Survey began to represent those routes on its maps. From the late 1980s, the Countryside Commission started a campaign to bring all rights of way into good order. Together these represented a huge step forward for recreation, particularly for walkers in England. The access provisions of the 1949 Act have had a more chequered history. The legislation currently proposed by the Government on access to open countryside, will at last fulfil what was promised in 1949 and first sought more than a century ago.

Do these aspirations for rights of way and access to open countryside, meet the recreational needs of today, or are they a recreational agenda which belongs to the pre-war era? Walking in the countryside remains hugely popular. Walking and mountaineering, the traditional activities, have grown in popularity over the last decade. The hills of the Lake District are busier than ever before. But there has also been a growth of other activities: off-road cycling, horse riding, off-road vehicles, trips to 'visitor attractions' such as gardens and rural theme parks.

Visiting the countryside remains important socially (both for those who visit and for local communities), economically and environmentally. Many countryside recreation sites, because they require low intensity management help sustain, rather than threaten, an environmental resource. Recreational opportunities need to be of high quality (few people enjoy overgrown footpaths). They need to offer an assured experience where people can go in confidence, to be convenient and accessible and to be flexible in relation to changing demands. The requirements of sustainability, both environmental and social, point to the importance of recreation close to where people live and available by non-motorised travel.

While the universal rights of way system meets some of these requirements well, its overall standard remains low or at least unpredictable. It is much better at catering for the needs of walkers than of horse riders and cyclists. It needs to be enhanced, particularly close to cities and in popular recreational areas, by routes managed to a higher standard with few physical barriers and greater ease of access. This is what the 'Greenways' and 'Quiet Roads' currently being developed by the Countryside Agency and local authorities in many parts of the country seek to achieve. Access to water, whether for boating, fishing, picnics or other uses has not generally received the same attention as access to land, yet it too has its fair share of management problems. So legislation today might build on the rights of way legislation, empowering local authorities to designate routes for non-motorised travel, both on and off public roads, with accompanying high standards of maintenance and publicity.

What of access to open countryside? It will be fascinating to see whether the Scottish approach or the England and Wales approach proves to be the more viable. In England and Wales, the somewhat artificial separation of land types, deriving from the 1949 Act, may prove difficult to implement in practice. It implies that some types of countryside are suitable for recreation and others are not. 90% of the mapping should prove no problem, and when complete will at least provide greater certainty both for the recreational user and for the landowner. But I have some misgivings about the definitional work needed and about the notion of a two-tier countryside that it implies.

The Scottish approach based on, for example, Danish and German experience looks interesting. The confirmation that people are free to go anywhere in the countryside, except in crops and near to buildings, but coupled with a duty of care, looks to be a sensible way forward. However, if it is not linked to more specific provisions to facilitate public access, whether linear or area-wide, it could remain a noble statement of principle which has limited practical value except for the more determined hill-walkers.

CONCLUSION

In summary, what might be the main features of a Countryside Act for the new Millennium?

- First, there would be a legal underpinning for the concepts of Countryside Character and Environmental Capital.
- Second, there would be with a re-definition of the role of town and country planning, sharpening its contribution to sustainable development.
- Third, there would be fresh provision for multi-sector conservation Boards to set strategy and carry out management activity in specific areas of countryside, with long-term sustainability objectives.
- Fourth, there would be a stronger commitment to use fiscal instruments and other regulatory and incentive mechanisms to guide consumer decisions towards sustainability objectives; for example, visitor taxes or car use charges.
- Fifth, there would be a duty of care on farmers to maintain the quality of the countryside.
- Sixth, there would be a new power and duty on local authorities to define networks of routes for non-motorised travel based on rights of way and parts of the minor road network.
- Seventh, there would be new provision for a legal right of access to the countryside for recreation, coupled with a duty of care on recreational users.

In conclusion, the countryside remains important as a national as well as a local asset, contributing to the economic, social and environmental well-being of us all. The spirit of 1949 remains relevant: the means of channelling it into legislation and practice has changed. The countryside is also a European asset. The European Landscape Convention now in preparation will give recognition to the importance of all our countryside, not only to those parts which we have defined as special places.

FURTHER READING

Blunden, John and Curry, Nigel (1990). *A People's Charter? Forty years of the National Parks and Access to the Countryside Act 1949.* HMSO, London.

Edwards, Ron (1991). *Fit for the Future; report of the National Parks Review Panel.* Countryside Commission, Cheltenham.

MacEwen, Ann and Malcolm (1987). *Greenprints for the countryside?: the story of Britain's National Parks.* Allen and Unwin, London.

Sheail, John (1998). *Nature Conservation in Britain: the formative years.* The Stationery Office, London.

17

Delivering Benefits Globally, Nationally and Locally

Roger Crofts

INTRODUCTION

THE ACHIEVEMENT OF sustainable development offers a major opportunity for the statutory conservation agencies in Britain. I argue that the environment is a key element of sustainable development and that environmental interests must play a more active part in achieving sustainable development. The key is integration. To paraphrase the title of the conference, two connections are needed: to link *nature* and *landscape* together and to link both with *people*. Both of these connections must be at the heart of new approaches locally, nationally and globally. The old adage 'think global, not local' remains relevant, but I argue that when we act globally we should be influenced by experience and practice locally and nationally.

I shall examine the 'lessons from the past' and draw out from them four challenges of sustainable development for environmental interests. I shall then examine 'visions for the future' and set out four further challenges of sustainable development which these visions present. I will then examine new approaches underway in Scotland, in which Scottish Natural Heritage has a key role. In each one I shall set out the expected sustainable development benefits and assess the extent to which each is addressing the eight challenges identified earlier in the paper.

Throughout the paper I shall use the definition of sustainable development as the total integration of the trilogy of increasing economic prosperity, achieving social well-being and equality, and improving the stewardship of the environment.

I take the dividing point between the past and the future as 1992. This was the period when the aims and purposes of statutory nature and landscape conservation and the means of achieving them were redefined and new institutional structures were put in place. It was also the period when new visions were set globally at the UN Conference on Environment and Development in Rio which are now being actioned nationally and locally.

LESSONS FROM THE PAST

When one hears of nature conservation experts being burnt in effigy or reads headlines such as 'Birds halt development', 'People should come first', 'Industry fears over nature reserve plan', it is clear that nature and people are seen as opposites. There are many and complex reasons for this stand-off. I will summarise those most pertinent to the achievement of a more integrated approach which the sustainable development agenda demands.

Sectoral policies and the deployment of resources have tended to be the order of the day. There has been insufficient attention given to the impacts on the environment of policies and resource deployment for housing, enterprise, energy, transport, agriculture, forestry, fisheries and even the environment itself. Improvements are certainly noticeable, especially in forestry and, more recently, in transport and agriculture. However, many areas of policy and resource deployment remain woefully short of a multi-objective approach which recognises the environment as an intrinsic element of equal standing with economic and social elements. Take, for example, where the Common Agriculture Policy ensures economic and efficient production of food but fails to secure either a high level of environmental stewardship or the provision of social benefits to rural communities. Even when the environment is considered, it is often marginal. All too often, environmental policy and environmental resources are expected to mitigate the effects of what are seen as environmental problems. An excellent example is the lack of integration of agricultural and environmental policy when applied to the management of wild geese on intensively farmed land; an increase in over-wintering populations is seen both as an agricultural problem and a conservation success.

The separation of nature conservation from landscape conservation and access to the countryside in policy, resource deployment and institutional structures existed for over 40 years. It is pertinent to ask how can environmental interests expect other sectors to embrace a more integrated approach when none existed in the natural heritage sector?

The *institutional structure* which develops, approves and puts these policies into action is frequently insular and confrontational (what is now called the 'silo mentality'). Each functional sector has developed its own *institutional ethos and culture,* and, as a result, a certain *professional preciousness.* Attempts to merge cultures and to bring about a more flexible approach to decision-making have in the past been woefully lacking. More complex structures and more flexible working practices are an essential element in achieving sustainable development.

Many attempts to place environmental considerations at the heart of decision making have been made through the use of *environmental evaluation methodologies.* But there has been limited acceptance of them. It is recognised that the values which society might place on the functions and services provided by the environment for society are rarely easy to measure or compatible with tried and tested economic measurement techniques. Those who seek to measure everything in monetary terms do place environmental considerations at a disadvantage and this means that progress is often slow. Much good work is now being undertaken by ecologists and economists in this very complex field (see Vaze, 1998). And there is now a stronger political will, as exemplified by the publication of headline and core indicators by the UK Government embracing environmental, economic and social factors (DETR, 1999). There remains the need to speed up the development and use of new techniques. This is best achieved through collaboration between academic disciplines and sponsorship by a variety of agencies with different functions. Hopefully, the result will be that the outcomes are accepted and used by decision-makers, whatever their sector of operation.

The poor *communication* between environmental experts and others has been a handicap. There are inevitably, for instance, communication difficulties between the language of science and that of economists. The position has been exacerbated by the capacity of technical experts to confuse their knowledge with their own *value systems.* On all too many occasions, we have seen in the past information and knowledge being confused and mixed up with a set of personal values which can sometimes detract from the argument for change. For example, arguments concerning potential collapses in wild species populations often ignore the underpinning objective population viability analyses. Similarly, arguments about job losses due to the designation of a wildlife site frequently ignore the economic benefits which the site can provide. The media in its normal conflict-seeking mode of operation has sought to exploit and, indeed, exaggerate, differences between the 'sides'. More collaborative working is necessary, using everyday language within the context that experts identify the shared values which the sustainable development ethic demands.

The *skills* required to deal with the complexities of the environment within the wider context of sustainable development are extraordinarily wide. Traditionally, environmental organisations have tended to employ experts on, for example, species populations, habitat monitoring and management, and landscape aesthetics. These experts are still needed. In addition, there is the need to engage those with skills in community participation, project management, resource planning, economic evaluation and analysis of economic forces, amongst others. Environmental organisations, therefore, must ensure that they employ, or have access to, the requisite range of skills. In addition, management should ensure that existing staff have the capabilities to do the job now required of them.

The pressures on the statutory conservation agencies since their establishment fifty years ago have changed. One of the most significant changes, in the context of sustainable development, is the *balance of effort* between protected areas and work in the wider countryside. The impact of post-war policies, fuelled particularly by the EU Common Agricultural Policy, has meant very substantial losses in biodiversity since 1945 (Wynne, et al., 1995), when Sir Arthur Tansley wrote his seminal book *Our Heritage of Wild Nature*. Protected areas have become an even more important instrument of environmental policy (IUCN, 1997). The amount and rigour of legislation attached to them has increased accordingly, especially under the EU Habitats and Species Directive and the enabling UK Regulations. In this context, the ability of the statutory agencies to engage effectively with *key stakeholders* has been hindered by imposed timescales. As a result, there are all too many examples of conflict between the local community and environmental organisations when there should be shared recognition benefits which the environment can bring to the local communities (The Scottish Office, 1998). Positive approaches to stimulate financially new forms of management are beneficial but clash with the now out-moded compensatory regime born of the 'voluntary principle'. Pressures to maintain the current status of ecological health ignore the natural, and often unpredictable, dynamics of natural systems. Scientific analysis is not always in a position to provide guidance on management solutions. Much excellent policy advice on the wider countryside has been given over many years by the current statutory conservation bodies and their predecessors but resource restrictions have meant fire-fighting on protected areas has tended to be the order of the day. New approaches to help cope with this situation, embracing ecosystem management at different geographical scales (see below), have been introduced by a number of agencies (Crofts *et al*, 2000).

A variety of approaches by the statutory conservation agencies would help to address these points. Successful argument for using a complementary range of Government policies and resource mechanisms to achieve society's objectives for protected areas is essential. More people-friendly and inclusive approaches to conservation are required, both set down in statute and applied in practice. More training in collaborative working with people is needed. More scientific endeavour orientated to the understanding of natural processes and functions and the implications for managing and manipulating them would also help.

Finally, in this brief survey, is the issue of how *society*, and communities and individuals within it, *value* the environment. Reference to any opinion polls shows consistently that health, education and employment are top of the poll and as a result are highest on the political agenda. Environment has a generally low rating. Those environmental issues undertaken by the statutory conservation agencies tend to be lower than those of the statutory environmental protection agencies. A clear connection between environmental protection and human health and well-being is an important part of the explanation. And yet individual incidents concerning wildlife – a stranded sperm whale, persecution of hen harriers or peregrine falcons, reappearance of otters in rivers, or ospreys nesting in the Highlands of Scotland – evoke a strong, and positive, public and media reaction. At the same time, we are still bedevilled by the uninformed views of those who wish to intervene to 're-balance nature' by removing some species in order to support economic ends, or those who wish to preserve and protect the furry and the cuddly and ignore the natural imbalances which do occur when society intervenes in natural systems. Perhaps the lesson is for the environmental movement to act in a more concerted way across the voluntary groups and within Government agencies and through integrating organisations such as IUCN. The action is to demonstrate good practice on the ground in order to increase understanding of the value and benefits to people of a well-stewarded environment.

Figure 1. Protected areas in Scotland

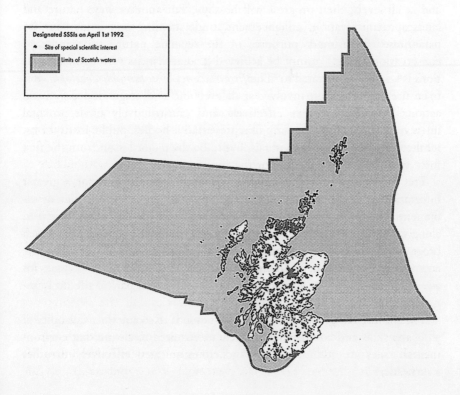

Designated SSSIs on April 1st 1992

* Site of special scientific interest

Limits of Scottish waters

Perhaps these issues are best epitomised by just two illustrations. On the map of the whole of Scotland (Figure 1) the marine environment is by far the largest area and yet there has been little activity in terms of protected areas work by conservation agencies there; the concentration of effort has been on the terrestrial protected areas. The consequence was that, unfortunately, the public perception was negative. Newspaper headlines with which we are all so familiar claim that: 'People should come first', 'The Chief Constable is driven from his home by a plague of bats', etc. The notion that people are really the endangered species, therefore, grew in force during the period.

There are many lessons which can be drawn for the environment and environmental bodies from this rapid review of forty years. I have identified four lessons which I style *challenges of sustainable development*.

The key challenge from the writer's perspective (having been engaged in re-defining the objectives for institutional structures and the culture of statutory conservation, and then leading their implementation in Scotland) is to ensure that *people* are fundamental. Society can have all of the appropriate policies, all of the relevant scientific knowledge, all of the necessary fiscal instruments but unless people are involved in the decision-making about the environment, who are committed to it at all stages and at all levels, then progress will be slow. Put another way, nature and landscape conservation, enhancement, understanding and enjoyment (to paraphrase the primary purposes of the separate nature and landscape conservation bodies) cannot be achieved if society in its various manifestations is ignored or dictated to. The *first challenge of sustainable development* is to ensure that people are involved at all levels and at all stages in decision and action. Bringing together effectively and constructively environmental interests with others in the form of representative bodies, public institutions, local communities and individuals, has to be the major lesson from the first forty years and the challenge for the future.

The *second challenge of sustainable development* is to press for a greater integration of environmental, social and economic interests in policy development and resource deployment. Programmes with multiple objectives, along with the strategic assessment of the environmental component of each programme, are critical features if the challenge is to be met. Ensuring the acceptance of environmental considerations means that the methodologies for assessing and appraising a policy need to be an integral part of the decision-making process.

The *third challenge of sustainable development* is to secure the availability of all of the skills and competencies which are required to ensure that environmental issues are addressed fully and communicated effectively to other stakeholders.

The *fourth challenge of sustainable development* is to ensure that wildlife and landscape protection and enhancement is undertaken everywhere, and is not restricted to protected areas.

In summary, the first four challenges of sustainable development are:

- ensuring that people (representative bodies, public institutions, local communities and individuals) are involved at all levels and at all stages in making decisions,
- pressing for a greater integration of environmental, social and economic interests in policy development and resource deployment,
- securing the availability of necessary skills and competencies, and
- ensuring that wildlife and landscape protection and enhancement are undertaken everywhere, and not restricted to protected areas.

VISIONS FOR THE FUTURE

The 'Visions for the future' are, perhaps ironically, those determined at the Rio Earth Summit in 1992. They were the culmination of a formative period of intellectual activity. The World Conservation Strategy of 1980, perhaps the seminal environmental document of the twentieth century, argued for a new approach based on the key objectives of maintenance of essential ecological processes and life-support systems, preservation of genetic diversity, and ensuring the sustainable utilisation of species and ecosystems (IUCN/ UNEP/WWF, 1980). These concepts were developed and encapsulated ultimately in the Convention on Biological Diversity with its key objectives of the conservation of biological diversity, the sustainable use of its components, and the fair and equitable sharing of the benefits arising from the use of genetic resources (Glowka *et al*, 1994).

Parallel and complementary thinking was being developed, stimulated by the desire of some industrial nations to bridge the 'North/South gap' and the recognition that western industrialised nations' values were always being imposed on developing countries. The Report of the World Commission on Environment and Development (WCED, 1987) placed people at the heart of the agenda and coined the term 'sustainable development' – bringing together the environment and development with the focus clearly on people 'whose well-being is the ultimate goal of all environment and development policies'. This is epitomised in the sub-title of the Commission's Report 'From one earth to one world', signalling integration and cohesion of the key issues affecting human survival on the planet. This carefully analysed and argued vision, along with the further work by the environmental movement in the form of *Caring for the Earth* (IUCN/UNEP/WWF, 1991), provided the basis for the Rio Declaration on Environment and Development which set out 27 principles (UNCED, 1992). This suite of agreements set a new vision, a new baseline and a new challenge for everyone: integrating people and their environment globally, nationally and locally.

In Europe, the European Union responded with the signing of the Amsterdam Treaty with its provisions on sustainable development and environmental assessment at the heart of decision-making. The EU Council of Ministers approved the EU Biodiversity Strategy. The Council of Europe set in train the pan-European Biological and Landscape Diversity Strategy. In the UK, the Government published strategies on sustainable development (DoE, 1994a), biodiversity (DoE, 1994b) and climatic change, established round tables, panels and advisory groups on sustainable development to stimulate debate and lead to action: the former easy, the latter at times intractable, especially where there was a lack of political will.

In Scotland, a new statutory agency was established in 1992 (Rifkind, 1991; SDD, 1991). Scottish Natural Heritage was formed in the context of new international thinking on Sustainable Development (SNH, 1993). The key drivers were: to bring decision-making on Scotland to Scotland, to integrate nature conservation with landscape conservation and access, to provide a more cohesive approach to the natural heritage, to create opportunities for positive action for the natural heritage, and to provide a greater understanding of the processes affecting the natural heritage and its better management (see Crofts, 1994a and 1994b; SDD, 1991).

Its remit has three significant elements as far as sustainable development is concerned. First, the enabling statute brings together for the first time the protection and enhancement of nature and landscape. Second, it has a specific remit on sustainable development: 'SNH shall have regard to the desirability of securing that everything done, whether by SNH or any other person, in relation to the natural heritage of Scotland is undertaken in a manner that is sustainable' (Natural Heritage (Scotland) Act, 1991, Section 1(1)). This was a first for a statutory body in the UK. And, third, it has a specific focus on people as encapsulated in its balancing duties 'to take into account as may be appropriate in the circumstances of: the needs of agriculture, fisheries and forestry; the need for social and economic development in Scotland or any part of Scotland; the interests of owners and occupiers of land and the interests of local communities' (Natural Heritage (Scotland) Act, 1991, Section 3 (1)). This is most pointedly emphasised in its mission statement: 'working with Scotland's people to care for our natural heritage'. In the words of its founder Chairman, Magnus Magnusson, 'Our task is to secure the conservation and enhancement of Scotland's unique and precious natural heritage, and to help people to enjoy it responsibly, understand it more fully and use it more sensibly and sensitively, so that it can be sustained for future generations' (SNH, 1994). He also emphasised that 'Conservation and development are interdependent. Conservation keeps our actions within the earth's carrying capacity; development enables people everywhere to enjoy healthy and fulfilling lives. As we strive to achieve a proper balance between the two, our partners in action are farmers, crofters, foresters, land owners, planners, local communities, conservation bodies, recreation groups . . . for environmental issues there is no 'them' and 'us': we are all in this together' (SNH, 1992).

In 1999, natural heritage policy and action was devolved to the Scottish Parliament, and also to the Welsh Assembly. This creates the opportunity for tailor-made solutions for addressing nature and landscape and people in each country. At the same time, it also presents the challenge of ensuring there is due recognition of the international value and importance of the environment in the constituent parts of the UK.

To summarise, the essence of the new accords is a vision for the future which calls for a world:

- where human society and its natural environment are accepted to be interdependent,
- where people are an intrinsic part of the environment,
- where the environment is recognised as a capital asset for society, and
- where the environment can be used for human benefit provided that this is within its carrying capacity, that undue risks are not taken and that the functioning of natural systems is not significantly impaired.

The institutional, legal and administrative mechanisms were set in place in the early 1990s to support the achievement of these ideals. Making them a reality, however, is not a straightforward task (Crofts, 1991). To assume that the new international accords of 1992 were all about human benefit and that the environment was purely for human exploitation would be a fundamental mistake. For those people who think the accords were all about a 'sustainable economy' and a 'sustainable society' and not a 'sustainable environment' then I am afraid they have got it wrong. And, therefore, it was very encouraging for us working in Scotland to find in the 'Partnership for Scotland', the coalition document between the Liberal Democrat and Labour Parties, the phrase 'environmental sustainability'. A number of new approaches are being promoted which should help to deliver the vision in practice (Holdgate, 1996).

Biodiversity has become a major theme. The 59–point *Biodiversity: the UK*

Action Plan (DoE, 1994b) touched all parts of Government which it needed
to and was, at the time, a major step forward. In practice, however, most
progress has been made by Government and non-government environmental
bodies working together. Those aspects which could be delivered by this
sector were the order of the day and countless Species Action Plans were at the
forefront of endeavour. Only recently have Habitat Action Plans begun to
take a more prominent role. I am of the view that a vast number of Species
Action Plans and a few Habitat Action Plans do not make a Biodiversity
Action Plan. Even now some key elements of the Convention on Biological
Diversity have insufficient attention paid to them: genetic diversity (as
opposed purely to species and habitat diversity defined on a largely non-
genetic basis), sustainable use of key biological resources, such as fish and
wood, and the role of protected areas. A broadening of action by Government
and its agencies is urgently needed. Fundamentally, this must result in the
local biodiversity action plans and the processes associated with their development feeding into and influencing local Agenda 21 plans. If they do not,
then I consider it will be a major failure.

Soil, air and water provide a resource base for civil society and they can also
provide specific **environmental services and functions** for society: the living,
natural capital. Take, for example, wetlands (mires, fens, salt marshes and river
floodplains) and their role in the UK. They are part of functioning natural
systems. Unfortunately, they are too often regarded as a hindrance to farming
or house construction or other development, which need to be controlled
through drainage. Stopping floodplains flooding to protect arable farmland
means that the run-off in the channels will be faster and that flood banks
downstream are likely to be overwhelmed causing substantial damage with a
high cost of reinstatement. Wetlands are, therefore, important natural
regulators of water movement. They also serve as sinks for waste, as well
as wildlife sanctuaries providing both spiritual refreshment and recreational
enjoyment. Defining such functions and services and ascribing a monetary
value to them provides the basis for a new way of assessing the environment
alongside those features which are more susceptible to measurement by
normal economic indicators (Costanza *et al*, 1997, Daily, 1998). The same
approach can be taken for many other services (see table below) such as
erosion control, soil formation, genetic resources, food production and
recreation. It is possible to analyse the interaction and dependencies between
the various components of an ecosystem, and to ascribe quantative and non-
quantative values for society. Such approaches provide an aid to understanding the complex dependencies of society on the functioning of natural
systems. More engagement on these approaches would yield benefits to
decision-makers.

KEY ECOSYSTEM SERVICES AND FUNCTIONS

Ecosystem service	Ecosystem Function	Society Benefit
Soil formation	Support soil formation processes	Long term natural capital for food and fibre maintained
Erosion control	Retain soil within system	Greater natural production capacity, less use of artificial production stimulants
Water regulation	Regulation of hydrological flows	Reduced flood risk to farmland and settlements, provision of wildlife sanctuaries and recreational use, waste sink
Landscape and biological diversity	Retain diversity of life forms and landscapes	Emotional, health, recreational, and economic benefits and more wildlife

The basic scientific approach which calls for individual elements of the environment to be reorganised as part of wider functioning systems was recognised recently in the Fountainbleu Accord (IUCN, 1998). It is welcome news that there is a renewed interest in *understanding ecosystems* as an intrinsic element of planning and managing the natural dynamics of the environment (Budianski, 1996; Maltby, 1999). The ecosystem approach, as it is now labelled, is 'a method for sustaining or restoring natural systems and their functions and values. It is goal driven, and is based on a collaboratively developed vision of desired future conditions which integrates ecological, economical and social factors. It is applied within a geographic framework defined primarily by ecological boundaries' (U.S. Inter-agency Ecosystem Management Task Force, 1995). In our visions for the future we are prompted, therefore, to ensure that the dynamics of natural systems, including the fact that they are inherently unstable and have a value for society, are taken into account when society seeks to intervene.

It is important to address the functioning of environment systems at the appropriate *geographical scale*. This has become known as the 'bioregional approach' (Miller, 1996 and 2000). It is defined as dealing with the functioning of ecosystems, which includes people, at an appropriate geographical scale. It has been applied to the Central American Cordillera, the Serengeti and nearer home is being applied to the Tweed basin, the Loch Leven catchment in Fife, the whole of Scotland and also in many European countries (Crofts *et al*, 2000). The bioregional approach seeks to lessen the isolation of protected areas by recognising that every part of a region plays a different part in the functioning of the whole, and should not have an adverse effect on the whole. It recognises that there are gradations in the protection for species, habitats and landscapes from core zones of high protection, through buffers, to corridors which connect them, and placed within a wider matrix (Figure 2). Human settlements and economic activity are embraced within the bioregion to ensure that there is a connection between human needs and the functions and services provided by the environment within the region.

Figure 2.   Schematic Diagram of Integrated Planning

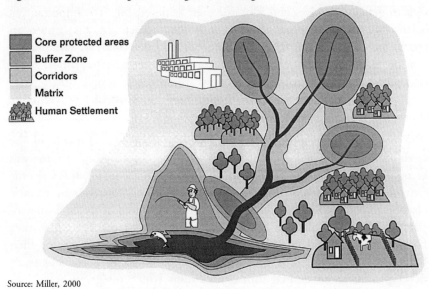

Source: Miller, 2000

A critical aspect of ecosystem management at different geographical scales, as now practised, is that humans are integral components of the ecosystem: they influence the system while also being affected by it (McNeely, 2000). This has very substantial implications for the processes of deciding on objectives and outcomes, and determining strategies and plans. People as key stakeholders can no longer be ignored. Although engagement of stake-holders prolongs the decision-making process, it provides long-lasting results compared with possible immediate but short-lived gains if there is no engagement. Defining who the stakeholders are is crucial – local communities, owners of land and other property, organisations with statutory responsi-bilities, and democratically-elected representatives of the people. Local inter-ests, although vitally important, are not the only legitimate stakeholders. National government and its agencies, along with representative and member-ship organisations with specific interests and responsibilities are equally important. Effective processes which allow for the full engagement of these stakeholders must be part of the approach. In turn, stakeholders should accept that the achievement of shared objectives and outcomes must be part of the deal of engagement.

Defining agreed objectives and sharing desired outcomes amongst stakeholder interests is a critical part of the sustainable development agenda. The broader the objectives and outcomes, then the wider the stakeholder base must be, and so the more challenging it becomes. It is essential to identify the values which are shared and those which are not, and from the common values seek to define objectives and monitor their achievement. It is important to balance the three elements of sustainable development in this context to ensure that one does not take over the others. Recognition that some values can be mutually supportive is also important, such as aesthetics with naturalness, enhancement and restoration with local economic worth.

A managed approach, which allows reaction to particular problems or allows adaption to reach desired end points, is necessary. This cannot be undertaken without adequate scientific information and knowledge of the environment and informed interpretation of the status and trends of the constituent parts. Taking full account of the dynamics of the environment at different spatial scales, and identifying the limits of acceptable change and carrying capacities of the environment, are all critical.

To arrive at desired outcomes, there must first be discussion and agreement on the action required and the means of taking it forward. The full engagement of those stakeholders with the ability to deliver new approaches and mechanisms and their political willingness to adapt to changing circumstances are essential components. A variety of measures, with fiscal instruments arguably the most powerful, alongside regulation, statutory duties, statutory or voluntary codes of practice, must all be part of the toolkit.

From this review of the visions for the future to achieve sustainable development there are a number of key lessons: promote environmental functions and services, engage all stakeholders throughout the process of decision-making and action, have clear goals and the means of achieving them, aided by the use of the best available knowledge and information, obtain quickly the necessary knowledge and information where there is a critical gap, use flexibly different tools and mechanisms, and work at the appropriate geographical scale.

From these points I draw four further challenges of sustainable development:

- The *fifth challenge of sustainable development* is to establish frameworks for decision-making and action at the appropriate geographical scale which bring together all of the elements of the environment, including nature and landscape, protected areas and the wider countryside.

- The *sixth challenge of sustainable development* is to ensure that the strategies within each geographical area have clear goals and meaningful indicators to measure progress and that they are shared by all stakeholders.
- The *seventh challenge of sustainable development* is to ensure that the services and functions which the environment provides for society are better understood and accepted.
- The *eighth challenge of sustainable development* is to ensure that appropriate scientific knowledge of the environment is available and accessible to all.

PUTTING THE IDEAL INTO PRACTICE

The eight challenges of sustainable development from an environmental perspective form the basis for reviewing practice. A great number of initiatives are in place in many countries. Five of these which are led, facilitated or involve Scottish Natural Heritage are reviewed here. In each case, the contribution to sustainable development and the processes and mechanisms used are described briefly. The outcomes to date are then assessed against the eight challenges: Figure 3 summarises the assessment.

I. NATURAL HERITAGE ZONES

A new framework for the delivery of SNH's work locally and nationally is currently being developed – styled Natural Heritage Zones. The planned benefits for sustainable development from this programme will be: to clarify the environmental contribution to sustainable development locally through the local Agenda 21 process, local Biodiversity Action Plans and Community Plans; to identify environmental opportunities which will bring social and economic benefits locally; and to engage stakeholders in vision and objective setting and ensuing action.

Scotland has been sub-divided into 21 zones (Fig. 4) which have similar natural and cultural attributes. Each zone has been defined on the basis of a variety of factors, including species distribution, climate, soils, topography and landscape character (Mather and Gunson, 1995; SNH, 1998a; Usher and Balharry, 1996). For each zone, all relevant data are analysed in order to aid the development of a vision for the next quarter of a century and the opportunities for and means of achieving it. From this material a prospectus for each zone is drafted. Thereafter, engagement with key stakeholders is undertaken. Simultaneously, national assessments of the status of key elements of the natural heritage are developed. The material from these assessments and from the zonal prospectuses is then used to identify national policy objectives. Again, engagement of key stakeholders is an important part of the process of agreeing these objectives.

Figure 3. Natural Heritage initiatives in Scotland: A sustainable development assessment

Challenges of Sustainable Development	Natural Heritage Zones	Loch Leven	The Cairngorms	The Firths	Duthchas
1. Engagement of people and stakeholders	?	✓	✓	✓	✓
2. Integrated policy and resources	X	✓	✓	✓	?
3. All skills and competencies engaged	✓	✓	✓	✓	✓
4. Embracing whole landscape	✓	✓	✓	✓	✓
5. Integrated framework at appropriate scale	✓	✓	✓	✓	✓
6. Goals identified and indicators defined	✓	✓	✓	✓	?
7. Environmental services contribution identified	✓	✓	X	?	?
8. Appropriate environmental knowledge available	✓	✓	✓	✓	?

Response to "challenge"

✓ wholly met   ✓ met in part   ? not tested   X not met

Figure 4. Natural Heritage Zones: integrated planning and decision-making

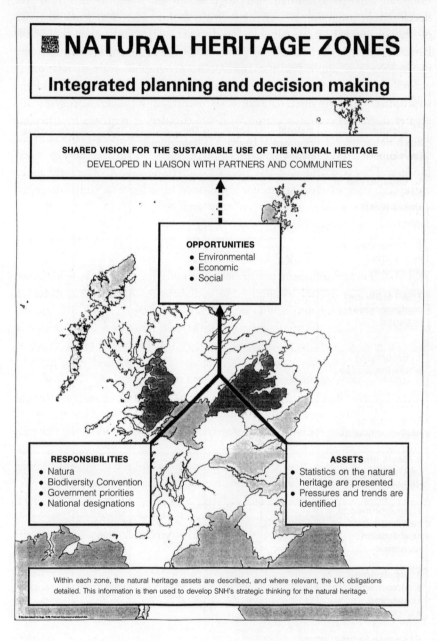

Only an interim assessment of progress can be made as this four-year development programme is at the half-way point. The clear gains in terms of the challenges of sustainable development are: embracing the whole landscape in which the role of protected areas is given a wider context; the approach is applied at the appropriate geographic scale in relation to natural features, deliverable solutions and stakeholder perception; and the appropriate environmental data has been assembled. It is acknowledged that a greater degree of communication with stakeholders is required to articulate clearly the goals and the means of achieving those goals. More critical in the development work is the engagement of people – including the key stake-holders. This is essential if the policies and resources of others are to be harnessed, and where appropriate modified, to achieve a truly integrated approach: this activity is still at an early stage.

2. LOCH LEVEN CATCHMENT

The Loch Leven catchment in Fife has local value for recreation, wildlife and its contribution to the economy. It is internationally significant for its breeding, migratory and wintering wildlife, particularly wildfowl, and its brown trout fishery. Nutrient enrichment through phosphorous deposition in the loch itself demanded action within the catchment. Although some action had been underway for two decades, statutory agencies and local interests recognised that a more concerted effort was required.

The planned benefits for sustainable development were to achieve sustainable management within the catchment through the development of an integrated catchment management plan with the specific objective of reducing phosphorous input.

The process used was to establish a steering committee of key stakeholder interests and for the public agencies to join together and appoint a project officer. Four working groups, dealing with water quality, river management, planning and development, and agriculture and forestry, were established with representation of key stakeholder interests. Extensive consultations were carried out leading ultimately to the publishing of a catchment management plan (Loch Leven Catchment Management Project, 1999). The plan includes 62 recommendations with planned implementation directed at key statutory bodies. The clear outcome is an agreed plan by the stakeholder interests as a framework for future action.

An assessment against the eight challenges of sustainable development shows that all of the challenges have been met and that implementation of the strategy will ensure action agreed by the parties is undertaken and progress monitored. The quality of the local environment has been recognised as important in its own right. All stakeholders have recognised that they have a role to play in improving environmental quality. The integrated approach as an effective means of dealing with the issues has been recognised and acted upon. Finally, there is a recognition that to achieve the desired outcomes requires effort by all stakeholders committed over a long period of time.

3. THE CAIRNGORMS

The need for an integrated approach to the management of the Cairngorms Mountains and their surrounding glens and straths has been recognised for a long period of time. In 1991 the Government began a new initiative which, through various manifestations, is ongoing. The planned benefits for sustainable development are the reversal of environmental, and specifically ecological, degradation and the delivery of benefits to local communities without damaging the environment. Better protection was required for key environmental assets, especially in the montane and sub-montane zones and in the native woodland zones. Opportunities also needed to be provided for economic development within the context of a high quality environment. All thinking and action had to engage the key constituencies of interest.

Government determined that action was required and established a Working Party comprising key stakeholder interests and supported by technical experts. After an intensive period of activity, the outcome was a detailed analysis of the situation and a shared vision (Cairngorms Working Party, 1992). Following a hiatus in decision-making, the Government established a Cairngorms Partnership but took a rather more detached role in the identification of the key stakeholders. After an intensive period of data gathering, analysis (Cairngorms Partnership, 1996) and consultation throughout the area and further afield, a Management Strategy was drawn up and agreed (Cairngorms Partnership, 1997). Following a further delay, a new Partnership was eventually established with the remit to deliver the Management Strategy. It is too early to judge the outcome of this stage, suffice to note that there are many actions underway some of which stem from the Management Strategy.

Parallel with the establishment of the second Partnership was work undertaken by SNH, at the request of Government, to draw up detailed proposals for the establishment of a National Park for the Cairngorms. In addition to gathering the best available experience from other developed countries (Bishop, et al., 1998), extensive consultation exercises were held, consultation papers drawn up (SNH, 1998b) and circulated widely, and meetings and seminars undertaken. The outcome was a clearly stated aim that the purposes of a Cairngorms National Park should be environmental, social and economic and that all of these could be developed in a coordinated and integrated manner, with the proviso that in the case of dispute, long-term conservation of the natural resources would be favoured (SNH, 1999).

Assessing progress against the eight challenges of sustainable development shows a reasonably positive picture. The one key missing element is the recognition of the provision of environmental services and functions, although work on landscape sensitivity and planned work on water should go some way to filling this gap. There remains a need to ensure a real balance of interests and not just to provide something for each constituency. A clearer definition of the area is essential which is geographically integral, only then can coherent policies and actions be delivered. The need for a clear mandate to the given to the new Partnership as a whole for the delivery of the agreed strategy, building in all stakeholders, is also needed. Strategic actions flowing from the management strategy rather than specific disconnected projects is also critical.

4. FOCUS ON FIRTHS

In Scotland, as in other parts of the UK, the maritime environment has been given little attention as an asset and until quite recently virtually ignored from an environmental management viewpoint. The major Firths are areas of high environmental quality, have internationally significant concentrations of wildlife, a diversity of economic activity and dependent social communities. The planned benefits of sustainable development are to promote a joint approach for the delivery and implementation of marine protected areas under the EU Habitats and Species Directive and the EU Birds Directive, to bring about a shared approach to economic benefit through tourism, and where appropriate, for industry, and to maintain traditional fishing activities. The UK Biodiversity Action Plan, published in 1994 (DoE, 1994b), identified a target for the drawing up of strategies for the key Scottish firths: Moray, Forth and Solway, by the end of 1998.

A series of fora were established for each of the three firths, together with subsidiary fora for the inner firths for the Moray Firth: Dornoch and Cromarty (SNH, 1995). The fora comprised initially of the core constituents but these were extended progressively as more stakeholders opted in to the process. In each case a full time project officer was appointed, initially funded by key public sector interests led by SNH. Newsletters to communicate progress, and topic papers to seek views on key activities, functions and other issues were produced.

The outcome is that strategies have been achieved (e.g. Solway Firth Partnership, 1998), or were in an advanced state by the deadline (e.g. Forth Estuary Forum, 1998). The pace of activity has been high and has engaged many interests in a productive way. The rate of progress has varied due to local circumstances dependent upon the perceived degree of threat to specific interests of this more planned approach, the size and complexity of the stakeholder interests and the size of the area.

Good progress has been made when assessed against the eight challenges of sustainable development. The key message is that a good deal of time is required to address new areas and topics and to bring together stakeholders who would not normally work together. Now the challenge is to ensure that the strategies are transformed into action plans with required changes in policy and the disposition of resources, and clearly defined measures of measuring progress put in place. The services which the environment can provide have not been fully built in to the strategies and this remains a worthwhile challenge to be met.

5. DUTHCHAS

The Highlands and Islands of Scotland is perhaps the most challenging area for achieving sustainable development. The aim is to help to bridge the gulf which often is perceived to exist between protection of the environment and securing development to benefit local communities. An experimental approach is currently underway partly funded by the EU LIFE Environment programme. It is entitled 'Duthchas' – emphasising the place of communities in their future and the connection of people with their land. The planned benefits for sustainable development are to find practical solutions for achieving development in remote rural communities based on the natural and cultural heritage resources.

The initiative is being undertaken in four locations, representing different community and heritage circumstances. In each, a full-time project officer has been appointed as a facilitator. The project is overseen by a Partnership of nineteen public bodies and is led by a full-time Project Co-ordinator. The plan is for all interests to work together, assess assets, focus on key issues, plan for the future and undertake actions.

The project itself is only just a year old and it is too early to check progress against the eight challenges of sustainable development. Integration of policies and resources, definition of goals and means of their achievements, contribution of environmental services and functions, and availability of appropriate environmental know-how have still not yet been tested. The project itself was born out of a long process of progressive engagement between the key stakeholders and agreement of the objectives and means of implementation. Already key issues which have to be resolved have been identified. Local participation has to be supported by the provision of hard social, economic and environmental information if the definition of objectives is to be well founded. Aligning the strategies of public bodies which work at a national level so that they support the local processes remains a challenge. A process to resolve inevitable differences in view between local people, and between local interests and public agencies, is essential. All of this takes a great amount of time and effort. Pushing forward faster than key stakeholders wish risks undermining the process and failing to achieve the benefits.

CONCLUSION

International experience and recent experience in Scotland shows that there are a number of critical factors for the success of initiatives which seek to place the environment, alongside social and economic aspects, to deliver sustainable development in practice (Figure 5). There needs to be flexibility of policies and associated instruments for delivering them and a need to modify institutional structures and to evolve the cultures of the organisations and the staff within them. There is a need to plan and manage at the appropriate geographical scale bearing in mind environmental functions, services and dynamics. Engagement of stakeholders in determining outcomes and the means of achieving them is vital, with an inclusive process throughout. Best available knowledge and information should be used at all times. Focused and strategic effort on key knowledge gaps where these are impeding advancement is required. Adaptive management is usually the best approach, with a process of monitoring and scientific assessment of the outcomes against the values and objectives being a critical part of the process.

Good progress has been made in a short time. There remains a need for greater effort to focus on environmental resources as an essential and dynamic asset in the sustainable development equation. The need for shared visions and outcomes for the use and management of the environment is critical. In addition to improved methods of evaluating the environment, we also need to apply structured and integrated approaches to ecosystem dynamics, functions and services at appropriate geographical scales. There are many challenges but it is clear that if we can move towards meeting these then the environment will become the essential practical element of sustainable development and, thereby, provide benefits locally, nationally and globally.

In Scotland, sustainable development with environmental sustainability as a key element has been agreed as a priority by the Scottish Executive for the Scottish Parliament. New machinery is required to follow up the work of the Advisory Group on Sustainable Development (AGSD, 1999) and take the agenda forward with the active engagement of all interests, including statutory environmental bodies.

Figure 5.   Diagrammatic Views of Sustainable Development

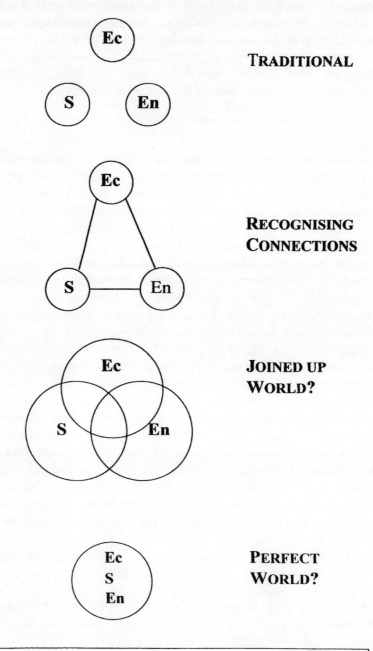

Overall, as T.C. Smout (2000) put it so appositely in his recent Ford's lecture: '. . . changes, however, will demand more than political determination, important though that is. They also demand a reduction of the sense of aggrieved self-righteousness on all sides'.

REFERENCES

Advisory Group on Sustainable Development (1999). *Scotland The Sustainable.* Secretary of State for Scotland's Advisory Group on Sustainable Development, The Scottish Office, Edinburgh.
Bishop, K., Green, M., and Phillips, A. (1998). *Models of National Parks.* SNH Review, 105.
Budiansky, S. (1996). *Nature's keepers: the new science of nature management.* Phoenix, London.
Cairngorms Partnership (1996). *The Cairngorms Assets.* Cairngorms Partnership, Grantown.
Cairngorms Partnership (1997). *Managing the Cairngorms.* Cairngorms Partnership, Grantown.
Cairngorms Working Party (1992*). Common sense and Sustainability: a partnership for the Cairngorms.* The Scottish Office, Edinburgh.
Costanza, Robert *et al.* (1997). *The value of the world's ecosystem services and natural capital.* Nature, 387, 253–260.
Crofts, R. (1991). Can we make sustainable development work in practice?, in LeRoy, M. (ed), *Regional development around the North Atlantic rim.* Volume 1, International Society for the Study of Marginal Regions, Nova Scotia, 77–92.
Crofts, R. (1994a). Sustaining the earth's resources, in O'Halloran, D., Green, S., Harley, M., Stanley, M. and Knill, J. (eds), *Geological and Landscape Assessment.* Geological Society, London, 7–10.
Crofts R. (1994b). An integrated natural heritage organisation in Scotland, paper presented to conference on 'Merits of Merger'. Cardiff, Wales.
Crofts, R., Maltby, E., Smith, R. and MacLean, L. (2000), *Integrated planning: international perspectives.* Scottish Natural Heritage, Edinburgh.
Daily, G.C. (ed) (1997). *Nature's services: societal dependence on natural ecosystems.* Island Press, Washington D.C.
Department of the Environment (1994a). *Sustainable Development: The UK Strategy.* HMSO, London.
Department of the Environment (1994b). *Biodiversity: The UK Action Plan.* HMSO, London.
Department of the Environment, Transport and the Regions (1999). *Sustainable development indicators.* DETR, London.
Forth Estuary Forum (1998). *The Forth: the way forward.* Forth Estuary Forum, Edinburgh.
Glowka, L., Burhenne-Guilmin, F. and Synge, H. (1994). *A guide to the convention on Biological Diversity.* IUCN Environmental Policy and Law Paper, 30.
Holdgate, M. (1996). *From care to action: making a sustainable world.* Earth Scan, London.
IUCN (1997). *Action for protected areas in the UK.* IUCN, UK, London.
IUCN (1998). *Imagine tomorrow's world.* IUCN, Gland, Switzerland.
IUCN/UNEP/WWF (1980). *World Conservation Strategy.* IUCN, Gland, Switzerland.
IUCN/UNEP/WWF (1991). *Caring for the Earth.* IUCN, Gland, Switzerland.
Loch Leven Catchment Management Project (1999). *The Loch Leven Catchment Management Plan.* Scottish Natural Heritage, Edinburgh.
McNeely, J.A. (2000). Bioregional planning and ecosystem-based management: commonalities, contrasts, constraints and convergencies, in Crofts *et al. Integrated planning: international perspectives.* SNH, Edinburgh.
Maltby, E. (1999). Some European perspectives on the ecosystem approach, unpublished manuscript. Royal Holloway Institute for Environmental Research, London.

Mather, A.S. and Gunson, A.R. (1995). *A review of biogeographical zones in Scotland.* SNH Review, 40.

Miller, K.R. (1996). *Balancing the scales: Guidelines for increasing biodiversity's chances through bioregional management.* World Resources Institute, Washington D.C.

Miller, K.R. (2000). What is bioregional planning? in Crofts *et al. Integrated planning: international perspectives.* SNH, Edinburgh.

Rifkind, M. (1991). The Government's proposals for the natural heritage in Scotland. Paper presented to the Royal Society of Edinburgh Conference on NCC/CCS merger, Edinburgh.

Scottish Development Department (1991). *Scotland's Natural Heritage – The Way Ahead.* SDD, Edinburgh.

Scottish Natural Heritage (1992). Launch Brochure. SNH, Edinburgh.

Scottish Natural Heritage (1993). *Sustainable Development and the Natural Heritage: the SNH approach.* SNH, Edinburgh.

Scottish Natural Heritage (1994). *Annual Report 1992/3.* SNH , Edinburgh.

Scottish Natural Heritage (1995). *Focus on Firths.* SNH, Edinburgh.

Scottish Natural Heritage (1998a). *Natural Heritage Zones: An introductory briefing.* SNH, Edinburgh.

Scottish Natural Heritage (1998b). *National Parks for Scotland: a consultation paper.* SNH, Edinburgh.

Scottish Natural Heritage (1999). *National Parks: SNH's advice to Government.* SNH, Edinburgh.

Smout, T.C. (2000). *Nature Contested: Environmental History in Scotland and Northern England.* Edinburgh University Press.

Solway Firth Partnership (1998). Solway Firth Partnership, Dumfries.

The Scottish Office (1998). *People and Nature.* HMSO, Edinburgh.

Tansley, A. (1946). *Our heritage of wild nature: A plea for organised nature conservation.* Cambridge University Press, Cambridge.

United Nations (1992). *Conference on Environment and Development.* UN, New York.

US Interagency Ecosystem Management Task Force (1995). *Ecosystem Management.* Washington D.C.

Usher, M. B. and Balharry, D. (1996). *Biogeographical Zonation of Scotland.* SNH, Edinburgh.

Vaze, P. (1998). *UK Environmental Accounts 1998.* HMSO, London.

World Commission on Environment and Development (1987). *Our Common Future.* Oxford University Press, Oxford.

Wynne, G. *et al.* (1995). *Biodiversity Challenge* (second edition). RSPB, Sandy, England.

18

Vision and Reality: A Perspective of Conservation Past, Present and To Come

Martin Holdgate

THE COMPLEX ROOTS OF CONSERVATION

IT IS A truism that people and nature are inseparable. In many communities, especially of hunter/gatherers directly dependent on the productivity of natural and semi-natural ecosystems, 'caring for the Earth is born when you are born' (Gilday, 1994). Such interdependence is reflected in culture and language: the Yamana of Tierra del Fuego, castigated by Darwin in *The Voyage of the Beagle* as living at the lowest limits of human savagery, had a language extraordinarily rich in nouns descriptive of the coasts and beaches so vital to their existence as canoe-based nomads (Darwin, 1845; Bridges, 1948), and the Inuit have a similar diversity of words for snow. Reverence for nature lies deep within many cultures: there have been sacred groves in places as far apart as the Pacific Islands, West Africa and northern Europe from the dawn of history (Fraser, 1987; Holdgate 1999).

Human history over much of the Earth has been a story of a rise to pandominance, made possible by agriculture which secured and increased the food supply and in turn supported increasingly diverse urban cultures. The human species is now said to appropriate, use, or waste about 40% of primary productivity on land (Vitousek *et al.*, 1986). Most historians trace the origins of European and Middle-Eastern civilization to the 'fertile crescent' of Syria, Iraq and Iran, some 5000 years ago (Leakey, 1981). That was also the birthplace of the Judaeo-Christian religion, whose definition of the human relationship with nature as one of supremacy, or at best, of responsible stewardship, fits a society that needs to intervene in ecological systems, managing crops and herds and defending them against wild predators and competitors.

The modern conservation movement is very much a creature of western European and North American culture, even though it was exported by Europeans to many distant lands during the colonial era (Crosby, 1986; Holdgate, 1999). I suggest that deep within its foundations there are fundamental antitheses – or even contradictions – that have affected the developments reviewed in this meeting, and still affect policies today. The consequences are very evident at global level in the General Assemblies and Congresses of the World Conservation Union (IUCN).

The essential antitheses – which overlap – can be summarized as:

- nature as God's world   *versus* nature as a human possession
- reverence for nature   *versus* economic valuation of nature as a resource
- nature's rights   *versus* the rights of the human user
- nature as a universal possession *versus* nature as private property

The left hand column can be said to define 'nature-centred' conservation, and that on the right 'people-centred' conservation. Devotees of the former defend nature for itself, while those in the second camp are strongly motivated by self-interest.

The 'nature-centred' approach was anciently manifest in sacred groves and divinities of place, and was rediscovered by romantic philosophers, such as Rousseau (who taught that nature is inherently good, and that the closer people are to nature the freer and happier they become) and Ernst Haeckel, founder of ecology, whose doctrine of monism stressed that humanity was part of nature and that nature was beauty and order (Bramwell, 1989). Poets and writers including Emerson, Wordsworth and Thoreau sang the same song. Thoreau wrote that 'in wildness is the preservation of the world' (Shabecoff, 1993). The pioneer of the North American National Parks movement, John Muir, argued that 'while God's glory was written over all his works, in the wilderness the letters were capitalized' (McCormick, 1989).

From early times, nature protection has involved actions designed to safeguard both sites and species. Site conservation began with sanctuaries and refuges closed to hunting, and in Europe these can be traced back to the sixteenth century. The first modern-style bird sanctuary in England was created at Walton Park by Charles Waterton in 1826 (Holdgate, 1999). Many people credit Wordsworth with first formulating the concept of National Parks, because he argued that the Lake District should be treated as 'a sort of national property, in which every man has a right and an interest, who has an eye to see and a heart to enjoy' (Wordsworth, 1810). The world's first true National Park was created in North America, at Yellowstone, in 1872 and it matched John Muir's vision of such parks as unpeopled wilderness – though Gustavus Doane, who advised Congress to create it, also stressed its research potential (Nicholson, 1997).

Species conservation has both altruistic and utilitarian roots. Bird Protection Societies appeared from 1875 onwards, starting in Germany. The excessive slaughter of seabirds for 'sport' off the British coast in the 1860s inspired the first Act of Parliament to protect wild birds in 1869. Twenty years later, there was similar revulsion against the killing of birds to provide fashionable plumes – which, as recently as 1905, were worth twice their weight in gold (Allen, 1987). But the earliest species conservation measures were adopted for reasons of human self-interest. Some may stretch back into the dim past of hunter/ gatherer cultures, where the devastating consequences of the 'overkill' of large mammals (Martin, 1971) may have stimulated the evolution of traditional practices that curbed excessive slaughter (Kemf, 1993). In medieval Europe control of hunting in so-called 'forests' was achieved by vesting exclusive rights in kings or powerful magnates. Kings and emperors had their hunting preserves in Asia too (Holdgate, 1999). In North America, with its more egalitarian culture and with the unchecked slaughter of bison and extermination of the passenger pigeon as salutary reminders, hunters themselves came to recognize that future sport would be better if they conserved quarry species and their habitats. Societies like the Boone and Crockett Club and the More Game Birds Foundation (later known as Ducks Unlimited), whose members were hunters but whose aim was the conservation of quarry species were established (Shabecoff, 1993). In the UK, WAGBI, the Wildfowlers Association of Great Britain and Northern Ireland, was cast in the same mould. Other Societies – including some for bird protection – were created because of fear over the loss of species useful to agriculture.

Both nature-centred and people-centred conservation gained strength in North America during the Presidency of Theodore Roosevelt, between 1901 and 1909 (Shabecoff, 1993). Roosevelt was close to John Muir and, perhaps partly through his influence, created a number of National Parks, National Monuments and Wildlife Reserves. On the other hand, his principal adviser on conservation was Gifford Pinchot, a forester who found Muir's almost mystical attitude to nature hard to grasp. Instead Pinchot proposed three principles: 'the use of existing resources for the present generation, the prevention of waste, and the development of natural resources for the many rather than the few' (McCormick, 1989; Shabecoff, 1993). He was concerned with the optimal use of all living resources – in exploited forests and farmlands as well as in the wilderness. He could be described as the pioneer of sustainable development.

Science has also played an important part. The description of the fascinating diversity of nature by travellers like Humboldt, Darwin and Hooker helped stimulate the nineteenth-century explosion of interest in natural history which led inevitably to calls for nature protection. The science of ecology, as it developed from Haeckel's original quasi-philosophical publications into a science led by people like Davenport, Clements, Shelford, Tansley and Leopold, gave new insights into the inter-relationships of all life forms and especially into the origins, distributions and functioning of plant and animal communities. The work of Aldo Leopold led to the conclusion that species could only be understood and protected when their habitats were also understood, and that in an environment dominated by people, humans had to act to maintain ecological balance (Leopold, 1933). Ecologists appeared to hold the key to the *how* of conservation: how to achieve the perpetuation of species, their habitats and their productivity, whatever the altruistic or materialistic reason *why* conservation was to be pursued. But ecology went wider: it was applicable to the sustainable use of living natural resources on lands and waters managed for agriculture, forestry and fisheries as well as those set aside as national parks and nature reserves. Ecology was a holistic science, and had holistic relevance because it appeared to provide a new basis for the wise use of environmental resources.

VISION AND REALITY IN THE POST-WAR WORLD

These historical strands are evident in the processes that led to the 1949 Act in the United Kingdom (Sheail, 1998), and to the creation and development of the International Union for Protection of Nature (now IUCN) in 1948 (Holdgate, 1999). The UK had had animal- and nature-protection societies for many decades, beginning with what became the RSPCA in 1824 and continuing through the RSPB, the National Trust, the Society for the Promotion of Nature Reserves and the CPRE and its Scottish and Welsh counterparts. The SPNR, led by Charles Rothschild, drew up the first list of 273 potential nature reserves (Rothschild and Marren, 1997) and its collaboration with the British Ecological Society (Sheail, 1987) culminated in the proposals for national parks and nature reserves in the Dower Report and by the National Parks Committee, Nature Reserves Investigation Committee and Wild Life Conservation Special Committee (Sheail, 1998).

But a people-centred concept of conservation became increasingly evident in the period between 1920 and 1950. One strand was the emergence of town and country planning as a discipline concerned to regulate and optimize the conversion of greenfield to brownfield uses in the inter-war period in Britain (Sheail, 1981). Another was the increasing recognition by people like Arthur Tansley and Julian Huxley that more was needed than the protection of key sites as nature reserves. Like Aldo Leopold and Fairfield Osborn in the United States, they and the other members of the Committees they chaired were convinced of the potential importance of ecology as a foundation for the development of natural resources. Tansley, by 1947, had come to see both farming and forestry as areas of applied ecology: to quote John Sheail 'the ecologist's holistic view would encompass both intensively used land and areas of semi-natural and natural vegetation' (Sheail, 1998).

Tansley, Huxley, Dower and their colleagues mapped out an approach that would have applied the discipline of ecology and the practices of town and country planning to the whole countryside. The biological service they advocated would have developed research and provide advice on the conservation, regulation, control and management of plant and animal populations. It would have administered national nature reserves and could well, also, have guided the administration of national parks. It would have provided Ministers with the expert foundations for a unified rural policy encompassing landscape, wildlife and recreation. It would have lifted conservation above nature protection, seen in the public mind as a minority eccentricity (Anon, 1946) – and would, in effect, have placed what today we call sustainable development at the heart of national policy. Much that appeared in Agenda 21 (UN, 1992) is a logical development – and not too novel a development – of what Tansley, Huxley and their colleagues were advocating in 1947.

The vision was ahead of its time. As John Sheail has demonstrated (Sheail, 1998) it was constrained by established sectoral interests and institutions. This is a familiar event in Governments, whose sectoral Departments have immense cultural inertia, distrust innovation and loathe superimposed co-ordination. A whole series of such bodies reacted with suspicion to the idea of a cross-cutting new authority or 'board'. The agriculture departments and Agricultural Research Council were anxious about duplication of responsibility. Scottish interests feared subordination to England. The National Parks interests wanted to run their own show. This sectoralism may explain why the conservation units established under the 1949 Act lacked obvious procedural or administrative inter-connections (Mercer, this volume).

The Nature Conservancy and National Parks Commission established by the 1949 Act were therefore already narrowed-down versions of the initial concept. The Nature Conservancy was limited to the provision of scientific advice on the conservation and control of the natural flora and fauna of Great Britain (but not Northern Ireland), the establishment and management of nature reserves, and the organization of research and scientific services related to those objectives. And from the outset it was stalked by predators. The Treasury was not sure that a new body was needed, and constrained its budget and its ability to purchase land and research stations (Sheail, 1998). Having hemmed the Conservancy into a narrow space and limited its growth, established interests found it easy then to question whether it was worth having at all. It can be hypothesised that it survived largely because its second Director General, Max Nicholson, was himself a senior Civil Servant with wide contacts in Parliament and the official world, and adept at playing what are euphemistically called 'Whitehall games'.

Similar tensions were evident at international level. Here nature-centred initiatives predominated in the early stages. Before the second World War there had only been two efforts to establish global machinery for nature conservation as a whole – a Consultative Commission for the International Protection of Nature constituted in 1914 as a result of initiatives by a Swiss, Paul Sarasin, and an International Office for the Protection of Nature established in the Netherlands by Pieter van Tienhoven in 1928 (Holdgate, 1999). By 1946, as the surge of post-war reconstruction began, the former was defunct and the latter gravely weakened. Only the International Council for Bird Preservation, founded in 1922, was functioning effectively, and that (as its title implies), had limited coverage.

A major people-centred initiative nearly happened in 1944. President Franklin Delano Roosevelt had become convinced of the importance of conservation of natural resources as a foundation for lasting peace, and proposed an international conference on the subject (Shabecoff, 1996). But his death brought that to nothing, and the rationale for the new international organization for the protection of nature proposed by Charles Bernard and Johann Büttikofer of the Ligue Suisse pour la Conservation de la Nature lay very much at the 'nature-centred' end of the spectrum (Büttikofer, 1947; Holdgate, 1999). The UK and USA were unenthusiastic, the former because their priorities lay at home where Huxley and Tansley were busily at work, and perhaps because they considered the protectionist approach of the Swiss outdated (Holdgate, 1999). But Julian Huxley's appointment as the first Director General of UNESCO changed things. Thanks especially to UN-ESCO sponsorship, and despite the familiar governmental resistance to any financial commitments, the International Union for the Protection of Nature was founded at Fontainebleau in 1948.

From its beginning, IUPN's programme belied its name, for it was concerned with nature as a resource as well as nature as an object of devotion. Like the Nature Conservancy in Britain, it stressed the essential role of education and public information. Like the NC, it synthesised the best available research and looked at future problems: it is noteworthy that it debated the possible impacts of pesticides on nature at the Conference it organized jointly with UNESCO at Lake Success in 1949 (IUPN/UNESCO, 1949). In fact the first IUPN programme had six themes: safeguarding endangered habitats and species; disseminating existing knowledge; augmenting knowledge through research; disseminating information likely to promote conservation; educating adults and children about the dangers posed by the modification of natural resources; and promoting international agreements on nature protection. The parallels with the programme of the British Nature Conservancy are close, although IUPN was not an executive agency: it worked by convening technical meetings, promoting information exchange and so helping its governmental and non-governmental members to do their own work better (Holdgate, 1999).

The pendulum of international conservation swung strongly towards science in 1956, when the IUPN General Assembly met in Edinburgh with a programme greatly influenced by the Nature Conservancy (and especially by Max Nicholson and John Berry, who persuaded national bodies concerned with the use of environmental resources to become involved). Under strong Anglo-American pressure it changed its name to International Union for *Conservation* of Nature *and Natural Resources,* and emphasised its mandate as the application of ecological knowledge for the safeguarding of species and habitats and the sound management of species, rangelands and other biological resources used by people. From then until the early 1970s the outlook and programmes of IUCN and the Nature Conservancy moved very much in parallel, except that IUCN covered national parks as well as nature reserves (it soon became responsible for preparing a World List of National Parks and equivalent protected areas, under mandate from the United Nations).

VISION AND REALITY: FIFTY YEARS OF CHANGE

Over the past fifty years, national and international conservation have, therefore, gone through several phases. In Britain there has been a progressive erosion of the original vision of a holistic, science based, nationwide biological service. Both in Britain and internationally, conservation has been overwhelmed and transformed by the 'environmental revolution' of the 1960s and 1970s. As a consequence, new mechanisms for conservation at global, national and local levels have emerged.

In Britain, although the 1949 legislators jibbed at giving it a mandate to spearhead ecological applications in agriculture, forestry and fisheries, and although it had a traumatic infancy, the Nature Conservancy of the 1950s and 1960s expressed many of the visions of the founding fathers. It spanned nature-centred and people-centred conservation (although it did not have responsibility for landscape, which fell to the National Parks Commission, whose role was advisory rather than executive). It had the status of an independent Research Council and developed a substantial research wing. It pioneered research into the impact on wildlife of toxic chemicals, especially pesticides, at a time when these 'wonder chemicals' could do no ill in the eyes of the agricultural world – which did its utmost to denigrate the Conservancy's work. It appreciated the importance of education and public information, and supported postgraduate research studentships that brought many outstanding ecologists into the profession. It was scientifically holistic and territorially almost nationwide. Despite prevailing sectoralism in the structure of Government, the Conservancy built bridges, for example working with MAFF to create the Farming and Wildlife Advisory Groups and collaborating with enlightened hunting organizations like WAGBI and with foresters, landowners and educationalists. It adopted a regional structure which allowed the contacts with local authorities, rural communities and local individuals that are now accepted as essential for effective conservation anywhere in the world. It balanced the need to safeguard species and habitats in their own right with the need to establish conservation as a wider area of social policy. Furthermore, to quote Michael Dower (this volume), its staff were a multidisciplinary team of enthusiasts.

By 1965, the Nature Conservancy was an outstanding success and had gained well-deserved international regard. On any rational expectation, it could and should have evolved into a powerful nationwide environmental agency. Why did this not happen ? I do not believe that the prime cause was the intense politicisation of the environmental world in the late 1960s and early 1970s, and consequent changes in the machinery of government, because the Nature Conservancy had already been swept into the Natural Environment Research Council, NERC, before the 'environmental revolution' really got under way. I think that one problem was that the incorporation of the Conservancy as a component of NERC impeded its response to the rapid changes of the day. On the positive side, that incorporation had reaffirmed the scientific character of the Conservancy and its independence from day to day political pressures. On the other hand it implied that the Conservancy was primarily a research body – part of the science sector, not the planning sector, of government (Sheail, this volume). Although the NERC of the day had many distinguished scientists with a strong commitment to conservation among its members, the Conservancy's field conservation programmes, its land acquisition and its visible and distinctive public profile jarred on senior NERC Headquarters staff and on some members of its Council. These tensions intensified once the landscape of environmental politics was transformed.

The 'new environmentalism' had a different focus from any preceding movement. It was concerned especially with pollution and the excessive consumption of natural resources, and it traced both back to the exponential increase in human numbers. Rachel Carson's alarm call about the potential ecological impact of pesticides (Carson, 1967); Barry Commoner's prediction of catastrophic resource depletion (Commoner, 1971) and Ehrlich's 'population bomb' (Ehrlich, 1968) caught public imagination. These new concerns had three immediate consequences. First, they took nature conservation in the narrower sense – the establishment of nature reserves and the protection of wild species – back to where it had been as a minority interest. Second, their calls for major constraints on industry and for community action to curb population growth made environmental affairs vastly more political. Third, they made environment an international business.

In the United Kingdom, the 'new environmentalism' stimulated a ferment of action. The Nature Conservancy made a major contribution to the Countryside in 1970 Conference and to European Conservation Year (Boote, this volume). Government acted in October 1969 to establish three new institutions. An 'overlord' Secretary of State for Local Government and Regional Planning, Anthony Crosland, was given cross-departmental responsibility for coordinating activity to combat pollution. A Central Scientific Unit on Environmental Pollution was established as part of the Secretary of State's office, to provide the information on which that coordinated action should be based. And a Standing Royal Commission on Environmental Pollution was created as an independent, authoritative, adviser on pollution control policy. These cross-cutting functions survived (albeit somewhat curbed and constrained) when the 'overlord' Secretary of State was replaced by a Secretary of State for the Environment in 1970.

DOE was the lead department for international conservation, and led the UK input to the United Nations Conference on the Human Environment – the Stockholm Conference – in 1972. It led in the negotiation of three major international Conventions – Oslo, London and Paris – dealing with the prevention of marine pollution, especially from the dumping of wastes (Holdgate, 1979). It was also the planning Department, and the Countryside Commission (as the National Parks Commission had become in 1968) answered to DOE ministers. It appeared logical, especially after Stockholm, that nature conservation policy should answer in the same way. Viewed from this standpoint, it made sense for the Nature Conservancy to be removed from NERC and be reconstituted as an agency supported through, and answering to, DOE.

As is well known, this was achieved at the price of splitting the conservation branch from the research that was designed to underpin it. I believe that such a split was almost inevitable in the political circumstances of the time: the period of the Rothschild report and its advocacy of the customer-contractor principle. But although both the twins born from this embryonic fission, the Nature Conservancy Council and the Institute of Terrestrial Ecology, have undoubtedly been success stories, these changes marked another erosion of the original holistic vision of a nationwide biological service, strong both in research and its application. The NCC, inevitably, gained a higher political profile following the 1981 Wild Life and Countryside Act, not least because of protracted argument as that measure passed through Parliament, and the strengthening of protection given to SSSIs which it provided. The Act also broke new ground in its provision for marine nature reserves, although entrenched rights of navigation and fisheries doomed their designation to protracted wrangling (Warren, this volume).

One step leads to another. A further consequence of the 1981 Act was that the Secretary of State for the Environment, whose responsibility for deciding the most contentious planning cases was otherwise limited to England, found himself embroiled in highly controversial issues in Scotland, like proposals for afforestation on Creag Megaidh and peat cutting at Duich Moss on Islay. This jarred especially on Nicholas Ridley, who felt that the arrangement was constitutionally wrong. He also felt personal sympathy for landowners whose rights he saw eroded by the NCC's team of nature protectionists. His personal concerns led fairly directly to the 1991 Act and the further reconstruction and devolution of the conservation agencies in the United Kingdom. It left the Joint Nature Conservation Committee as the vestigial shadow of Tansley and Huxley's vision of a holistic nationwide biological service.

THE BROADER PICTURE: INTERNATIONAL CONSERVATION

The rise of the 'new environmentalism' also had major international consequences. As in the UK, it left nature conservation, represented by IUCN and by WWF (founded in 1961 essentially as champion and fund raiser for nature) to one side of the action which was spearheaded by dynamic new bodies such as Friends of the Earth and Greenpeace. Another consequence was a new 'north-south' tension between developed and developing countries. The latter viewed the new environmentalism's preoccupation with pollution and resource depletion as very much the business of the North. Many developing countries criticised the Stockholm agenda for focussing too much on the concerns of rich countries – who had the resources to put those problems right if they wished – and for ignoring the 'pollution of poverty' and underdevelopment from which they suffered (Holdgate, Kassas and White, 1982).

In a sense this North-South debate was another manifestation of the argument between nature-centred and people-centred conservation. Nature-centred conservation implies that nature needs to be safeguarded against humanity. For many people that conclusion is counter-cultural, or even ludicrous, in a world where a billion people live near or below the threshold of absolute poverty and where expanding settlements can only feed themselves by finding new land to cultivate. This north-south polarization can be expressed as two additional antitheses:

- nature's rights   *versus*   the rights of the poor
- developed country rights   *versus*   rights of the South

This is, at bottom, a debate about sovereignty, ownership and power. Many in the developing world resent the way the champions of conservation in the rich countries demand that poor countries stop clearing tropical forests, encroaching on the world's remaining wilderness and using wildlife commercially (Ramachandra, 1963). They condemn the export of the 'Yellowstone model' of protected area to places like the Serengeti or Ngorongoro, with the alienation, and sometimes the displacement, of the people who live there.

However bitter it has been at times, the debate has been valuable because it led to recognition, in both North and South, of the need to judge conservation in its social context – which means, inevitably, the context of local communities. The problems and opportunities of regions, countries and localities differ. The conservation policies of developing countries have had to blend respect for nature with economic self-interest. Julius Nyerere, at the celebrated Arusha Conference of 1963 at which he enunciated the 'Arusha Declaration,' made it clear that he was motivated to conserve wildlife largely because of the economic value of ecotourism to countries like Tanzania (Grzimek, 1961). And problems have to be addressed at the right level. Crocodile ranching and programmes of controlled wildlife use like the CAMPFIRE project in Zimbabwe have aided conservation because local communities derive economic benefit from wild species and have an incentive to retain them. In more and more countries it has become obvious that nature-centred and people-centred conservation have to come together (Holdgate, 1999).

THE WAY AHEAD

We have, it seems to me, come full-circle since 1949. The visionaries behind the 1949 Act saw conservation – as most of us here do – as a central component of public policy: a means of ensuring harmony between human communities and the wider ecological systems on which they depend. Today's catch-phrase 'sustainable development' : meeting the needs of the present without compromising the ability of future generations to meet their own needs, is only achievable through conservation, as Julian Huxley and Max Nicholson interpreted the concept.

In one sense, conservation has succeeded, because sustainable development is now global policy. As Norman Moore (this volume) has put it, conservation has become a central ingredient of modern life. We are all concerned about the multiple purposes of land and water use, and many policies have an almost Utopian goal of bringing agriculture, forestry, fisheries, recreation and the maintenance of a diverse wildlife together within a diverse, beautiful landscape occupied by prosperous local communities. European and British agriculture and forestry have broadened their goals, and incorporated much more conservationist thinking (Dwyer and Hodge, this volume: Mutch, this volume). But practical action depends on getting the balance of a series of alternatives (and additives) right:

- holistic   *versus*/and   specific
- central   *versus*/and   decentralized
- agency-centred   *versus*/and   community centred
- science-based   *versus*/and   value-based

The United Nations and many international organizations have been established because of a belief that the economic, social, political and environmental problems facing the world community are so all-pervasive that global debate and global consensus on action are imperative. Similar assumptions are reflected in many recent conservation documents, including the *World Conservation Strategy* (IUCN/UNEP/WWF, 1980) and its more people-centred successor, *Caring for the Earth* (IUCN/UNEP/WWF, 1991). The Stockholm Declaration and Action Plan, the Rio Declaration and Agenda 21 endorsed by the 1992 UN Conference on Environment and Development, and the steadily swelling series of international environmental conventions (IUCN, 1993) are expressions of this desire for global action.

The global agenda demands national and local action. The Stockholm Conference called for national State of the Environment reports. The World Conservation Strategy urged countries to prepare National Conservation Strategies. The World Bank has made the preparation of National Environmental Action Plans a condition for some of its loans. Rio repeated the demand for national action. Many countries have responded: the UK, for example, has prepared the White Paper *This Common Inheritance* (UK, 1990), the UK Strategy for Sustainable Development (UK, 1994a) and the national Biodiversity Conservation Action Plan (UK, 1994b).

Caring for the Earth and Agenda 21 both recognize the need to go further, reaching down to sub-national and local levels. Moreover, because conservation must be expressed through a wide range of policies, it needs a wide range of allies. The Fourth World Congress on National Parks and Protected Areas, meeting at Caracas, Venezuela, in 1992, stressed the need to view protected areas in a wider social context. It emphasized that long-term success depended on securing the active support of a wide range of stakeholders, and demonstrating that a protected area was beneficial to the community in whose area it was situated (McNeely, 1993). The adage 'think globally, act locally' is only half correct, because global thinking has to be informed by local thinking, local values and experiences (Crofts, this volume). Conservation action is most likely to succeed if there is a vertical flow of ideas and knowledge from the local to the global and back again, and lateral interchange between all sectors of the community.

This perspective is clearly of great importance in the United Kingdom where the ferment of the 1990s affected all the national conservation agencies (Phillips, this volume) and the new millennium is beginning with new, devolved, governance structures (Curry, this volume). In this context the break-up of the Nature Conservancy Council in 1990 may prove pre-adaptive, for in Scotland and Wales integrated landscape and nature conservation entities await the new political systems. In looking forward over the next fifty years it may be pertinent to bear in mind the five priorities for conservation enunciated in November 1998 at Fontainebleau, where IUCN celebrated its 50th anniversary (McNeely, 1999). These five priorities are:

- intensify efforts for conservation, since national and international action are lagging behind rhetoric and biodiversity is being lost;
- accelerate action, because environmental and social changes are accelerating, making adaptive action more urgent and difficult;
- involve all sectors of society and all stakeholders, and use economic means as well as laws and regulations to achieve action;
- provide persuasive information, in forms useful to those who will carry the action forward, presented in ways that will cut through today's 'data overload';
- recognize that while many problems may be ecological, the solutions lie outside the traditional roles of the conservation and environment movements and will have to be socially and politically holistic.

Fifty years on from the 1949 Act, we have a dual challenge. We must match action to need and circumstance on the ground (and in the sea); to local ecology and local human priorities. But there is need also for a broader view of both spatial and temporal dimensions. Long-termism needs to replace or counter-balance short-termism.

This is well illustrated by climate change, which will affect the whole planet on a time scale of centuries. It demands global commitment, for which the Convention on Climate Change provides the framework. But the implementation of the Convention depends on action that involves citizens and companies within national and local communities. Very similarly, biodiversity losses are a global concern – but each country and sub-national region has primary responsibility for its own distinctive species and plant and animal communities (Langslow, this volume). Again, knowledge will always be incomplete – but we can optimize what we have by integrating our research and sharing information across the national, continental and global board.

One thing that has become clear is the changing status of science. As Charles Gimingham and Michael Usher (this volume) have pointed out, in the 1970s new ideas emerged, but in the 1980s major questions came to the fore. We are now challenged to use science to predict the consequences of major environmental and social trends. There are many success stories (Thomas, this volume). But at the same time, public regard for science, and especially for regulations based on science, has diminished. It is healthy that scientists and scientific pronouncements are no longer treated with awed reverence. But scientific method – based on the continuing questioning of hypotheses, demand for reproducibility of experiments, and insistence that the science rather than the scientist is what counts – remains essential if we are to respond rationally to environmental and social challenges.

That does not mean that we should treat science – as we did thirty years ago – as the dominant determinant of public policy. As Robin Grove-White (this volume) has emphasized, environmentalism has achieved a cultural significance in the contemporary world which the languages of science and economics cannot fully express. The social values of the wider community will have a determining influence on policy. It follows that science has to contribute to a wider debate, and to the evolution of those social values and demands. But if the role of science is to inject more and better information into the debate, it follows that there must be a willingness to adjust policies and positions in its light, and in some circumstances NIMBY may need to become YIMBY. The precautionary principle (Tait, this volume) was developed partly as a response to uncertain risk, and as the margins of uncertainty narrow so the position of the advocates of extreme precaution is eroded. The key lies in connections, which help people to understand where others are coming from and provide a framework for equitable debate (Royal Commission, 1998).

What would Julian Huxley and Arthur Tansley would be urging if they standing before us now? I suspect that they would be urging the new, decentralized, conservation agencies in the United Kingdom to recognize the need for dialogue, for inter-connections, for common endeavour, and for strong research. They might well endorse Roger Clarke's call (this volume) for flexible adjustment of the instruments for conservation in response to changing social demands and needs. I suspect that they might urge a strengthening of the central machinery for synthesis, making the Joint Nature Conservation Committee an Ecological Advisory Council with its own Accounting Officer and distinct grant-in-aid, drawing on the totality of available knowledge and applying it for national biodiversity conservation and national sustainable development. They might well support Norman Moore's call (this volume) for a Watchdog Unit, evaluating the effectiveness of conservation action in the light of the best available science. Perhaps they would also remind us that, as the Nature Conservancy recognised from the outset, conservation is a social policy and requires social enlightenment – which depends on communication to the community at large. Perhaps Huxley would re-echo some words his brother Aldous wrote to him in January 1948 (Huxley, 1948):

> We need to philosophize and poetize the conservationist's doctrine and to incorporate it into the general thought and sentiment of our age. As things stand, hardly any attention is paid in schools or universities (outside the specialist fields) to the practical and, much less, to the philosophical implications of conservationism on the one hand and our current destructionism on the other. If we don't do something about it pretty soon we shall find that, even if we escape atomic warfare, we shall destroy our civilization by destroying the cosmic capital on which we live. Our relation to the earth is not that of mutually beneficial symbiosis: we have become the kind of parasite that kills its host even at the risk of killing itself.

Perhaps less has changed since 1948 than we like to think.

REFERENCES

Allen, T. B. (1987). *Guardians of the Wild. The Story of the National Wildlife Federation.* Bloomington and Indianapolis: Indiana University Press.

Anon (1946). Nature conservation in England and Wales. *Nature,* 157, 277–80.

Bramwell, A. (1989). *Ecology in the 20th Century.* New Haven: Yale University Press.

Bridges, Lucas (1948). *Uttermost Part of the Earth.* London:Hodder and Stoughton.

Büttikofer, J. (1947). Statement on the international protection of nature. In Büttikofer, J. *International Conference for the Protection of Nature.* Basel: Swiss League for the Protection of Nature.

Carson, R. (1963). *Silent Spring.* London: Hamish Hamilton.

Commoner, B. (1971). *The Closing Circle.* New York: Alfred Knopf.

Crosby, A. W. (1986). *Ecological Imperialism. The Biological Expansion of Europe, 900–1900.* Cambridge: University Press.

Darwin, C. (1845). *The Voyage of the Beagle.* Everyman edition. London: Dent, 1955.

Ehrlich, P. S. (1968). *The Population Bomb* New York: Ballantine.

Fraser, J. G. (1987). *The Golden Bough. A Study in Magic and Religion.* Abridged edition. London: Papermac.

Gilday, C. K. (1994). Comment. In *IUCN Bulletin,* 2/94 p. 20.

Grzimek, B. (1961). Winning the Fight for Africa's Game. *Daily Telegraph, 21 August 1961.* Cited in Holdgate (1999).

Holdgate, M. W. (1979). *A Perspective of Environmental Pollution.* Cambridge: University Press.

Holdgate, M. W. (1996). *From Care to Action. Making a Sustainable World.* London: Earthscan.

Holdgate, M. W. (1999). *The Green Web. A Union for World Conservation.* London: Earthscan.

Holdgate, M. W. , Kassas, M. and White, G. F. (Eds) (1982). *The World Environment, 1972–1982. A Report by UNEP* Dublin: Tycooly International.

Huxley, A. (1948). Letter from Aldous Huxley to Julian Huxley. Quoted in Holdgate (1999).

Huxley, J. (1973). *Memories* New York: Harper and Roe.

Huxley, J. (1948). Notes for the opening of the Fontainebleau Conference. Cited in Holdgate (1999).

UNESCO (1950). *International Technical Conference on the Protection of Nature, Lake Success, 22–29 August 1949.* Paris and Brussels: UNESCO.

IUCN/UNEP/WWF (1980). *The World Conservation Strategy: Living Resource Conservation for Sustainable Development.* Gland, Switzerland: IUCN.

IUCN/UNEP/WWF (1991). *Caring for the Earth: A Strategy for Sustainable Living.* Gland, Switzerland: IUCN.

IUCN (1993). *Status of Multilateral Treaties in the Field of Environmental Conservation.* IUCN Policy and Law Occasional paper no 1. Bonn: IUCN Environmental Law Centre.

Kemf, E. (ed) (1993). *The Law of the Mother. Protecting indigenous peoples in Protected Areas.* San Francisco: Sierra Club.

Leakey, R. B. (1981). *The Making of Mankind.* London: Michael Joseph.

Leopold, A. (1933). *Game Management* New York: Scribner.

McCormick, J. (1989). *The Global Environmental Movement. Reclaiming Paradise.* London: Belhaven Press.

Mc Neely, J. A. (1993). (ed) *Parks for Life. Report of the Fourth World Congress on National Parks and Protected Areas.* Gland, Switzerland: IUCN.

McNeely, J. A. (1998). Conclusions. A New sense of Urgency. *World Conservation,* 1/99, March 1999.

Martin, P. S. (1971). Prehistoric overkill. *In* Detwyler, T. R. *Man's Impact on Environment.* New York: McGraw Hill.

Nicholson, E. M. (1997). The Challenge for a New Renaissance. Lecture, September 1997.

Ramachandra, G. (1997). The authoritarian biologist and the arrogance of anti-humanism. Wildlife Conservation in the Third World. *The Ecologist,* vol 27, no 1, 14–20.

Rothschild, M. and Marren, P. (1997). *Rothschild's Reserves. Time and Fragile Nature.* Colchester: Harley Books.

Royal Commission (1998). *Setting Environmental Standards. 21st Report of the Royal Commission on Environmental Pollution.*

Shabecoff, P. (1993). *A Fierce Green Fire. The American Environmental Movement.* New York: Hill and Wang.

Shabecoff, P. (1996). *A New Name for Peace. International Environmentalism, Sustainable Development and Democracy.* New England: University Press.

Sheail, J. (1981). *Rural Conservation in Inter-war Britain.* Oxford: Clarendon Press.

Sheail, J. (1987). *Seventy five years in Ecology. The British Ecological Society.* Oxford: Blackwell Scientific Publications.

Sheail, J. (1998). *Nature Conservation in Britain. The formative years* London: The Stationery Office.

UK (1990). *This Common Inheritance. Britain's Environmental Strategy.* Cm 1200. London: HMSO.

UK (1994a). *Sustainable Development: The UK Strategy.* Cm 2426. London: HMSO.

UK (1994b). *Biodiversity. The UK Action Plan.* Cm 2428. London: HMSO.

UN (1993). *Report of the United Nations Conference on Environment and Development, Rio de Janeiro, 3–14 June 1992. Volume I: Resolutions adopted by the Conference.* New York: United Nations publications, E,93.I.8.

Vitousek, P. M., Ehrlich, P. R., Ehrlich, A. H., and Matson, P. A. (1986). Human appropriation of the products of photosynthesis. *Bioscience,* 36, No 6, 368–373.

Wordsworth, W. (1810). *A Guide through the District of the Lakes in the North of England.* Fifth Edition. Kendal: Hudson and Nicholson.

Index

Access to open countryside, xiv, 172, 191–3

Acidification of land and water, 89

Adaptive strategies in animals and plants, 81, 82–3

Agenda 2000, 122–3, 129

Agenda 21, 208, 230

Agri-environment schemes, 125–6, 131, 167, 177

Agriculture
  impact on environment, 124–5
  industry and change, xiii, 53, 117–34
  mechanisation and effect on landscape, 117
  policy and effect on landscape, 117–18
  policy in Switzerland, 130–31
  pressures for change, 120-23
  sustainable development in, 190
  technology, developments in, 118

Agriculture Act 1947, xiii, 99, 117

Agriculture Act 1986, 167

Areas of Outstanding Natural Beauty (AONBs), 57, 65

Biodiversity, xii, 91–2, 93, 103, 112–13, 114, 202, 203–4
  Action Plan, 92, 101, 152–3, 167–8, 184, 208, 230
  definition of, 113
  future of, 181–5
  Strategy (EU), 202

Biogeography, island, 82

Biological invasions, 80, 87–8

Bioregional approach to environmental systems, 205–6

Biotechnology, social attitudes towards, 135–49

British Plant Communities (5 vols., by J. S. Rodwell), 84

Broads Grazing Marshes Scheme, 63, 125

Cairngorms, 212–13

Campaigning, 20–22, 23, 46, 62

Caring for the Earth, 230

Climate change, 46, 89–90, 103, 184, 202

Common Agricultural Policy (CAP), 58, 122, 196, 198

Common land, 41

Community participation, 164–6, 168
  and Millennium Greens, 170
  and provision of urban open spaces, 169
  and rights of way, 169–70

Community Woodland Supplement, 169

Conservation
  and conflict, 30, 196–7, 220
  biology, 91
  Boards, 189–90
  early history of, 1–3, 220–22
  inclusive approach to, 198, 200
  (Natural Habitats, etc.) Regulations 1994, 114, 115
  public perception of, xii, 97–105, 196–7
  threats to research within, 23

Convention on Biological Diversity, 201

Council for the Preservation of Rural England, 2

Counter-urbanisation, 119

Country parks, 37–38, 55–56

Countryside
  Act 1968, 37, 64, 162
  and Rights of Way Act 2000, 116, 129
  as a marketable commodity, 61
  benefiting from 'area of natural beauty' designation, 188–9
  character and quality, 187–9
  management of, xi, 52–69
  Premium Scheme, 63
  (Scotland) Act 1967, 8–10, 64
  Stewardship scheme, 63, 65, 167
  wider, and SSSIs, 16–17

Countryside Commissions, xi, 37, 53, 55–56, 67
  Recreation 2000 documents of, 41

'Countryside in 1970' Movement, 14–15,
    21, 34–35, 45, 52–54
  Study Group, report of the, 10

Diversity, genetic, 91
Dower, John, 3
'Duthchas' sustainable development project,
    214–15

EC Habitats Directive, 113–14, 167, 198
  see also Special Areas of Conservation
Ecological
  conservation, public perception of, 97–
    105
  dynamics, 90–91
  genetics, 80, 85, 91
  modelling, 91
  research, 92
  theory, global perspectives and
    biogeography in relation to, 81–2

Ecology
  and multivariate data analysis, 81, 84
  history of, in relation to wildlife
    conservation, xi, 79–81
  landscape, 92
Ecosystems
  bioregional approach to, 205–6
  key services and functions of, 205
  mechanisms at work in, 80, 81, 91, 92,
    151–2
  restoration of, 156–9
  understanding, as element of managing
    natural dynamics of the environment,
    205
Edinburgh, HRH The Duke of, 21
Environmental change, 89–90
Environmental decision-making and
    stakeholder input, 206–7
Environmental impact of agriculture
  'input model', 124
  'output model', 124–5
Environmental movement
  and relationship with new social
    movements, 48
  early history of, 45
  growth of, xi, 44–51
Environmental Protection Act 1990, 52,
    171
Environmental services and functions, 204–
    205
Environmentally Sensitive Areas (ESAs),
    63, 167

European
  Conservation Year 1970, 11, 17, 21, 54
  Marine Sites, 114, 115
  model of agriculture, 130
  Regional Development aid, 126
  Union, 45, 52, 58, 183
Eutrophication, 90

Farm Biodiversity Action Plans, 167–8
Farmer as land manager, 123–4, 191
Farming and Wildlife Advisory Groups,
    58–9, 166–7
Firths, environmental management of the
    Scottish, 213–14
Food production, postwar, 118
Forestry, xi, 65, 70–78
  and peatlands, 72–3
  broadleaved, 75
  current practice in, 73
  diversity of planting in, 75
  genetic considerations, 74
  harvesting, 75-6
  landscape considerations in, 74
  large-scale management in, 76, 77
  multi-purpose, 77, 183
  non-commercial, 76
  ploughing in relation to, 72-3
  tax-breaks, 73-4
  thinning practice, 74,
  Treasury borrowing rate, effect of on, 72
  tree improvement, 74
Forestry Commission, xi, xii, 55, 70-71,
    73
  and nature conservation, 71
  origins, 70
Forests
  Community, 169, 190
  National, 169, 190
'Free market' in agriculture, 120–22, 123,
    148

Genetically modified (GM) crops, 136,
    140–48, 184
Genetics, ecological, 80, 85, 91
Green Party, 46, 64

Habitat
  loss, 118
  recreation, 150–60
  Teams, 16
Habitats
  Directive, EC, 113–14, 167, 198
  Scheme, 167, 183

Hedgerows
  destruction of, 26, 118
  protection of, 129
  role of in the countryside, 18
Huxley, Sir Julian, 5, 99, 107, 224

Institute for Environmental History,
    University of St Andrews, ix
Institute of Terrestrial Ecology, 8, 18, 85
Integrated rural development (IRD), 126
Intensive farming, ecological impact of, 50
International collaboration in conservation,
    82
International Union for the Protection of
    Nature, 224–5

Key sites, 15

Land
  classes classification, 85
  ownership, rights of, 127, 128
Landscapes, dynamics of, 92
Large Blue butterfly, re-establishment of,
    155-6
Leisure facilities
  constraints on use of, 39–40
  in urban areas, 37, 41
  Recreation 2000, 41
  see also Recreation in the countryside
Loch Leven catchment, 211–12
Loch Lomond, ix

Man and Environment (by R. E. Boote), 21
Managing the countryside, xi
Marine conservation, xii, 106–116
Marine Conservation Society, 109
Marine Nature Conservation Review
    (MNCR), 113
Marine nature reserves (MNR), 109–112,
    114–15
Maximum tolerable population size (MTP),
    87
Minimum viable population size (MVP), 86
Monks Wood Experimental Station, 18,
    25
Moorland Scheme, 167
Moorlands Association, 41-2
Multipurpose land use, 123
Multivariate methods of data analysis, 81,
    84–5

National Heritage (Scotland) Act 1991,
    171

National Nature Reserves (NNR), 15, 222
  management of, 7, 16, 107
  role of, 4, 5, 99
  threats to, 23
National Park Policies Review Committee,
    57
National Parks, ix, x, 32
  changing role of, x, 38, 41
  country parks in relation to, 38
  in Scotland, proposals for, 57–8, 65
  Loch Lomond, 9
  management of, 57, 189
  origin of, 3–4, 32–33
  threats to, 57
  three main purposes of, 42
National Parks and Access to the
    Countryside Act 1949, ix, x, 1–12,
    97, 99, 106, 186
National Parks Committee, 5
National Trust, 55, 56
National Vegetation Classification, 84
Natura 2000, 114, 116
Natural Environment Research Council, 8
Natural Heritage Zones, 208–11
Nature Conservancy, ix, x, xi, 6–8, 13–24,
    53, 99, 152
  founding of, 6
  hostility towards, 13–14, 223
  relationships within the, 19–20
  research within the, 17–19, 28, 151
  role of, 6, 16
  Scientific Policy Committee, 7
  Toxic Chemicals and Wildlife Section,
    25, 28
Nature Conservancy Council, 8, 18, 46,
    58, 66
Nature conservation, relationships between
    interests within, 19
New Agricultural Landscapes Programme,
    58
New Towns Act 1946, 2
NIABY concept, 135
NIMBY concept and its limitations, 135–
    6
Non-native species, 80, 87–8, 113
Norfolk Broads, 63–5
Nuclear power, 50

Objectives 5b, 1 and 2, European Regional
    Development aid, 126, 169
Outdoor recreation, 8–10, 100
  see also Recreation in the countryside

Pesticide Safety Precautions Scheme, 26
Pesticides, 14, 18, 21, 25–31, 143
    effect on wildlife of, 26, 118
    publicity concerning, 26
    regulation, 137–8
Picnic sites, 37, 55
Planning
    as tool for long-term sustainability, 188
    in relation to countryside character, 187–
        8, 222
    system and agriculture, 127–8
Ploughing, in relation to forestry, 72
Pollution, 14, 50, 89–90, 112, 124
Population
    persistence, 86–7
    viability analysis (PVA), 86
Property rights, 127–30

Quality of life indicators, 183

Reith, Lord, 2
Recreation
    at sea, 114
    in the countryside, x, 32–43, 54–56,
        99–100, 161–80, 191–3
    see also Leisure facilities
Reintroduction of vanished species, xiii
    see also Species re-establishment
Remote sensing, 85
Research funding and dominant interests,
    50
Rights of way, 60, 162, 163, 169, 173,
    177, 191–2
Rio Earth Summit 1992, 46, 64, 112–13,
    162, 195, 201
Risk
    assessment, 86, 136
    regulation, precautionary, 138–45
    regulation, reactive/preventive 137–8
Ritchie, James, 5, 107
Rothschild, Charles, 150–51, 222
Royal Society for the Protection of Birds,
    62
Royal Society of Edinburgh, ix
Rural services, decline in, 119, 124

Science, changing status of, 232
Scottish National Countryside Monitoring
    Scheme, 85
Scottish Natural Heritage, origins and
    remit, 202
Silent Spring (by Rachel Carson), 14, 25
Sites of Special Scientific Interest (SSSIs),

    17, 107, 129, 170–71, 182
    in Scotland, 199
    threats to, 23, 171–2
Socio-economic change, nature of, xi
Special Areas of Conservation (SACs), 113,
    114–16
    selection of, 115
Species
    categories (SNH), 88
    decline, 181–2, 198
    re-establishment, 150, 153–6, 182–3
Sports Council, 37
Sustainable development, 46, 51, 64, 65–6,
    68, 82, 120, 123, 183, 188, 190,
    195–218
    challenges of, 200–201, 207–8
    definition of, 195
    key factors in, 215–17

Thinning practice in forestry, 74
The Theft of the Countryside (by M.
    Shoard), 46
Torrey Canyon oil tanker spill, 108
Tourism
    and car use, 34
    as generator of rural income, 163, 191
    increase in, 9, 34
Town and Country Planning Act 1947, 2,
    99, 127
Town and Country Planning Act 1968, 57
Town and Country Planning Act 1990,
    127
Tree improvement, 74

Voluntary bodies
    diversification in, 62
    growth in membership of, in 1980s, 62
    importance of, to nature conservation,
        24

'Watchdog unit', need for a, 29
Wild Life Conservation Special
    Committees, 5, 6, 222
Wildlife and Countryside Act 1981, 17,
    46, 58, 102, 109, 110–11, 170
Wildlife Enhancement Scheme (WES;
    English Nature), 171
Woodland Grant Scheme, 169
World Conservation Strategy, 113, 230
World Trade Conference, Seattle 1999, xi

Yorkshire Naturalists' Union, 1